114

DISTANT SOVEREIGNTY

DISTANT SOVEREIGNTY

National Imperialism and the Origins of British India

SUDIPTA SEN

Routledge
Taylor & Francis Group
NEW YORK AND LONDON

Published in 2002 by
Routledge
29 West 35th Street
New York, NY 10001
www.routledge-ny.com

Published in Great Britain by
Routledge
11 New Fetter Lane
London EC4P 4EE
www.routledge.co.uk

Routledge is an imprint of the Taylor & Francis Group.
Copyright © 2002 by Taylor & Francis Books, Inc.

Printed in the United States of America on acid-free paper.

10 9 8 7 6 5 4 3 2 1

Library of Congress Cataloging-in-Publication Data is available from the Library of Congress.

Distant Sovereignty / Sudipta Sen
  ISBN 0-415-92953-9—ISBN 0-415-92954-7 (pbk.)

For
Phil Corrigan

Contents

Illustrations

Foreword

T his book owes its origins to the friendship and encouragement of members of the Discussion Group on the Formation of the English State, St. Peter's College, Oxford University, where I first presented a paper in April 1993 at the insistence of Bernard Cohn. My introduction to the group and subsequently to the *Journal of Historical Sociology* (*JHS*) seems in retrospect, to have been a catalytic experience, in the sense that it forced me to consider the history of colonial India in the light of the domestic history of England and come to terms with an archival methodology that has lately been christened as the "new imperial history." There is nothing here that is particularly radical in this for those of us who had the privilege to work with Barney Cohn, who had almost single-handedly initiated this mode of inquiry for an entire generation.

I am also indebted beyond words to Philip Corrigan for his amazing generosity, his critical eye, and his bibliomania, all which have enriched my life as a historian and as a human being ever since I met him. I wish to thank others associated with the Oxford group and the *JHS*, especially Derek Sayer, Gavin Williams, Joanna Innes, Martha Lampland, Bruce Curtis, John Gillingham, Sir Gerald Aylmer, and Daniel Nugent; it is indeed difficult to accept that the last two are now no more. I would also like to thank here a mentor from my student days in Calcutta, Rudrangshu Mukherjee, who introduced me to the history of England and urged me towards further exploration of colonial Indian history. Among friends who have helped to sustain my interests over the years, I cannot forget Antoinette Burton, Philippa Levine, and Faisal Devji. Others who have directly or indirectly commented on aspects of this work are Uday Singh Mehta, Thomas R. Metcalf, Elizabeth Helsinger, Jean Comaroff, Paul Jaskot, Ian Barrow, Urmila Dé, Jeremy Black, Mary Poovey, Richard Cullen Rath, Michael

Fisher, Durba Ghosh, Prasannan Parthasarathi, Paul Greenough, Gautam Bhadra, Barun Dé, Sanjay Srivastava, and Kevin Grant. Research for this volume was conducted at the Oriental and India Office Collections at the British Library, the Widener Library at Harvard University, the Bird Library Special Collections at Syracuse University, the Olin Library at Cornell University, and the West Bengal State Archives at Kolkata. A special note of thanks goes to Susan Bean and the staff of the Duncan Philips Library at the Peabody Essex Museum, Salem, where, searching for something quite else, I stumbled upon some of the printed pamphlets discussed here. I do not have the space here to acknowledge all the conferences and venues where I have presented various chapters and sections of this book. I must thank, however, the following for agreeing to the publication of revised versions of articles in this book: the *JHS* and *South Asia* (the South Asian Studies Association of Australia).

Thanks are also due to Minara Mollah for her detective work with footnotes and bibliography and to Vik Mukhija for his helpful editorial interventions and remarkably friendly policing of deadlines; finally, my gratitude to L, D, and M for putting up with the research and writing of this book.

Introduction

RESTORING THE MUGHAL EMPIRE

By the summer of 1813 it had become clear to residents of Delhi and to observers of public affairs in northern India that the great Mughal emperor had been made a virtual prisoner on his throne by the British. In that year the dowager queen and the heir apparent had traveled east to seek the counsel of Awadh, a provincial regime humbled by the East India Company, in the dispute that was brewing over royal succession. The Company did not approve of the emperor's choice of prince regent and took exception to the fact that the prince had deceived the British Resident by pretending to attend a wedding and by falsely claiming that the governor-general in Calcutta had issued leave for their travel. The Company found these actions "disgraceful" and in subsequent letters of complaint accused the royal family of having brought "injurious insinuations against the justice and liberality of the British government"; it also reprimanded the emperor on his behavior in the matter of succession to the throne as a sign of his "ingratitude and deceit."[1]

After the Battle of Delhi in 1803, in which the Marathas were repulsed, the emperor had all but surrendered to the British forces. The facts that he was financially beholden to the East India Company, confined to the walls of the Red Fort, its court, and its bazaar, did not retain regular troops in his pay, and required written permission of the British Resident to move about freely were a testimony to the undeclared political mastery of the British at the heart of the subcontinent. But it is also clear that the British were eager to preserve remnants of the Mughal empire and the royal family as a necessary bastion of their newly acquired territorial and military power. They viewed themselves in this capacity as a "subject of jealous observation" by other potentially hostile states and chieftains in India and did not wish to dissolve their relationship to Delhi until such time when the "security and tranquility" of the Company's dominions in India had been secured.[2] The Residence of Delhi in the early years of the nineteenth century was seen as an important and delicate office on which hung the political interests and indeed the "national objects" of the Company. It required familiarity and extensive intercourse with the natives of India, especially those who were known for their "spirit of military enterprise, turbulence and insubordination."[3] Enemies abounded near Delhi and across the northwest; the Marathas still roamed free in the countryside.

The aura of the Mughals would continue to haunt the political climate of northern India for a long time to come. Any association to Delhi in the eighteenth century was a valuable tool for aspiring regimes and military fortune seekers. Lord Lake, the British commander who had retrieved Emperor Shah Alam in 1803 from dangerous collusion with the Maratha chief Daulat Rao Sindhia (who was advised by the French), considered the Mughals as integral to the future security of British possessions on the northwest frontiers.[4] Just as the Marathas were dispersing after their loss to the British in August 1803, Lake was contemplating measures by which the royal family would be brought under permanent custody with "every possible mark of honor and respect."[5] Governor General Lord Wellesley also wrote to the emperor, pledging that the Company would deliver him and his household from the indignities to which they had so long been subjected "by the violence, injustice and rapacity of those who have forgotten the reverence due" to his royal person and illustrious house.[6] The success of British arms, he added, had proven to be "the happy instrument of your Majesty's restoration to a state of dignity and tranquility under the protection of the British power. . . ."[7] In 1809 the British were defraying expenses for the repair of the palace gates of Delhi—carved wood with iron inlay and European-style flowers designed by Italian artists—which had been damaged by a recent uprising. The broken columns were not only a sad and unseemly sight but "inconsistent with the dignity of government."[8]

The political relationship between the British in India and the ruling house of Timur continued to be fraught with inconsistency and ambiguity in subsequent decades. The contradictions of legitimacy would be resolved only after the mutiny and rebellion of 1857, when the last emperor, Bahadur Shah, was tried as "a subject of the British Government in India," and a "false traitor against the State" who had proclaimed himself as the "reigning King and Sovereign of India" and taken "unlawful possession" of the city of Delhi.[9] And yet this was the very same empire that had bestowed on the English the revenues of Bengal after the battle of Plassey, favoring Clive with gifts and the title of "Flower of the Empire, Defender of the Country, the Brave, Firm in War (*sabit-jang*)" as an honorary officer.[10] It was also the authority from which the Company derived its formal position of *divan* on August 19, 1765 enabling it to collect the extensive revenues of Bengal,

Bihar, and Orissa—a windfall that bailed out its monopoly trade—in exchange for an annual tribute of 26,00,000 rupees.

Just within a few years, however, the subordinate position of the British would become suspect. In 1772, when the emperor threw himself in the hands of the Marathas, the payment of this tribute was promptly withheld, a decision upheld by the Court of Directors the next year.[11] In 1807 the dynastic custom of bestowing ceremonial robes (*khilat*s) on all principle chiefs attending the court of Delhi, including the British governor-general and the Resident, was revoked as "an exercise of the imperial authority, the object of which was to obtain a public acknowledgement of Vassalage and submission to the throne of Delhi on the part of the British government."[12] The Mughal emperor had in the past sent presents to the king of England and in letters addressed His Majesty as an equal in terms such as: "our dear brother King George."[13] But in 1823 the letter intended for England congratulating the new king on his accession was declined by the Company, which saw it as "inadmissible whether considered with reference to the constitutional character of the British Government in this country, or the circumstances or the situation of the Delhi Court in relation to that government."[14] In 1825 the ancient rites of prestation (*nazar*) to the throne were abolished because "they implied a recognition of the sovereignty of the crown of Delhi over the Company's possessions in India."[15] In 1828 the emperor was forbidden to correspond any further with the governor-general or native princes and chiefs because of the Mughal imperial seal, which ascribed to the British "the humiliating designation" of vassalage (*fidvi*) to the throne.[16] This, according to the Company, was a "sufficient acknowledgement by the Court of Delhi, that the relation of Sovereign and Vassal had ceased between the representative of the house of Timur and the British government in India."[17] There were no more audiences with subordinate princes, no coins struck in the name of the emperor in Delhi, no benediction for chiefs or nobles in the few provinces left in his realm. A few thousand descendants of royal blood, linear and collateral, remained within the walls of the palace.[18] In 1814, during Metcalfe's residency, the key to the palace gates had been taken away on charges of the murder of an illegitimate infant.[19]

This gradual peeling away of Mughal regalia provides the immediate historical context for this book. It indicates that sovereignty was ill defined and jealously guarded in the new regime established in India by the English East India Company; although many contemporaries saw the restoration of the Mughal house as a sham or a fiction, the British were careful not to break off their ties to it in public till it had become virtually impossible to continue the relationship in 1858, after the Mutiny. It is my argument that in the eighteenth century, and perhaps even in the early nineteenth, the self-image of British rule in India could not be fully or comfortably unfastened from the nominal regality of the Mughals. The British did not wish to be seen as an Indian power and they did not wish to assume indiscreetly the mantle of a sovereign authority in India.

By the mid-eighteenth century, the British had become deeply entangled with Indian politics, society, habits, customs, and manners. Yet at the same time, the imperial ambitions of the East India Company demanded a measured distance from its Indian subjects. At the heart of this seeming paradox was the fact that the Anglo-Indian company-state derived its autonomy and political structure from historical developments that took place far away in the British Isles, while it sought the trappings of an Indian polity familiar to its hastily acquired subjects. Moreover, the Company was not quite prepared to set up a full-fledged extraterritorial state. "A trading and a fighting Company" wrote Jonathan Holwell, an eyewitness to the Battle of Plassey "is a two headed monster in nature, that cannot exist for long."[20] It could not represent England in India comfortably, nor did it seek to represent the people of India who fought its wars and paid its taxes.

THE ENIGMA OF SOVEREIGNTY

The initial rule of the East India Company in India had little constitutional precedent. The royal charters of Cromwell, Charles II, and Queen Anne did grant the company leave, as they did most overseas joint-stock corporations, to safeguard sea-lanes, set up trading and manufacture on foreign soil, run mints, raise armies, sign treaties, and mete out limited civil and criminal justice.[21] But these charters did not stipulate much in regard to the diplomatic and political relationship with Indian powers or to the peculiar mosaic of Indian territorial arrangements that had surfaced with the decrepitude of the Mughal Empire. For the greater part of the eighteenth century the British acquiesced in the idea that the ruling house of Timur, despite its state of utter disrepair, was a source of visible, if not always legitimate, authority. Robert Orme's official history of British conquests in India, published in 1782, was called the *Historical Fragments of the Mogul Empire,* and James Rennell's first atlas of India was in many respects a map of the old empire and its new successor kingdoms. Such a situation remained in effect as long as the Company believed that its territorial acquisitions in India were not the results of concerted wars of aggression but were inadvertent offshoots of the defense of its strategic and corporate interests.

Before the era of military engagements it was common enough among servants of the Company to try to comprehend something called a "constitution of the Empire of Indostan," in which the "Great Mogul" was seen as the "sole proprietor" of all land and all countries "absolutely subjected."[22] He retained the exclusive right to grant such lands at will to feudatories as revenues for life and to deputies (nabobs) in lieu of pensions. The confirmation and signature of the emperor was required in all grants of territory. It was also understood that such rights had been infringed with the decline of the empire, dislocation of the royal family, and fall in the revenue yield from the provinces. Regional "nabobs" such as the one in Bengal, who had been formerly subject to the control of the diwans (revenue officers), had now taken advantage of the weakness of Delhi and had replaced the payment of regular revenue with a nominal tribute.[23] British obeisance to the Mughals was however, short-lived. Lord Clive would state in his speech to the House of Commons in 1769 that the British conquest of Bengal had made a mockery of it all; the Great Mogul was now the "*de jure* Mogul, *de facto* nobody at all, . . ." and the nabob just a servant of the Company.[24]

A precise definition of sovereignty had always been elusive. Clive had initially tried to solve the problem by claiming that he had "established the power of the Great Mogul" and thus had effectively restored his rights in 1765.[25] He based his theory on the "masked system" of administering Bengal in the interests of the Company while leaving undisturbed the acknowledged sovereignty of the Mughals, but it was difficult to maintain this arrangement as long as the French remained in India as a national threat. Edmund Burke went much further than his contemporaries in identifying the fundamentally dual source of the political authority of the Company. The first derived from the charter by which it was endowed by the Crown and authorized by act of Parliament; the second derived from the collective charters and grants bestowed on the Company by the Mughal emperor, particularly the "great Charter by which they acquired the High Stewardship of the Kingdoms of Bengal, Bahar and Orissa in 1765."[26] To Burke this duality was not an inherent contradiction. He held the sovereignty of the Mughals sacred and inalienable, and considered the duty and responsibility of the English Company towards the subjects of the Mughal empire valid even after its loss of effective power:

> For when the Company acquired that office in India, an English Corporation became an integral part of the Mogul Empire. When Great Britain assented to that grant virtually, and afterwards took advantage of it, Great Britain made a virtual act of union with that country, by which they bound themselves as securities for their subjects, to preserve the people in all rights, laws and liberties, which their natural original Sovereign was bound to enforce, if he had been in a condition to enforce it. So that the two duties flowing from two different sources are now united in one. . . .[27]

Burke had thus made a remarkable case for the natural and common source of rights and obligations for a possible constitutional arrangement of British India, which would, of course, never come to fruition. A few years earlier, in 1767, during the Chatham (Pitt the elder) ministry, Parliament had made an attempt to secure for the nation at home a rightful share of the revenues of eastern India collected by the East India Company, to establish a firm constitutional arrangement between the English and the company-state, and to declare the Crown's right to the revenue of India.[28] The plan was eventually abandoned in the face of opposition from constituencies that saw in it the overreach of king and Parliament into the proprietary rights of chartered corporations. In fact the whole question of territorial rights acquired by conquest or gift and the precise legality of the Company's possessions in relation to the Crown were never to be addressed fully.

Years later, in 1829, Rammohan Roy, the noted Bengali scholar and social reformer, traveled to England as an agent of the king of Delhi to deliver a letter of complaint to the king of Great Britain regarding the financial state and upkeep of the royal family. The Mughal emperor had conferred on him the title of "Rajah" (king) to elevate him in rank above that of the officials of the East India Company, an act that annoyed the governor-general in Calcutta, who refused to recognize the envoy and his title.[29] The Court of Directors of the Company, having considered the claims of the king of Delhi, referred the papers back to the Board of Control, insisting that the matter be settled by the appropriate authority in India.[30] It is likely that the Company did not wish to see the issue become public knowledge. This was considered a secret matter, and there were allegations that Roy had somehow gotten hold of official documents in a clandestine fashion, a charge that led to the resignation of his friend and deputy envoy to England, William Montgomery Martin.[31]

Roy was pleading for a reconsideration of the stipend allowed to the emperor and his family in Delhi in support of "fallen royalty." He presented the case as concerning both "national character" and "public justice," asserting that the natives of India were entitled to appeal directly to justice of the British Crown as British subjects under its protection, which was recognized by Parliament and by the fact that the Board of Control had been created in the first place to bring Indian affairs under the direct supervision of the ministry.[32]

Roy pointed out that the Company government had agreed in 1827 that it did not recognize the "right of the throne of Delhi to confer honorary distinctions on any *but* the Royal servants." The royal house of Timur had exercised such a right from time immemorial, often in favor of the Company's own servants and Residents, and thus the refusal was an "unmerited insult," a violation of the assurances given by Wellesley in 1804. Roy detected a great deal of unease in the attitude of the directors of the Company:

> These various obstructions and the direct breach of their own engagements, rules and regulations on the part of the local government can only be ascribed to their anxious solicitude to prevent an appeal to England; from a well founded apprehension that their treatment of the King of Delhi would not meet with the approval of a high minded nation.[33]

In contrast to the public concern regarding India in parliament, Roy found the Court of Directors to be indifferent to the grievances of the natives of India and felt they hardly inspired "confidence in the justice and protection of the British Government."[34] He found the board much more willing than the court to accept the authenticity of his nomination and receive him into the audience of the British sovereign "as a subject of His Majesty's remote dominions" representing the Indian emperor, whose sovereignty was still dependent on the British Crown. Some of the native subjects of British India, he reminded Charles Grant, president of the Board of Control, were now "capable of appreciating the character of the local government as well as the nature of the British Constitution, and the relation subsisting between them," unlike the masses, who thought that the "Company was a venerable and old lady who sent out her favorite sons successively to take charge of the country."[35] In India the Company had assumed a sovereign power that tolerated little expression of public opinion, emboldened by the vast distance between itself and the British Parliament. A denial of appeals from Indian subjects, Roy argued, would imply that they were "virtually excluded from the benefits of the British Constitution."[36]

Although the board would eventually uphold the authority of the Indian government on this matter,[37] the appeal of the king of Delhi made board members edgy. They were obliged to restate that the Indian government had the right vested in it by Parliament (through the valid portions of its original charter) to confer titles and distinctions on the natives, to make war and peace, to enter into treaties with the native states of India, and to make rules and regulations for the governance of native subjects.[38] They also contended that the right of the Crown to interfere in Indian affairs was restricted by law. The ability to endow native chiefs and states with honorary distinctions was seen as qualitatively distinct from those conferred by the crown on "the European part of its subjects."[39] Natives and Europeans were subject to two different sets of laws—British and British-Indian. It was the East India Company in whose name the administration of India was vested and upon which the natives were "taught to look as the sole governing party" exercising the power of life and death over them.

Rammohan Roy, who died shortly afterwards, in 1833, and was buried in Bristol,[40] did not live to see any agreeable resolution to the questions he had raised, but much like Burke, he had arrived at the conclusion that the privilege and obligation of sovereignty joined the Mughal emperor and the king of Britain, and that Lord Wellesley's promise to Delhi was a binding contract and "a plain question of national faith."[41] He was quick to grasp that without a concession of minimal rights flowing from the Crown of England to subjects of the East India Company's empire, their right to property, and clearly the title of the king of Delhi to his estate, patrimonial inheritance, and share of revenues from former dominions, were indeed based on an insecure and even invalid, constitutional agreement.

CONSTITUTING THE COMPANY RAJ

Rammohan Roy's critical remarks provide a point of departure for my contention in this book that a distant and disputed sovereignty was part and parcel of the body politic of the early British Empire in India. Going by prevalent constitutional ruling as well as natural law—to paraphrase Henry Hallam (1827)[42]—as an independent sovereign the Mughal emperor was not amenable to the jurisdiction of the Company as long as he was considered supreme within his own territory. Under usual circumstances sovereigns were considered inviolable if they exercised any measure of dominion, and this would have pertained to the Mughal emperor as well, for he had not been dethroned, neither had he abdicated.[43]

There were other equally vexatious instances of Indian potentates who had emerged in the eighteenth century independent of the influence of Delhi. One case in point had been the so-called "puppet" nawabs of Bengal, where the British were in charge of the former ruling family's keep and the upkeep and appearance of the fort at Murshidabad, including expenses for servants and the female quarters which the Resident described disparagingly as indulgence toward "eastern luxury" that would not bear scrutiny in a full public audit.[44] In matters of revenue and the judiciary, there continued to be legal wrangling over the nature of the Nawab's sovereignty, for there was considerable debate as to whether he was indeed, as Hastings termed it, "a mere pageant" or still the master of his own fate, *princeps sui juris*.[45] Agents (supravisors) appointed to collect land revenue in the Bengal countryside found themselves subordinate in rank to the Resident at the nawab's court, which complicated the pecking order of civil servants in the employ of the Company as nominal protectors of the local ruling house.[46] And yet in 1807, the Company spent more than half a million rupees to build a new palace in Murshidabad and protect it against the encroachment of the river, "to contribute to [the Nawab's] comfort and convenience, as well as to promote the dignity of his situation."[47]

An even more troubling diplomatic and military entanglement for the Company was the ruling house of Hyder Ali in Mysore, which would become the sworn national enemy of the British by the end of the century. The dissolution of Tipu Sultan's household and the careful sequestration of his children illustrate the inordinate delicacy with which the matter of native regal authority was handled in British India during this period. The changing attitude toward Indian monarchy and sovereignty thus reveals the refashioning of an expatriate British regal identity, however deficient or plagued with contradiction and inconsistency.

John Kaye, historian of the Indian mutiny summed up the relationship between the Company and the Mughals till 1857 as a "political paradox" in which the Mughal emperor was a "pensioner, a pageant, and a puppet . . . a King, yet no King—a something and yet a nothing—a reality and a sham at the same time."[48] Monarchy as an institution could not be dispensed with nonchalantly in India. Coins bore the name of the Mughal emperor in India until at least 1835, and the governor-general and even lesser British officials who ruled in his name continued to accept ritual gifts of obeisance from their Indian subjects. Such displays were crucial to the fabrication of the new dependency in India. Here too, just as in England, to follow Walter Bagehot, the "efficient" parts of the constitution could only follow from the "dignified" parts. Bagehot has argued: "every constitution must first gain authority, and then use authority; it must first win the loyalty and confidence of mankind, and then employ that homage in the work of government."[49] Given the circumstances of imperial expansion, whether such a view applies *mutatis mutandis* to the foundation of Company rule in India is subject to debate. But the appeal of a "fountain of majesty," considered by Bagehot as the most popular and common aspect of the English constitution, with its drama, pageantry, and awe, and one that inspired an "instinctive sentiment of hereditary loyalty" among the subjects, provided the British in India with a much-needed political idiom.[50]

During the period under consideration, the concept of sovereignty in England had become thoroughly assimilated under the rubric of the "king in Parliament," leading to idea of an absolute dominion superceding traditional medieval ideals of liberty, property, and customary rights inherent in the commonwealth.[51] How far the Hobbesian characterization of absolute monarchy as habitual obedience constituting the bond of subject and sovereign applied to Parliament at this very time can be disputed, but of the three possible contenders for sovereignty (to invoke Maitland)—the king, the king in Parliament, and the law—the writ of the "king and Parliament" had become without question the preeminent foundation of authority.[52] More important for our purposes is the fact that in the first half of the eighteenth century the old Whig theory of an Ancient Constitution was being revived and manipulated by Whigs and Tories alike, popularized by opportunists such as Bolingbroke, who promoted the appealing idea of a "patriot king" (*Remarks on the History of England*).[53] This would eventually lead to the widespread notion that the history of England was a natural progression on the path of liberty, where the Norman yoke and Stuart despotism were episodes in the long struggle against tyranny culminating in the heroic and dramatic Revolution of 1688. This assertion of a triumphal march of the English constitution can be seen clearly in the context of dissenting opinion, most notably that of Hume, who refused to concede that a pristine ancient English constitution had been handed down unchanged from generation to generation.[54]

The restoration of legitimate monarchy in England as historical precedent is a subject of peculiar relevance to the formation of British rule in India. The titular and sumptuary obligations of the British in India were not just ornamental, nor were they merely self-serving. Even if the rights and liberties of Indian subjects did not pose a serious threat to the legitimacy of rule, the consecration of the newly founded empire-state remained deeply problematic. Here it was the history of Indian conquest that provided a legible case for the architects of the company Raj, rather than English common law. Although there was no one written corpus that would suffice as the working constitution of the company-state, there evolved nonetheless a constitutional language and style in which the British treated the extent and limits of Indian powers and their various ranks of subordination to the new regime, secured by contractual treaties. The government, property, and land tenure of the Mughals became subjects of great importance during the experiments of the land settlements of Bengal, which exhumed a whole corpus of historical credentials. These papers became the basis on which a virtual constitution of the Mughals was resurrected, what Alexander Dow described as "the despotism of the house of Timur . . . circumscribed by established forms and regulations, which greatly tempered the rigid severity of that form of government."[55] A similar exposition can be traced to a founding collection of documents on the system of land tenure, judiciary, and police in British India that was commissioned by Parliament in 1812—the much-circulated Fifth Report from the Select Committee of the House of Commons regarding the affairs of the Company in India.[56] Robert Grant, addressing proprietors of the India Stock during debates that took place in India House over the renewal of the Company's charter, insisted that there was indeed a constitution of India just as there was in England—the work of ages and the "wonder of the world." The Indian "constitution," in the words of Grant, was:

> the slow creation of years . . . which has not, indeed, attained theoretical perfection, perhaps not even all the practical perfection of which it is capable . . . but of which I will yet be bold to say, that, considering the peculiar circumstances of the country; considering the nature and political capacity of the natives; considering the relations subsisting between the two countries, it is scarcely a less important achievement, than the British constitution itself.[57]

Such rhetoric seems a little premature, especially during a period in which the military and political future of British India had hardly been settled. But it illustrates that the India of the early company Raj had already assumed the appearance of a substantive body politic, endowed with a constitutional history of its own.

Walter K. Firminger, archdeacon of Calcutta and president of the Royal Historical Society, is one historian among a few who tried to show the natural development of such a constitution. In his extensive preface (1917) to the Fifth Report and its supporting documents Firminger furnished a succinct account of the constitutional foundations of British India. He argued that the servants of the Company had put together an internal government in Bengal in the eighteenth century under the "plea that they were acting within the constitution of the Mughal Empire," but in reality, although not fully acknowledged, it was the sword of conquest "that lay behind the civil settlements of the English."[58] By curtailing step by step the military strength on which the native government of Bengal was based, and through the gradual increment of troops and garrisons, which was possible because of their monopoly of land revenue, the British succeeded in forging a series of treaties with the nawabs of Bengal (1757, 1760, 1763, 1765). These, according to Firminger, mark the stages of the advancement of British political intentions. It was useful for the Company to deny the acquisition of "sovereign rights" and to assert that their rule was "within, and not imposed over and above, the Mughal constitution"; it was a posture to keep the French at bay and appease critics back in England who would not tolerate the violation of a cardinal principle of English constitutional law, which stated that British subjects could not acquire territories independently of the crown.[59] The sovereign status of the Company was thus implicated in the very fabrication of its history.

THE MANTLE OF AUTHORITY

A quick glance at the official portraiture of the East India Company makes it clear that the British regarded the representative image of their legitimacy with great concern. Artists who were commissioned to depict events of national importance, such as the conferral of the title of diwan by the Mughal Emperor Shah Alam in 1765 (painted by Benjamin West), a triumphal moment for Clive, or the encounter between the Clive and Mir Jafar after the victory of Plassey, did so with great care and an eye towards historical authenticity. Arthur William Devis completed the painting of Lord Cornwallis receiving the sons of the slain ruler of Mysore, Tipu Sultan, in England in 1803, assembling the sketches and portraits of the princes and their attendants as well as notable British officers who attended the governor-general as a "Historical Picture" for public exhibition.[60] Even the "meanest attendant" was rendered faithfully; dresses and distinctions were painted as observed. Details were drawn, among other sources, from Major John Dirom's *Narrative of the Campaign,* an account that recorded faithfully how Lord Cornwallis had "received the Boys as if they had been his own sons" as well as their melancholy appearance following the death of their father at the gates of the fort and of their mother, who died a few days later "of fright and apprehension."[61] It was a painting that attracted particular notice, for there had been no instance in British history of a prince being delivered as hostage to comply with the terms of a treaty. The details of another remarkable painting by Devis, *Finding the Body of Tippoo,* demonstrates the value of historical accuracy in the memorialization of the moment of conquest and the British regicidal conscience. This was based on the eyewitness account of General Baird, who was in charge of scouring the palace and finding Tipu, the dreaded adversary of Mysore. Baird's account of proceeding to the gateway covered with the bodies of the fallen in battle, exudes the high drama of conquest and deserves to be quoted at length:

> The numbers of the dead, and the darkness of the palace, made it difficult to distinguish one person from another, and the scene was altogether shocking; but aware of the great political importance of ascertaining, beyond the possibility of a doubt, the death of Tippoo, the bodies were ordered to be dragged out, and the Killedar [keeper of the castle] and two other persons were desired to examine them one after another. . . . By a faint glimmering light it was difficult for the Killedar to recognize the features, but the body being brought out, and satisfactorily proved to be that of the Sultan was conveyed in a Palankeen to the Palace where it was again recognized by the eunuchs and other servants of the Family . . . brought from under the gateway, his eyes were open and the body was so warm, that for a moment Col. Wellesley and myself were doubtful whether he was not alive. . . .[62]

Robert Kerr Porter would paint the same scene again as *The Discovery of the Body of Tipu Sultan* (1802). Colonel Mark Wilks, one of the first major British historians of southern India, in his account of the Sultan's death adds further that the sons who had surrendered to General Harris were also asked to identify their father's body, which was thereafter interred on the same evening at their request. The funeral was arranged by Company officers. Tipu's remains were deposited next to his father, Hyder Ali, in the Lal Bag mausoleum "with all the splendour and distinction which the religious observance of Mahommedan rites, and the military honours of European sepulture could bestow."[63] Tipu's heir was not restored to the throne, for it was felt that the inevitable loss of power and territory to the English would have perpetuated the aversion of the house toward the English. The family was granted a fair payment for maintenance and discreetly removed from Mysore. An old Hindu family was restored to the throne of Mysore.

These accounts of Tipu's death reminds us how carefully the Company dealt with its deposed enemies in India, and indeed how precariously close the British were drawn to the indigenous idioms of kingship. Mather Brown's engraving, *Departure of the Sons of Tipu from the Zenana* (1793), captures a bit of the rue over the passing of indigenous royalty.

It is still difficult to determine exactly how the British viewed the question of Indian and oriental monarchy in the context of their empire, even if it is clear that they were aware that such monarchy had to be redefined and circumscribed in the context of the Company Raj. There was certainly recognition of sheer military prowess as a source of justifiable authority, which is one of the reasons why defeated enemies of the Company were easily assimilated into a national-imperial historical memory.

Historically, the "Great Mogul" had always been a subject of fancy along with Tamerlane and Kublai Khan. Dryden's *Aureng-Zebe,* first performed in 1675 at the Theatre Royal in Drury Lane, was closely based on Bernier's travel account, *Histoire de la dernière révolutions des états du grand mogul* (1670). In Dryden, quite unlike his portrait in Bernier, Prince Aurangzeb is introduced as a legitimate successor to the throne and not a usurper who deposes and murders his brothers in cold intrigue. His morality is exemplary, and his actions are dictated by courage and conscience. The sanctity of blood and righteous force constitute a legitimate monarchy:

> I know my fortune in extremes does lie:
> The sons of Indostan must reign or die;
> That desperate hazard courage does create
> As he plays frankly who has least estate. . . .[64]

Dryden and spectators of Restoration drama at Drury Lane worried little about the legality of oriental monarchs in the seventeenth century, and this unfamiliarity and theatrical license would perhaps have still been the case

almost a century later (1774), when a slightly different version of the play
was produced at the Covent Garden as *The Prince of Agra.*

But even the most careful scholars of India were captivated by the terrible legacy of the Islamic invaders of India. Sir William Jones, in his *Histoire
de Nader Chah* (an adaptation of Muhammad Mahdi's history), dedicated to
the king of Denmark, exhibits more than just scholarly enthusiasm for the
invader of Persia and India. While the text is a tribute to the greatness of
Nadir Shah, a hero, "roaring lion of the century . . . the mighty conqueror,
clement in justice," in his preface Jones presents Nadir Shah's bid for power
as the dramatic reversal of rightful sovereignty. It is nothing but an account
of terror and crime that leads this "famous warrior of fortune" to a perilous
precipice: a cautionary tale of power that spares only the "abject mouthed"
(*la bouche servile*) scribes who bestow the mantle of a "conqueror" and other
splendid titles on a scourge instead of an open condemnation of his injustice
and tyranny.[65] A more equivocal sentiment prevails in John Malcolm's ode
to Persia (1814) written after his journey to that country:

> The daring robber, born to high renown,
> First saves his country, and then grasps its crown. . . .
> A suffering world to Heaven for mercy calls;
> Beneath the dagger's point the Tyrant falls!
> Yet still his Persia boasts her NADIR's name,
> Whose genius rous'd her fallen sons to fame. . . .[66]

If Nadir Shah provided the most menacing image of despotism, easy to dismiss as the merciless plunderer of Delhi, Tamerlane (Timur Lang), from
whom the Indian Mughals drew some of their royal genealogy—an equally
vicious figure in history—was paid a more handsome, if grudging, tribute.
In his *History of Persia,* John Malcolm describes situation in India at the time
of the invasion of Timur:

> India had frequently been overrun by the hardy warriors of the north. Since the inva-
> sion of Ghizni, Hindoo princes had ceased to reign; and it had continued subject to dif-
> ferent dynasties of Mahommedan monarchs, who, in their turns, were overthrown by
> powerful conquerors. The destructive sword of Timour had desolated those fields,
> which, after a series of extraordinary revolutions, were destined to flourish under his
> descendents; and the scenes of his bloodiest and most inhuman massacres, by a strange
> vicissitude of fortune, became those in which his name, as the renowned ancestor of a
> long race of emperors, was most venerated.[67]

Such persistent engagement with royalty in India, howsoever unlawful or
despotic, can be explained in the context of the changing institution of kingship
back home in England. During the later part of the reign of George III, especially in the context of the Anglo-French struggle unfolding in the aftermath
of the French Revolution, the British monarchy, which had been steadily
stripped of the means of political absolutism, found a new basis in popular

imagination and reappeared as a national symbol. There has been some debate on the extent to which common patriotic sentiment grew around the figure of George III towards the end of the eighteenth century, but the domestic idealization of the royal family, paternal attributes of kingship, and the rise of public ceremony around royalty were certainly features of a new era of patriotic feeling.[68] It has been argued that the historic resilience of the institution of monarchy in England can be traced to the mythopoeic idea of the king's two bodies, as studied by Kantorowicz: the body corporeal and the body eternal.[69] While the institutions surrounding royalty were secularized, the central figure of the monarch reinvigorated the basis of authority in law, religion, and politics; while public and political alignments and sensibilities changed, new meanings were read into the traditional images of the Crown.[70]

The institution of kingship was seen as natural in a despotic society, and the perception that Indians were particularly amenable to a firm and paternalist monarchical rule, as Bernard Cohn has richly illustrated, was further confirmed during Victorian India, after the great rebellion of 1857.[71] Although a chartered corporation, the East India Company saw its territorial sovereignty in India through their very own idioms of royalty and subject-hood. Its tenure was marked by a struggle between the instinctive, national expressions of empire, and the more conscious attempt to make the foundations of British political supremacy legible to Indians.

THE RIDDLE OF "BRITISH INDIA"

The story of the British in India during the era of conquest and territorial expansion is a narrative split along two discrete historical registers. I reconsider in this book the relationship between these two pasts: the unremarked-upon complicity between the island history of the British Empire and the early history of British rule in India. Their entwined histories raise the question: How was the idea of Britain as a national and imperial entity articulated in the formation of the company-state? And what sort of historical mirror was it for Britain's political economy, public conduct, and national character?

In many instances, territorial expansion went ahead far too quickly for a mercantile corporation. It had to answer to Parliament for its military campaigns; it was often financially strapped, and strained to administer Indian territories. Company rule in India persevered because it was sustained by a burgeoning imperial nationalism. The director of the Company mused in 1821 that it was not easy to analyze "nature and sources of the British power in India," but that one of the principal elements was "our union, or the faculty of acting in concert under the guidance of a single mind."[72] It was not only the wisdom and energy of the councils, he asserted, but also surely the "intelligence, and vigor, and enterprise of the British character" that constituted a "solid foundation of strength" whose effect in India had been "heightened by the imagination."[73] Conquest clearly provided one of the enduring images of supremacy. In Sir John Malcom's description of the success of British exploits in India, the British army seemed to tower over its enemies, and move "amidst ten thousand of its rabble opponents like a giant with a thousand hands, which defend or strike according to the dictates of *one mind. . . .*"[74]

The history of Britain's commercial and political struggle for supremacy India in the later eighteenth century suggests a degree of anxiety about the tribulations of long-distance rule and its effect on the British character. Indian society presented Britons both apprehension and enticement along with the prospects of wealth. It was feared that young men with windfalls would turn into "nabobs" and dissipate their dignity and integrity in the luxuriant tropics. Religious sensibilities and moral fiber would become suspect in the wilderness of Indian idolatry. Such notions were reinforced by threats of war, disease, and untimely death. It was also dreaded that both manhood and blood would become suspect in the society of Indians and in cohabitation with women of a darker hue. The response to these worries in the long run was the gradual segregation of Britons and their Indian subjects, a distance that was made formal as the company-state became more firmly entrenched in the Indian soil. These measures ensured that India would never become a creole society or even a settler colony.

British India was thus removed from the history of the islands and remained distant from the common experience that is associated with patriotic sentiments at home. The most pronounced English prejudices were directed, as Michael Duffy has illustrated, against Europeans as foreigners, in the eighteenth century most commonly the French.[75] Indians hardly entered the popular historical imagination of Britons at home. If anything, in contrast to the empire closer to home in Scotland and Ireland or in North America, bits of India recovered from the native powers by war and treaty could only present the distorted specter of a nation unrealized, a relic of a bygone civilization, lacking patriotism, unity, and a moral coherence for its existence. And yet over time, the perception of India would acquire a new validity, fixity, and meaning and, in turn, in its very difference would contribute to new notions of belonging to Britain in the farthest recesses of the empire.

The history of British rule in India also provides glimpses of some of the most heroic and succinct expressions of Anglo-Briton political identity. One could still argue, surely, as Eric Stokes once did, that although India "undoubtedly hardened certain traits in the English culture" it still "played no central part in fashioning the distinctive qualities of English civilization," and that it was, rather, "a disturbing force, a magnetic power placed at the periphery tending to distort the natural development of Britain's character."[76] Stokes was echoing what John Seely had already articulated in the previous century, that during the first phase of British rule in India, a "mischevious reaction from India upon England was prevented."[77] England and the British Empire had managed to avert what the Romans could not—the nefarious effect of the cultures of colonized nations that could rot the core of the conquering, civilizing state:

> England on the other hand is not weakened at all by the virtue that goes out from her. She tries to raise India out of the medieval into the modern phase, and in the task she meets with difficulties and even incurs dangers, but she incurs no risk whatever of being drawn down by India towards her lower level, or even of being checked for a moment in her natural development.[78]

Such admissions in themselves are significant in that they find the idea of England, and thus of Britishness writ large, as a historically given, unchangeable substance, owing virtually nothing to the outer reaches of empire. Indeed, contemporaries saw these very same national qualities as a bastion against the cultural pull of India. Sir James Mackintosh, illustrious British historian and member of the House of Commons who began his Indian career as chief justice in the court of vice-admiralty in Bombay in 1804, urged the grand jury in his first charge (July 21, 1804) that their careers in India were a test of their patriotism:

> I am persuaded that your feelings would have entirely accorded with mine; convinced that, both as jurors and as private gentlemen, you will always consider yourselves as intrusted, in this remotest region of the earth, with the honor of that beloved country, which, I trust, becomes more dear to you, as I am sure it does to me, during every new moment of absence: that, in your intercourse with each other, as well as with the natives of India, you will *keep unspotted the ancient character of the British nation*. . . .[79]

Nationalism was thus reinforced in exile for those who took upon themselves the task of civilizing the distant outposts of empire.

In the light of a plethora of recent writing on its former colonies, it is becoming increasingly difficult to view the natural development of Britain in isolation from its imperial extension, the exclusive circle of nation from the great *orbis imperium*. Anthony Pagden argues that British imperial ventures of the eighteenth century were significantly different in conception from European exercises in the Americas in preceding centuries. British expansion in India and Africa took place in the period in which the ideology of universal empire, derived from the Roman *imperium* and its medieval survivals, had become patently moribund.[80] If this is true, then, notwithstanding the common historical analogy with Rome, the ideology of empire in India should have originated from within the imperial experience in Britain itself. David Armitage has recently suggested that there is indeed much to reconsider about the indigenous origins of British imperial ideas, the historiography of which needs to be considered more closely together with the national history of England, Ireland, and Scotland.[81] Yet, however valuable these revisions of imperial historiography may be, they leave little room for an exploration of the nature of the British Empire and the translation of its ideas of dominion and sovereignty from the Indian end of the spectrum, which, after all, belongs in the same historical epoch. This is not simply a plea to reinsert the Indian pale into the historiographical fray of empire, but rather to ask the question why India has remained such an exceptional case, an experience *sui generis,* and why the Indian archives of the East India Company have not been seen as witness to the same ideological formations that were played out in Britain itself. It is becoming increasingly clear to recent historians of the British Empire that there are indeed multiple archival traces of Britain that reflect the fragmented nature of the imperial venture, and that a new imperial historiography would have to contend squarely with the question of how such archives are to be sutured.[82]

It can well be argued that the British Empire in India is one of the earliest sites where distinctions between Britons and their Indian subjects were put on trial: a vortex much like the nefarious Black Hole of Calcutta, whose centripetal tendencies could draw out the most anxious, as well as the most confident, assertions of British exclusiveness and superiority. Homi Bhabha writes that the colonial difference is the "effect of uncertainty that afflicts the discourse of power" which also "estranges the familiar symbol of English 'national' authority."[83] At some point after the fact of conquest, the original designs of moral, enlightened rule were sullied in the habitual maintenance of the colonial order, a point where further representation would follow at the risk of mockery and of empty semblance. I find Bhabha's ruminations suggestive as they bear upon the compatibility of empire and nation and as they provide a mode of interrogation against the grain of received wisdom on the irreconcilable differences of race and culture as opaque categories. An unintended effect of colonial power, it can be argued, was the inevitable miscegenation of such categories, enabling subtler forms of subversion for the colonized. The quotidian realities of colonialism in the long term, following Bhaba, reduced the grand symbols of domination to an anxious sign, causing "a dominant discourse to split along the axis of its power to be representative, authoritative."[84]

While this account is informed by the expanding literature of critical, literary, and postcolonial theory, I suggest that the history of colonization in India splinters the normative binary of the self and the other in unexpectedly instructive ways. In part this is a quarrel with the way the scholarship on orientalism has reduced a whole array of discourses to the essential dyad of dominant and subordinate, colonizer and colonized. Notwithstanding the political acuity of such a perspective, such binaries in the end threaten to dissipate the very value of the psychosocial dimensions of colonialism that are explored with such sensitivity by Frantz Fanon.[85] More pertinently for our purpose, they do not leave much space for a more nuanced historical sociology of colonial rule. This is a study, thus, of the *skewed* correspondence between the conqueror and the conquered, where paradoxes of identity afflicted both, but in quite unequal measure.

I am indebted here to the feminist scholarship of recent years that has redrawn the boundaries of historical investigation by foregrounding the place, experience, and articulations of women within the passages of empire and by bringing the differences of gender most meaningfully into the debate over domestic, national, and colonial discourses.[86] Insofar as English*men* are key protagonists in this book, sections are devoted to a study of the forms of sociability, moral authority, and sexual conduct among traders and company servants. I view such aspects of the colonizing culture as pivotal to the beleaguered character of the civilizing agent. My examination of the forms of the colonial polity is informed by such attributes, and it extends and qualifies cultural approaches to English state formation suggested by Philip Corrigan and Derek Sayer in their classic commentary on the subject, *The Great Arch.*[87]

AN OUTLINE OF THE BOOK

English traders and Indian kingdoms had been interacting for almost a hundred years before wars for political and economic advantage were waged by the British in the second half of the eighteenth century. Trading settlements and manufactories, lodged in the cosmopolitan and mercantile fringes of the Mughal Empire and its successor states, brought people from the British Isles face-to-face with a very distinct culture even before the shape of Great Britain had fully emerged and before the place of divergent cultures, languages, and kingdoms within it had been fully determined. When the British were fending off the French in India and dislodging unfriendly Indian kingdoms, American colonies were in rebellion, Scotland had just been integrated into the kingdom with the suppression of the Highlanders, and Ireland was still in discontent.

Merchants, soldiers, ensigns, cadets, and adventurers in this period assimilated in many ways to indigenous culture, especially on the coasts of the Indian subcontinent. Trade depended on familiarity with local courts and patronage, middlemen and dependents, and Englishmen were drawn into Indian society through their native wives, mistresses, "natural children," and extended households. This book examines how and why, at the end of rivalry with other European trading companies and during the subjugation of native rulers, there was a sharp decline in intimacy between the British soldiers, merchants, and civil servants, and the Indians who would soon become their subjects. How was such social and political distance created? How was it maintained through the period of ascendancy of British rule in the subcontinent?

Ideas of racial and civilizational distinction and new modes of political and economic imagination, this book argues, became crucial to the distance that separated the Britons from Indians. At the same time, new forms of knowledge familiarized India and its inhabitants, reflecting contemporary disciplines of natural history and political economy. India and its inhabitants were thus transformed into objects of study, making it possible for politicians, financiers, and the educated at home to gain a common knowledge of the subcontinent that was not solely dependent on the incidental account of missionaries, travelers, and traders. India ceased to be just a frontier of mercantile adventurism. Subject to debate over the limits of the exercise of state power and the role of the East India Company, by the turn of the century, it had gained rapid visibility in Parliament and the in politics of Georgian England.

I contend that in the era of conflict over trade and expansion as well as the subsequent period of reform and regulation, during which a handful of Britons were put in a position of power over a vast dependency, new categories of distance and impartiality had to be invented in order to keep the rulers and the ruled in place. It is in this context that identities—patriotic, masculine, national, racial, and imperial—took shape. Much has been written in recent years on the representation of colonial subjects and the hegemonic framework of orientalist knowledge, but relatively few studies focus on an earlier moment in the formation of imperial rule in India, when the identities of the colonizer and colonized, the observers and the observed were much more fluid, historically contingent, and vulnerable to caprice.[88]

This book introduces two major propositions. The first is that the period of British ascendancy in India, roughly spanning a chronology of sixty-odd years (1770–1830) prior to the advent of the age of reform, entailed much more than military conquest, signing of treaties, monopolistic commerce, and acquisition of territory. In these years the East India Company not only waged a crucial battle for the legitimacy of rule but also articulated an expatriate sovereignty, civilization, and polity. The charter of this new colonial polity, as we have just seen, was not clear; it was not based on settlement but on the idea of custodianship of a vast, new, and alien subject body. The second proposition is that the acquisition of India—especially in the context of the loss of the American colonies, Anglo-French rivalry, and the Seven Years War—accentuated and cohered Anglo-British nationalism in the Indian empire. The most extruding accents of this imperial nation are to be found in very particular histories of institutions, disciplines, and practices that attended the formation of the colonial state, laid out in the first chapter. Through forms of the state derived from prevalent modes of statecraft in Georgian England, reigning notions of political economy and governance in England found their way into the Indian subcontinent.

Among the many forms of knowledge that came to the fore by which the British gained a new perspective of India as their own domain, I consider the discipline of history as perhaps the most significant. Early British historians of India, largely influenced by the Scottish moral enlightenment, discovered an ancient culture and a country that had been subject to many waves of conquest and eventually cleft into two distinct races, Hindu and Muslim. The Hindus were by nature and by virtue of their past subordinate to their Muslim conquerors, a fundamental fact that constituted the basis of despotism in India. Such representations of the Indian past, I suggest in the second chapter of the book, provided a source of manifest destiny for the British as the last conquerors of India, entrusted with a fallen civilization. The moral endorsement of history provided much more than legitimacy for the administrators of the East India Company.

In Chapter 3 I explore spatial incarnations of the state and its sovereignty through a study of imperial cartography and its iconic significance. I look at how British India as political space emerged as the result of an invasive perspective in which military surveys materialized over time into normative geographical images of India. The last two chapters concern emergent forms through which new modes of self and society were ordered in colonial India: domesticity and race. Chapter 4 takes up the issues of gender, charting the grammar of the masculine and feminine in the redefinition of ruler and subject and also in the inherent conceptions of domesticity in early ethnographies and travelogues. The first classification of Britain's Indian subjects can be found in these descriptions of domestic life, work, and bodies of the inhabitants of the Indian countryside in the period in which the company-state established its dominion. I examine the ambiguities and contradictions in the domestic ideology of the colonial state and the uncertain ordering of the gender and sexuality of its subjects. The history of colonial domesticity, I argue, is key to intrinsic idioms of British rule. The last chapter deals with questions of race and ethnicity, examining how notions and practices of sanguinary division between Britons and Indians came to be institutionalized. It considers the ideas of nationality and race as coextensive, which can be studied as a natural *taxon* that refracted the hierarchy of ruler and subject in early colonial India.

This book responds to a straightforward question: What should the historian of India endeavor to know of Britain's domestic past? Other questions follow. Where should one approach the common historical frontiers of the nation and empire? Where can be found the most crucial interlocutions between imperial and national identities for the new rulers of India? How vulnerable were their ideas of selfhood to cultural diffusion? I attempt to answer these questions by excavating the imperial strata of national characteristics: the skeins of language, race, nation, history, geography, habit, morality, and religion that precipitated Anglo-British identity in colonial India. The book reconsiders thus the very premise that essential facets of the British national character were fabricated at home or, at a stretch, in only Anglo-Saxon settler colonies.[89] Aspects of Britishness, as Linda Colley has demonstrated, fashioned in the aftermath of England's triumph during the Seven Years War, emerged also in relation to changing frontiers of empire and to new and competing nationalities within and without, such as the Scots, the Welsh, and the Americans.[90] It was also redefined and elaborated, I argue in this book, in less expected places such as India. The effect of the acquisition of Indian territories, another trophy of the extended conflict with the French, was, of course, not as clear.

Nevertheless, India provided the context for a new imperial nationalism. Whether or not articulations of Anglo-British character in India had a lasting impact on identities back in Britain is to some extent irrelevant to this exercise. I am primarily concerned here with the emergence of a more contingent nationalism that surfaced in India through the simultaneous inscription and effacement of its affinity with the subordinate culture. My task here has been to grasp the historical moment in which this distance was ritualized. The early British experience in India underscores the sheer contingency of the political regime in India, articulated in forms of the state and its political economy, in cartographic representation, in norms of domesticity, in racial distinctiveness, and, perhaps most important of all, in the narrative twists of history.

The conduct of English authority in India enables us to study closely within a relatively narrow compass the workings of an expatriate civilization, forced into months of exile on the sea and then years in an alien land, and pressed into the administration of a people little understood or even liked. An Indo-British perspective from around the turn of the century, which precipitated, in Bernard Cohn's phrase, "an idealized adolescent view," or perhaps an institutionalized memory, of British culture and society back home, provides clues to a very different historiography of empire.[91] One of the tasks of this book is to return some of the burden of authenticity to the agents of empire, rather than lay it once more on those who were subjected in various capacities, as a rejoinder in part to the ever-increasing volume of scholarship on the construction of national identity as indigenous responses to colonial rule.[92]

1

The State and Its Colonial Frontiers

THE GEORGIAN STATE IN INDIA

Histories of the British Empire and the Commonwealth have seldom wavered from the general rule that while the theater of empire is staged overseas, forces that shape the nation-state belong rightfully at home. This historiographical insularity of the English state is important not only for the purpose of a national historical narrative that would relegate empire to the peripheries, but also to perpetuate the idea that rule in the colonies was founded on the raw logic of economic exploitation, was reared on indigenous institutions and practices, and remained secluded from significant developments of the state and civil society on the domestic front. This chapter presents a view of the eighteenth-century English state from the colonial end of its compass, attempting to show how commercial expansionism in India during the Georgian period presupposed a more or less coherent ideology of rule. A particular incarnation of that state can be found in the beginnings of British dominion over India. Although this period has usually been seen as dominated by the concerns of trade and mercantilist expansion, it can be shown that the economic objectives of colonial rule, plainly manifest as they were for contemporaries, were never far from their juridical and moral implications. The early colonial regime attempted to replicate in India a political economy that would shore up Britain's long-standing pursuit of wealth and strategic advantage and secure the exclusion of national rivals on the European continent in that part of the hemisphere.

An argument for homologous state formation at home and in the colony may unsettle, perhaps, the given national boundaries of historical reckoning. Yet a reconsideration of the historiographical reach of Great Britain, long

1

after J. G. A. Pocock's invitation to a radical expansion of British history to involve the Scottish, the Irish, and the wider Atlantic world, would in itself be nothing new.[1] This, however, is part of an account of particular forms of knowledge and rule that traveled to later eighteenth-century India, pointing to an intimate connection that would, I hope, question and revise the division of historiographical labor between histories of England, the British Empire, and colonial India, and at a stretch, Ireland in the seventeenth and Scotland in the eighteenth century. This chapter concentrates on two related themes, namely, the English provenance[2] of the state established in eastern India by the East India Company, and implications of overseas imperial expansion for the nation-state at home.

Historians of the British Empire, even in recent times, have been rather hard put to reconcile specific interests of rule in the colony to the overall dictates of empire, or, to employ C. A. Bayly's terms, the "reactive and pragmatic aspects of colonial policy" to "authoritarian and ideological British imperialism."[3] Histories of the particular colonies, especially after the breakup of empire in the last century, have generally followed the outlines of the postcolonial nation-state, while wide-ranging histories of the British Empire have remained at odds with the domestic and national histories of England and Britain. A related problem has been that of chronology: Did colonial settlement precede or follow imperial objectives? In the case of India, which was never to become a settler colony, how did the contingencies of trade and war translate into the notion of a long-term dependency?

Such contradictions between the instrumentality of colonial rule and the ideology of empire, I shall argue, are not too difficult to reconcile. For one thing, empire, nation, and the monopoly of chartered corporations were implied *simultaneously* in colonial conquest. The attention in this chapter is thus on the infrastructure of the company-state itself, as a conduit of extraterritorial state-building. The viability of colonial expansion, particularly in the eighteenth century, cannot be conceived without the profound ideological and cultural mandate of the Hanoverian state, articulated and imposed—as Corrigan and Sayer demonstrate convincingly—through the institutions of parliamentary sovereignty, private and public property, natural rights of man, and the primacy of law.[4] My usage of the term "colonial," it should be added, thus follows not necessarily the linear chronology of military conquest and expansion, but along the terms of a certain regime of political reasoning inherent in the mercantilist commercial drive, a whole ensemble of articulations, measures, and policies both eristic and faithful to a certain vision of power and authority (what Foucault might call a *dispositif*) whose directions are marked at both ends: the parliamentary process in England as well as the quotidian administrative routines of the first phase of rule in the Indian interior.

The English settlement of eastern India, the Bengal presidency, founded along with its counterparts in Madras and Bombay, began to assert its political autonomy against indigenous powers during the first decades of the eighteenth century, and between 1757 and 1763 laid the early foundations of a mercantilist regime in defense of its commercial enterprise. In these years, during the much maligned rule of the East India Company in the chartered colony of Bengal, a certain species of statehood was undoubtedly being forged, although *within* the limits of what some contemporary observers regarded as "indirect rule." In the documentary thicket of debates on the legitimacy of rule, fair and free trade, monopolies and corruption, in parliamentary speeches and accusations, and in the endless number of pamphlets and petitions on foreign and inland trade, one can well detect the first drafts of a colonial state laid out by traders and financiers.

The Indian subcontinent, to be sure, was not the only place where a chartered company was operating from England and engaging in trade, pillage, and military confrontations with the indigenous population.[5] The specific history of the East India Company in India can be understood only in the broader transatlantic context of other competing overseas chartered corporations such as the Royal African Company, which dealt directly and indirectly in ivory and slaves on the African coasts, and the Hudson's Bay Company, which traded in fur in North America. Such products were thus in direct competition with spice, cloth, saltpeter, and indigo from India. The extension of the Seven Years War into the Indian Ocean and the subcontinent catapulted the East India Company and its army in India into political prominence. With the relinquishing of sovereignty to America and the fear of a national and imperial rival in France, questions of colonial possession and settlement in India took on a much-heightened importance for the British nation, especially in the last two decades of the eighteenth century, when the Indian seaboard became pivotal to imperial expansion in Asia and Africa.

Along with fields of national contention opened up by overseas ventures, the experience of the so-called "First Empire" at home would prove formative in India. The final union of Scotland, particularly the subjugation of the Highlands after Culloden, the military survey of William Roy (comparable to his colleague James Rennell's survey of India), and the passing of the Abolition of Heritable Jurisdiction Act in 1747, were thus events of paramount importance to the future of Britain's Indian possessions. Between 1784 and 1801, Henry Dundas, the law advocate of Scotland, became the unofficial secretary of state and whip hand on the Board of Control: a body consisting of six privy councillors appointed by the Crown that reserved all political power in India, including the privilege of recalling British officers, and oversaw annexation and possession abroad.[6] The exercise of patronage in India by the directors of the Company made it possible to recruit Scotsmen into the Indian service. Toward the end of the eighteenth century not only Dundas, but Charles Grant, Hugh Inglis, and David Scott were all responsible for providing many of Jacobite background with careers in India.[7]

Dundas, held culpable by many contemporaries for the "Scotticization of India," was singularly influential during the passage of Pitt's India Bill leading to the India Act of 1784, instrumental in the reception and management of administrative problems posed by early British India, and, as the "unofficial minister for India," was one of the main advocates of British imperial expansion.[8] The period of William Pitt's ministry was crucial to the outcome of debates about the nature of Crown and parliamentary control over Indian affairs. Much of this was a fight between Company directors and the board over the strings of patronage, and it was the fiercely defended monopoly of the Company that narrowly defeated Dundas's move to reduce the Company's army and send regular Crown troops to the east, although he adamantly declared that the board had the power to apply the entire revenue of India to its defense, leaving the Company "a sixpence for their investments."[9] Despite strong Whiggish currents in favor of direct accountability of rule and patronage in India to Parliament, during these years the task ruling of India was left in substance to the Court of Directors and the governor-general, while both were held directly answerable to the board. This was a lasting framework for the Indian empire in the years to come.

In India, notions of military, societal, and racial superiority on the part of East India Company administrators played a central role in the conception of a viable commercial system. What on the surface may appear as novel or deviant aspects of colonial administration thrust upon it by the force of circumstance turn out on closer inspection to be strikingly consistent with the overall paradigm of political culture in contemporary England. And further, the extended colonial sphere in effect lent an unprecedented coherence to some of the shared institutions of rule. The very context of an unfamiliar and alien society in which the East India Company ran its corporation and government thus throws into sharp relief the regulations, practices, signs, rituals, theorems, and documentary culture of the Georgian state in its struggle to incorporate the contingency of rule and administration in the distant colony.

CHARTERED RIGHTS

Ever since the declaration of a Commonwealth whose commercial interests at sea had to be defended from Continental powers, trade and settlement had been commanding a growing public and national interest in England. An act passed as early as the tenth year of Queen Anne's reign, for instance, was designed to encourage the East India Company "to proceed in their trade, and to make such lasting settlements for the support and maintenance thereof for the benefit of the nation."[10] During the period of colonial wars in the second half of the eighteenth century, as the East India question began to receive increasing attention in parliamentary politics, a prolonged battle of opinions raged about the precise relationship between the Company, Crown, parliament and nation, and the question of juridical precedent for territorial acquisitions overseas. The sovereignty of chartered corporations, especially in the aftermath of the American secession, had become a matter of intense debate.

The East India Company's monopoly of trade and territorial possessions in India had been historically obtained through letters patent under the royal seal, which granted it leave as a corporation to make requisite laws, constitutions, and ordinances for the effective and beneficial administration of its trading settlements. In his celebrated speech on the East India Bill, Burke described such patents as "public instruments" guaranteeing natural rights in the same manner as all "chartered rights of men" were sanctioned through inviolate historical examples such as the Magna Carta. More important, there was no confusion on the point that such rights had been rightfully purchased. As Burke saw it: "they belong to the Company in the surest manner; and they are secured to that body by every sort of public sanction. They are stamped by the faith of the King; they are stamped by the faith of the parliament; they have been bought for money, for money honestly and fairly paid. . . ."[11]

The monopoly of the Company was expected to yield for England an annual territorial revenue of seven million pounds sterling, command over an army of sixty thousand men, and disposal of the lives and fortunes of thirty million inhabitants. Hardinge, legal counsel for the directors, asserted that the exclusive trade and revenue was indeed the very property of the Company.[12] Territorial sovereignty in the colony, in the last instance, was contractual, held in return for public funds and trust, and the promise of revenue. In prevalent legal terms, the right of a corporation to hold territory overseas, granted by charter, was akin to the powers of "acquiring, purchasing, and possessing lands and hereditaments within the realm."[13]

Advocates of colonization, however, were not content with a mere contractual definition for rule or the conveyance of sovereignty. A far more grand historical and imperial precedent was the case of Classical Rome. Thomas Pownall, a prominent member of Parliament and onetime governor of Massachusetts Bay, cited as precedent the Roman Senate's declaration of responsibilities towards Macedonia and Illyricum.[14] Comparing clause by clause the letters patent for the Virginia and Rhode Island companies to the East India Company charter, he declared a general principle by which colonists had a natural and historical right to acquire, lawfully hold, and possess colonies, plantations, settlements, and factories on the edges or beyond the pale of known civilization (*in partibus exteris* and *caeteris*). Pownall, it should be pointed out, was one of the strongest advocates of a firm colonial policy and, along with Sir George Colebrooke (chairman of the Company) and Robert Clive, sought to bring Britain's North American and East Indian possessions within one consistent imperial policy.[15] There were many others who were skeptical of commitments beyond narrowly perceived speculative and financial concerns, but even these rested on written instruments of trade that clearly entailed rudiments of overseas administration and the possibility of forcible acquisition. Colonial trading corporations were given abundant leave to acquire, purchase, and possess lands, property, and stock, govern territories, regulate emigration and settlement, conduct war and peace with native adversaries, and run civil and military administration. The Tory radical William Cobbett railed against the augmented powers of the Company consolidated under Pitt and Dundas.[16] The Company, he argued, was allowed by charter to create a quantity of stock and thus make loans and pay in dividends the interest on money raised, just like the ministry. It had thus become, in fact, "a sort of under-government" aided by the India revenue, with its defense and administration under the supervision of "the mother government at Westminster."[17] "Thus set out in the world," Cobbett exhorted, "this company of sovereigns, furnished, at once, with dominions, subjects, taxes, and a funded debt."[18]

Attempts to vindicate or disprove the Company's right by charter thus provide a crucial trail of documents that ends in the Houses of Parliament and a certain trajectory of debates through which remote events of the Indian colony were periodically visited as routine and customary matters of the state, setting an imperial precedence for years to come. Thus, by the second half of the eighteenth century—ironically enough, at the height of the Company's notoriety—the moral-juridical discourse about the limits and responsibilities of colonial intervention had attained considerable maturity in the public eye. Without such a discursive arena, Burke's impassioned plea for a moral covenant between the nations of the colonizer and the colonized would have fallen on barren ground. Between Pitt's India Act of 1784 and the Regulating Act of 1814, Britain's imperial prospects had widened beyond common expectations, despite the loss of America. In this, India would come to occupy a preponderant position. After the era of parliamentary inquisition that saw the public censure of Clive and Hastings, much of the debate shrank to the mere principles of commercial operation: monopoly versus free trade. By the first decade of the nineteenth century, especially following the more aggressive military policies of Wellesley, the issue of Britain's Indian empire had become a reality regardless of Britain's engagement with European politics. Colonial frontiers of the state had by then already been naturalized.

POLITICS OF THE NATION

The Georgian period saw the consolidation of national identity in England. How far was the image of the nation implicated in colonial ventures, in the call for service, investment, and the promise of wealth? Drawing upon an older body of work—that of Dame Lucy Sutherland—it can be argued that the course of parliamentary politics was being increasingly affected by the remittance of wealth generated by prominent officials of the East India Company. Sutherland demonstrates in remarkably painstaking detail how the patronage and distribution of office was being directly mediated by Parliament, and how the Georgian state itself was clamoring for a much greater share over the revenue of the Company and trying to wield a direct influence over decisions about war and peace in the East Indies.[19] More recent reevaluations tend to confirm the picture of an irrevocable involvement of the state and Parliament in the affairs of the Company and the acknowledgment of the immense of value of its ventures in the revenue structure of the nation.[20]

Trade and war overseas, especially during and immediately following Clive's military triumphs in Bengal and the routing of the French in the Carnatic, had become recurrent national questions for the general reading public. The *Annual Register* in 1767 observed how the smallest details of the East India Company's activity in India and elsewhere had become the objects of interest to the public, and how their charters, possessions, rights, conduct, dispatches, and importance to the nation were "matters of eager and public discussion."[21] The annexation of Bengal, which yielded an unprecedented territorial revenue, and the colonial conflict with France featured prominently in the popular chronicles of the nation. Thomas Pownall, in a tract called *The Right, Interest, and Duty of the State as Concerned in the Affairs of the East Indies,* published in 1773, attempted to reveal this intimate connection:

> People now at last begin to view those Indian affairs, not simply as beneficial
> appendages connected to the empire; but from the participation of their revenues
> being wrought into the very composition and frame of our finances; from the com-
> merce of that country being indissolubly interwoven with our whole system of com-
> merce; from the intercommunion of funded property between the Company and the
> state—people in general from these views begin to see such an union of interest, such
> a co-existence between the two, that they tremble with horror even at the imagination
> of the downfall of this Indian part of our system; knowing that it must necessarily
> involve with this fall, the ruin of the whole edifice of the British Empire.[22]

Along with the concerns of profit and investment for corporations and spoils of trade and war overseas for individuals, colonial wars were certainly being projected, if not fought, as national wars. Between the war of American independence and the Continental struggle with France a certain palpable image of the nation was being forged.[23] India as an arena of struggle for colonial possession provided an equally significant imperial *and* patriotic arena for the realization of a Greater Britain. Without this wider geopolitical context, the complicity between the internal workings of the company-state and the development of the state in England may not be adequately fathomed.[24]

The battle launched against the nawabs of Bengal was seen as much as triumphs of intrigue as just retribution for the shame of the British nation in the sack and pillage of Calcutta and the widely reported infamous incident of the Black Hole. As the correspondence between the Company servants to the secretary of state and the Admiralty testifies, such actions on the part of the local rulers were seen as the "most violent breach of faith and of humanity" that cried out for a defense of the "honour of the English Nation."[25] On the eve of his expedition leading to the recovery of Calcutta and victory at the Battle of Plassey, Clive declared that he was "embarking on board his Majesty's squadron with a fine body of Europeans full of spirit and resentment of the insults and barbarities inflicted on so many British Subjects."[26]

Similar sentiments were expressed in the wars against local rulers such as Tipu Sultan in the south, who sought to collude with the French. Marquess Wellesley, flushed from victories against Tipu in Mysore (1799) and a treaty of great political advantage with the Mahrattas (1802), declared with much fanfare the ulterior and altruistic motives behind the military push towards the "natural frontiers" of India in his dispatch to the Court of Directors:

> We feel that it would not only be impolitic, but highly immoral to suppose that Providence has admitted of the establishment of the British power over the finest provinces of India, with any other view than that of its being conducive to the happiness of the people, as well as to our national advantage.[27]

In the popular press and the political rhetoric of the day, questions directed at national honor and shame were established tropes deployed to elicit patriotic response from audiences, especially in the Houses of Parliament. The "future government of our possessions in India," a contemporary pamphlet proclaimed, "deeply involves the credit of our Government, and the honour of our nation."[28] Nathaniel Halhed, noted scholar of Persian and close confidant of Warren Hastings, was a vocal critic of the conduct of the select committee appointed to investigate the state of the administration in India. He urged the committee to take seriously its responsibility—an inquiry into how the British possessions in the East Indies might be governed with the greatest security and advantage to Great Britain, and how the happiness of the native inhabitants might be best promoted[29] Britain's Indian empire, he thought, should attract the best of English politicians, lawyers, soldiers, and businessmen. For Halhed this was both a patriotic and a humanitarian task, one that connected the prosperity of England with the welfare of ten million newly acquired subjects, and the "honor of the British nation was staked on its impartial execution."[30]

A patriotic mandate behind the preservation of commercial advantages in the colony without doubt generated the requisite racial pride and commitment to rule that ensured the sustained interest (and ire) of the ruling elite in the conduct of the company-state. Intense debates that followed its administrative and financial travails, within and without Parliament, addressing specific questions about norms, conventions, and legalities of profit and rule, were, in the last instance, always argued in the larger interests of the nation. This was true in particular during the era of debates that took place during the renewal of the Company's charter in 1813. Cobbett wrote in the *Political Register* to vindicate the will of the people of England against the narrow self-interest of the ministers and exclusive trade of the Company:

> But, the *people*, if they have not been quite bereft of their reason by conflicting falsehoods, ought to consider the question as one in which *they* are opposed to this domi-

neering Company. It is with the *nation* that the Company has made a bargain; it is from the nation that they hold their Charter; and, it is for the nation to consider, whether that Charter shall be renewed; whether it shall again grant a monopoly of trade to select body of men, to the exclusion of all the rest of the King's subjects.[31]

The relationship between the Company and the composite nation-state of the British Isles remained fraught with inconsistency. At certain moments during the expansion of British rule in India, the Company appeared much larger than a mere corporation, eliciting patriotic sentiments against common enemies, especially France. During other times, the chartered monopoly struck critics as inimical to the spirit of liberty as enshrined in the British constitution. While the exact nature of the imperial nationalism remained in question, the company-state was busily if quietly replicating a set of rules, practices, laws, and constitutional frames that put the stamp of Georgian England on India.

ECONOMY OF ORDER

In this period of indirect rule the East India Company was often seen by many contemporaries at home as a mere corporation unfit to rule responsibly in the colonies. In the words of Adam Smith, it was a company of merchants "incapable of considering themselves as sovereigns," their mercantile habits compelling them to prefer the "little transitory profit of the monopolist, to the great and permanent revenue of the sovereign."[32]

This accusation was hardly isolated. Smith, along with other critics, had been pointing out that government policy in England in the matter of foreign trade had become the tool of mercantile interests, which were in the long run outdated and ruinous. For a growing number of free merchants at the turn of the century, the East India Company's monopoly of trade to India was odious to both the commerce and the glory of the nation, and its assumption of sovereignty in a distant land was deeply suspect. A pamphlet asked in 1807:

> Is it not a solecism in politics, to see a few merchants in Leadenhall Street, met in close divan, and manufacturing laws for the government and happiness of thirty million of their fellow creatures? Is not this system before unheard of in the history of legislation? Is not this *imperium in imperio,* this wheel within a wheel, a dangerous and alarming innovation in the science of politics?[33]

Yet, notwithstanding the potentially crippling criticism of the Company as a monopolistic corporation, its jealously preserved oligarchy, perpetuated through the ties of corruption, intrigue, and loyalty, could prove remarkably resourceful as a vehicle for imperial ambitions. The web of quasi-kin-based control over the mechanics of mercantile returns did, for better or worse, succeed in erecting a similar oligarchy overseas; and the policies of administration were not produced *ad libitum,* but came out of a much deeper and acquired sense of hierarchy and order: fiscal, military, and above all, documentary.

In the face of mounting criticism, especially after the period of the so called "abuse" of private trade and the alleged "rape of Bengal," the Company was quite amenable to an administration largely accountable to the king and Parliament and vindication of the royal charter. The period of greatest interference in internal trade by servants of the Company took place between 1757 and 1765, driven by the desire for quick profit and for supplementing their meager salaried incomes. This period also saw the last vestiges of resistance to the Company's ascendancy in Bengal on the part of its traditional rulers, the nawabs. The intrusion of Company servants into the internal commerce of India acknowledged soon after the acquisition of rule as being a "breach of all orders," "illegal traffick" leading to all the bloodshed, massacres, and confusion," and "in great measure the cause of the late wars."[34] To ensure the permanency of the newly conquered dominion and to draw upon its abundant resources, the Company administration sought to establish instruments of control, surveillance, and violence, and a set of rules and practices that would guarantee the opening up of commerce and extraction of territorial revenue. Such aims, I would argue, went far beyond the quotidian problems of maintaining a viable trade and financial operation. A whole array of legal, commercial, and administrative fictions was directly implied in the efforts to sustain a viable colonial administration.

These precedents hailed directly from reigning notions of political economy. In their discussion of the eighteenth-century English state, Corrigan and Sayer have observed how political economy "provided a moral rhetoric, a theatrical repertoire, a secular equivalent for religion that linked the facts of commerce to the promise of liberty."[35] Between the body of work produced by the Scottish moral philosophers and political arithmeticians, precursors of Smith, an economic system driven by the enduring (naturalistic) laws of the market had been discovered and established whose performance could be measured and diagnosed. The state and its administrative and legal machinery were enjoined to ensure its working. This analysis is particularly apt for an understanding of the colonial state run by the East India Company in Bengal, where such tenets were imposed on people who were not privy to this body of knowledge and where the ruler and the ruled by no means shared the "bonds of wealth and law" or the ideas of improvement promoted by the government.

The paternalist state in the eighteenth-century, empowered by tenets of mercantilism and political arithmetic, was destined for a prodigious lease of life in the colony, particularly as it was laid out through direct military conquest, and faced no significant dissent from within. Many of its ruling ideas could meet the needs of administering and reforming a vast population of newly found colonial subjects. J. Steuart, in his *Inquiry into the Principles of Political Economy,* laid out the agenda: "what economy is in the family, political oeconomy is in a state: with these essential differences, however, that in a state there are no servants, all are children."[36] John Bennet, in his discourse on commerce and colonies, advising on how to improve and regulate the trade and plantations of Great Britain, advocated that the polity was the father of a state, and trade and agriculture its nurse and mother.[37] From this perspective, the nature of public debate around the issue of "free trade" proves the point that although the sovereign power of a mercantile corporation was at stake, merchants in England wishing to enter the East Indian trade had already taken for granted a certain measure of administrative vigilance—a degree of state participation—to be able to protect their investment and profit in a lawful manner in a foreign land against breach of contract.

Keith Tribe's work has shown convincingly that the regulation of people and commerce, protection of property, and the general principles of statesmanship and legislation were the moving criteria of eighteenth-century political oeconomy.[38] Individual gain, profit of corporations, finance of the public, and revenue of the nation-state, in other words, constituted a proximate relationship, enabling a certain vision of economic order. Adam Smith himself, it might be argued, did not conceive of the realm of economic exchange in isolation from that of the state. From what has survived of his lectures at Glasgow, he seems to have considered justice, security, and revenue as the founding trinity of a conception of political economy.[39] This vision was based on a profound and implicit belief in the authority of a paternalist state, a belief that also contributed to the authoritarian ideology of the colonial state in India.

There were, of course, staunch critics of the autonomous pretensions of the company-state. In the Ninth Report of the Select Committee, drawn up in 1783, Burke insisted that the British government in India in the hands of the Company should be made directly accountable to Great Britain. In a passage of rhetorical flourish he suggested:

> The British Government in India, being a subordinate and delegated Power . . . is to be preserved in the strictest Obedience to the Government at Home. Administration in India, at an immense Distance from the Seat of the Supreme Authority, entrusted with the most extensive Powers, liable to the greatest Temptations, possessing the amplest Means of Abuse, ruling over a People guarded by no distinct, or well-ascertained Privileges, whose Language, Manners, and radical Prejudices, render not only Redress, but all Complaint on their Part, a Matter of extreme Difficulty. Such an Administration, it is evident, never can be made subservient to the Interests of Great Britain, or even tolerable to the Natives, but by the strictest Rigour in exacting Obedience to the Commands of the Authority lawfully set over it.[40]

Burke's was a distinctive plea, for he considered India to be a civilization quite apart, which should be held by Britain only through special mandate. But Burke was ahead of his time in contemplating seriously the consequence of the acquisition of a vast mass of subjects, including Asiatics, who did not speak English, were not Protestants or even Christians, and indeed belonged to a very different race. The plight of Indians was a question of the highest moral order, one that threatened the very dignity of the English polity. It is possible to see in Burke's exhortation an early instance of the case that the British Empire, including the Indian question in the late eighteenth century, had become, as Uday Mehta has recently put it, a mirror of British political thought.[41] Thus issues of popular sovereignty and limits on the exercise of power, which had been familiar liberal concerns, would now be raised in the context of the extended empire as well. Thus it is possible to suggest that problems of the formative state in India were not different in philosophy or in substance from problems of the state at home.

I am not suggesting, however, that the Georgian fiscal-military state was somehow a model simply plagiarized and transplanted to the distant colonies. In fact, given the North American experience, the fear was very much there that government so far away from metropolitan London would be prone to deviate from the norm. Yet, if the state sought by the English in India may be seen as a wider political process involving new technologies of rule and sociologies of knowledge, however much the Company innovated to keep its hold over the subcontinent, much of its foundation and authorship lay in Georgian England. In the realm of mercantile and military decision-making, which in this age of national aggression were tied together, it exhibited features very much in common with the British state.[42]

NATURAL ENDOWMENTS OF DOMINATION

A familiar historical reading of imperialism would tell us that military invasion and commercial exploitation were forces *a priori* that eventually led to larger purposes of rule, including its ultimate moral burden. Yet, if we understand the colonial state in India as the establishment of an ongoing exchange of dominance and subordination rather than a fixed empirical entity, this self-evident and functional view of rule cannot, at any instance, be taken as conclusive. Along with financial gain, eighteenth century mercantile expansionism was deeply impressed with the idea of freedom inherent in the *will* and *ability* to exploit and conquer.

The ideology of colonial domination was indebted to a reigning rational and moral climate in which distinctively racial hierarchies were being fashioned out of the old Great Chain of Being. Enlightenment humanism had bestowed the idea of natural history and the progress of civilization through successive stages of material experience and had opened up the evident possibility of encountering people of very different origins, in various conditions of savagery and unrefinement.[43] Even more central to racial and civilizational superiority was the idea that inequality between various parts of the inhabited world was the root and measure of all progress.[44] Such a thesis could easily lend itself to the commonsensical notion that agents of the civilized European world were historically destined to rule over the uncivilized. To this end, a great deal of attention was given to the "natural liberty" of the English male subject. This notion of liberty was crucial to the legal and moral tenets that made colonial rule acceptable, even desirable, for the good of the nation, and was endorsed by a cardinal principle of the British constitution. The link between the arrogance of liberty and the desire for conquest go well back to the vigorous naval and commercial policies of Restoration England. A pamphlet circulated in the 1720s asked:

> What is it has inspired the People of England with Courage and Magnanimity, beyond all other nations, but their Liberty? What is it has made us an Ingenious, Active, and Warlike Nation, our Liberty? What is it has rendered us a Great, Wealthy and Happy People, our Liberty? And what is it has made us Terrible to the whole World, but our English Liberty?[45]

Decades later, John Cartwright, championing the freeholders and the taxed householders of Boston, would invoke the same idea to defy and subvert the British Empire in North America, arguing that "political liberty" was the common right of all nations and of all men and that the political liberty of a nation inhered in its power of self-government, in its ability to make laws, and in the fair and substantial representation of its people in the legislature.[46] Such radical demands of the settler colony would indeed have to be ultimately resolved by war, but their legitimacy was not in question. In places like India during the expansion of British rule there were few partisans for such cause, and almost none from the ranks of native subjects.

The faith in individual liberty was generated, no doubt, through a profound historical relationship between property, patrimony, and patriarchal authority within the household. Many of these ideas were enshrined in legislation that reflected the intimate connections between liberty, private property, and law. By the eighteenth century, the gentry household had acquired a much sharper definition with the gradual decline of a wider clientage: retainers, servants, and tenants. The new patriarchal family was founded on a close adherence to property and the reinforcement of paternal authority. As Davidoff and Hall have shown, by the turn of the eighteenth century the landed estate and the commercial firm had contributed to the creation of a distinctive masculine economic agency.[47] Such a normative, paternalist, and propertied sense of agency was particularly instrumental in the colonial conception of rule, a theme I shall discuss at much greater length in a subsequent chapter.

The authoritarian family and the authoritarian nation-state were both results of a profound search for order in a world of rapid material change and uncertainty.[48] The anxieties of disorder that were reflected in the current doctrines of political economy also generated two inviolable and mutually dependent qualities in the conception of the civilized state of nations: liberty and property. In the age of British expansion, native populations brought under ethnological scrutiny were inevitably defined by the lack of these qualities. It was considered perfectly reasonable, for instance, to claim and annex territory where there were no "natural inhabitants," or inhabitants endowed with natural liberties. A pamphlet circulated in London illustrated the axiom that wherever trading settlements should come across territory with no fixed occupancy in land, or places where people did not mix their labors with the soil—wherever there was no established form of government or communion uniting the people into a collective body—the free subjects of England could claim the rights of possession.[49] This new reception of a Lockean idea of natural rights was supposed to apply to all the settlements in America and the coasts of Africa.

The old theorem of a sovereign commonwealth was thus applied to the colonial state and its effort to erect an autonomous and organized body politic on virgin territory. In this scheme, a peculiar union between the idea of liberty and dominion made it possible to override cognizable rights of native inhabitants. Conquest, consolidated into dominion, "vacated," "transferred," or "abolished" preexisting sovereignty.[50] We have seen in the introduction to this volume how the East India Company claimed what may be termed as a derivative dominion, deriving its status through its relationship with the Mughal Empire, whose deputy, the nawab of Bengal, was nominally in charge of the affairs of the kingdom. Despite such elaborate rituals of occupation, contemporary observers, especially the more trenchant critics of monopoly, admitted that the treaties drawn up after conquest were a farce and the rule of the native chief a mere fiction, and that the government of the country was effectively dissolved and sovereignty annihilated.[51] It was regarded as a "genuine stroke of politics" by which the Company succeeded in masquerading as an ally and protector of the native government while at the same time being the true landlord of the dominions of the state.[52]

This legal, contractual, and legitimizing idea of usurpation of freedom, particularly in the name of king and nation, was not novel to England or eighteenth century Europe in general. As Stephen Greenblatt has shown, Columbus's seizure of the lands of the Indians rested on natural and Roman law, especially on Justinian's pronouncement on the transfer of property with the consent of the owner, and the act of possession was sanctioned on the evidence that he had not been contradicted by the natives.[53] Further, according to medieval law, uninhabited land became the property of the first discoverers and claimants. British claims over the lands of India in the eighteenth century were qualified by such historical and juridical precedents, even though colonial rule was seen to have resulted from direct military conquest. In the age of mercantile corporations the annexation of overseas territory for commercial exploitation was routinely seen as natural and rightful. In his treatment of the history of commercial nations, Abbe Raynal considered such ventures as a matter of course:

> A free nation, which is its own master, is born to command the ocean; it cannot secure
> the dominion of the sea, without seizing upon the land, which belongs to the first pos-

sessor; that is, to him who is able to drive out the ancient inhabitants; who are, therefore, to be enslaved by force or fraud, and exterminated in order to get their possessions.[54]

To make a comparison with the Spanish case, it was not so much the savagery of the inhabitants but the belief in the decadence of oriental civilizations and the general state of unfreedom of the subjects who lived under despotic rule that justified annexation. Alexander Dalrymple, hydrographer to the Admiralty and the East India Company, a champion of the extension of the Company's commerce, expressed his reservations against the idea that natives of Hindoostan were fit to enjoy the fruits of freedom. His statement deserves to be quoted in full:

> I must insist that freedom can be enjoyed by men who *execute their own laws,* or *who live under equal laws of ancient usage:* it is impossible for that state to be free, where the inhabitants in general, have no share in Government and therefore no plan, to be executed by emperors only, can convey the *smallest part of freedom to the Indians.* . . . But admit for a moment, the possibility of communicating to the Indians, the *liberty* we enjoy; the consequence of that liberty must be that *force and elevation of mind* which has been so distinguishable in the British character . . . would the British with this spirit, submit to foreign rulers: grant his *principles,* he would not! And therefore making the Indians *free* we expel ourselves from India. . . . No legislative principles relating to common Government can be applied to the class of a *conquered* people, who *must* still be *slaves,* however light the yoke; slaves can only be Governed by despotic power, and they will be happily governed if that despotic power is constantly amenable to impartial justice and the Indians left to their own customs will enjoy perhaps all the liberty we can give them.[55]

This was not merely a rhetorical claim on the part of the stalwarts of the East India Company. The questions of freedom and unfreedom of subjects were crucial at this time when the contradiction between liberty and servitude was becoming sharper, particularly in the debates surrounding the whole institution and enterprise of chattel slavery.[56] By the second half of the eighteenth century the West Indian islands had been annexed, the British slave empire was thriving, and slave colonies were generating enormous amounts of profits for Atlantic merchants operating between Liverpool, Virginia, and the West Indies.[57] The relationship between various forms of servitude, both in the domestic arena and overseas, and the assimilation of diverse subject populations within a general racial and ethnological taxonomy is neither obvious or direct. The discourse of natural history, however, reinforced arguments about the diversity and difference within the ranks of mankind. As Arthur Lovejoy demonstrated succinctly in his genealogy of the idea of the Chain of Being, the eighteenth century privileged some of its principles over others, namely, the ideas of plenitude, continuity, and gradation, antecedent to latter-day theories of evolution.[58] And indeed, contemporary biological and anthropological reflection (following Kant's principle of inquiry into the order of nature) was preoccupied with taxonomy, and the specific relationship between man, anthropoids, and the lowest savage races.[59]

The general relationship between language, classification, and natural history, however, is not directly relevant to this discussion.[60] Colonial rule, it can be argued, produced unaccountable and exotic subjects at a fairly rapid pace, calling for a more immediate sociology of knowledge and new tools of understanding located in the general discursive climate of natural history, but it did not necessarily wait for conclusive philosophical endorsement of its findings. A hypothesis located in natural history that was instrumental to the colonial assimilation of diverse subjects and races was that of natural slavery. Anthony Pagden's study of natural law in the age of Spanish conquest has demonstrated the connections between enslavement, colonization, and proselytization, and especially how natural slavery of native inhabitants was conceived as the key political and juridical solution to the dilemma posed by the unprecedented acquisition of a vast body of pagan subjects through conquest.[61]

An enormous geographical and chronological divide separates the Spanish *encomienda* from the *indirect rule* of the Company in eastern India, yet, at the risk of simplification, I would suggest that the idea of natural servitude for various groups of colonial peoples in the age of British imperial expansion played an instrumental part in the conception of rule. One indication of this was the tautology of the Negro as the member of an inferior race and a natural slave.[62] And further, writers such as Lord Henry Home Kames could easily speculate on racial gradation in the creation of mankind and the origins of difference between Negroes, Hindus, and European. Such comparisons, needless to say, were indebted to the new geographical reach of the empire.[63] Racial epithets born out of confusion over the diverse origins of new British subjects, locating the African most of all as the stock in trade of human inferiority, had become commonplace toward the end of the eighteenth century. Pieter Camper's study of facial angles placing Negroes as the lowest form of humans, Moreau de Maupertuis's creationist theory of racial diversity, and Buffon's ideas of skin color as an affliction caused by tropical heat, all attempts to account for the evident lowliness of Africans as human beings of a radically different sort, had a cumulative effect on popular consciousness, especially in the context of the abolitionist debates.[64] Other norms of classification were even more uncharitable: James Burnett (Lord Monboddo) and Edward Long, author of the notorious *History of Jamaica* (1774), considered Africans to belong to a different species altogether.

The contradictions between mono- and polygenetic theories of racial origin in the context of India are more fully examined in a subsequent chapter of this book. It should suffice to remind the reader here that Africans were commonly regarded as the *ne plus ultra* of human savagery and bestiality, and further into the nineteenth century, the image of the "Negro," despite the redemptive language of abolition, framed all discussions of human classification.[65] In the eighteenth century Indian servants in Britain were commonly regarded as blacks or Negroes. Some had been brought back from the East Indies having been purchased as slaves, and Rozina Visram's account of Indian domestics in Britain, especially of advertisements in local papers of runaway "black boys" from India, indicates that Britons at home in this era saw Indians primarily as maids, servants, and slaves.[66] Slavery in fact was not uncommon in the British India of the late eighteenth and early nineteenth centuries. Slave boys and girls from both India and Africa served as pages and maids, and it was only in 1789 that the East India Company stopped transporting slaves from Africa to the Indian Malabar coast.[67] It is hardly surprising, then, that later in Victorian India racial epithets would still be tied to terms related to Africa and slavery. Thus John Beames, in his memoirs recounting his days at the East-India College in Haileybury, could remark quite offhandedly:

> If at any time one wanted to know what sort of place India was, or what one's future life or work there was to be like, it was impossible to find anyone who could give the requisite information. . . . All we knew was that it was "beastly hot" and that there were "niggers" there, and that it would be time enough to bother about it when you got there.[68]

The racial denotation of subjects deemed generally inferior to the English or Britons at large did not usually or necessarily follow the criteria adopted by naturalists or scientists of race. In the seventeenth century, English settlers encountering Native Americans in New England considered them to be wild people very similar to the Irish near home, and indeed referred to them as "Irish."[69] At the same time, Irishmen emigrating to North America were regarded for a long time as "white Negroes" or the "smoked Irish."[70] There was thus a degree of fluidity in the depiction of potential subjects during the age of imperial expansion and thus in the very criteria of racial inferiority. Such variability also helped fashion the attributes of the Company's colonial subjects in India.

"SOLE AND DESPOTIC DOMINION"

In the context of British rule in India, it was not enough merely to pronounce that the colonial subject was incapable of upholding the natural liberties with which the English were endowed. Meaningful administrative actions of the state could be conceived only through the production of a certain body of ethnographic and historical knowledge about Indian society. Seeing themselves as rightful successors to the Mughal emperors, and indeed holding the right to gather revenue on its behalf, Company administrators undertook an arduous inquiry into ruling institutions of the recent past. This struggle to grasp the continuity with and differences from previous modes of rule urged certain perceptions about the essential nature of Indians and their society.

What could have been the familiar models with which to relate indigenous society? Ranajit Guha, in his classic study, *A Rule of Property for Bengal,* suggested that colonial lawgivers, particularly during the era of Cornwallis as governor, viewed Indian society as essentially feudal and relied on physiocratic measures to sever the medieval and feudal ties of Indian society and create a new enterprise in landed property.[71]

It can also be argued that along with the idea that India was under a feudal yoke, there was an emerging consensus that the East India Company was a reluctant heir to a long tradition of oriental despotism, related to the history of Moorish or Islamic conquests and repeated invasions of the subcontinent. The unfreedom of the natural and original inhabitants, the Gentoos or Hindus, could thus be explained. Observers and critics of the Company's rule in Bengal attempted to explain at length the inherently despotic nature of Indian society. From Robert Orme in the eighteenth century to James Mill in the nineteenth, descriptions of India were replete with the charge of oriental despotism, which was seen as the principal malaise that had aborted the development of a proper relationship between state and civil society in India.

Luke Scrafton, in his *Reflections on the Government of Indostan* (1763), attempting to provide a short sketch of the religion, customs, and manner of government among the newly conquered Hindus, saw them as "a meek, superstitious charitable people," their character formed by their "temperance, customs and religion."[72] Their political ambition was severely restrained by their religion, which made them "strangers to that vigor of mind . . . virtues grafted on those passions" which animated an Englishman's restless and noble temperament. "Their temperance, and the enervating heat of the climate, starves all the natural passions," wrote Scrafton, leaving only avarice, a predisposition that was encouraged by "the oppression of the government. . . ."[73] Because of these fundamental flaws in the character of indigenous society, stymied by oriental despotism, Indians in general displayed no noble virtues of loyalty or patriotism, and thus the "mutual good faith, the bond of society, is broke. . . ."[74]

Other contemporary observers held the Mughal Empire patently responsible for the state of despotism prevalent in India. John Shore, a founding architect of the early settlement of land revenue in Bengal, held that the Mughal "dominion" was essentially a government subservient to the individual "discretion" of the emperor, and the "safety of the people, the security of their property, and the prosperity of the country, depended upon the personal character of the monarch."[75] In the epoch immediately prior to the introduction of British rule in India, a weak monarchy and a corrupt administration had encouraged widespread disorder. The institution of property and patronage had been abused, justice had been perverted, and "unrestrained oppression" had prevailed. Such a situation, according to Shore, was typical of Islamic governments, where "practice is for ever in opposition to the theory of morals."[76] A contemporary student of revenue management in the British Dominions of Bengal, concluded: "In the absolute Governments of Asia, it is not one great despot only that reigns—thousands of inferior degrees tyrannize in the subordinate spheres assigned to them, over a depressed and broken-minded people, habituated to the most abject servility for a series of ages."[77]

Burke showed much concern in his speeches for the "situation of the miserable natives" and held that it might be a task worthy of the benevolence of Britain to relieve them from "the bonds of mental slavery."[78] And yet, having lived under arbitrary and despotic authority, Indians were not prepared to receive the "beautiful and free system of British legislation," and all the British rulers could do was to "restore peace, order and unanimity to the extensive territories of India, by giving them the laws that they approved."[79] Robert Orme, official historian of the Company and one of the first writers to offer a considered ethnography of British subjects in India, declared that all prevalent customs and rites in the country derived from the "constant idea of subordination."[80] While the Moor was robust, stately, vain, fierce, oppressive and rapacious, the sway of despotic government and slavery had rendered the Gentoos naturally effeminate, patient and artful. William Watts, a contemporary of Orme, noted that the Gentoos were a mild, subtle, frugal race of men who were habituated to degrees of slavery.[81] Dalrymple noted the failure of the Company in delivering a code of laws that would regulate the manners and minds of the Indians, establish a new religion among them, destroy the divisions of caste, awaken a sense of industry, and give them new motives of action. Lack of liberty, despotism, and feudal anarchy together had made the society averse to rights based on civilized notions of property and contract.

This characterization of Indian society as inherently despotic can be seen in many ways as a projection of what Leonard Krieger has described as the eighteenth-century version of enlightened absolutism in Europe, a ruling legitimacy based on the principles of natural right.[82] The lengthy and tortuous discourse on the malaise of despotism was, as is explored in a later chapter, in part a projection of the deep unease of Britons who found the climate, morals, society, manners, and customs of India to be peculiarly corrupting. It also provided them with a substantive reason for paternalistic and authoritarian rule, leaving room for the liberal wish that one day, under British tutelage, Indians too would reap the fruits of liberty and property.

THE POSSESSIVE STATE

Property was, of course, one of the most fiercely defended institutions in eighteenth-century England. Adam Smith, lecturing to his students at Glasgow in 1763, defined property as belonging to a species of "real" rather than "personal" rights, which were both part of the "acquired rights" of mankind. Real rights consisted of property, servitude, pledge, and exclusive privilege. Of these, property was the most important:

> Property is acquired five ways. First, by occupation, or the taking possession of what formerly belonged to nobody. Second, by accession, when a man has a right to one thing in consequence of another, as of a horse's shoe along with the horse. Third, by prescription, which is a right to a thing belonging to another arising from long and uninterrupted possession. Fourth, by succession to our ancestors or any other person, whether by a will or without one. Fifth, by voluntary transference, when one man delivers over his right to another.[83]

Smith's students learned that these laws indeed varied according to the various stages of human history—hunting, pasturage, farming, and commerce. Thus agriculture once took over the former pastures and hunting grounds, and now commerce would take precedence over agriculture itself. Such had been the case in North America.[84]

The vision of a territorial possession, a dominion, and a conquered population was directly fastened to an absolute faith in defensible and bounded property. Landed property in particular, as John Brewer demonstrates, had become the backbone of the fiscal-military state in the Georgian period, and established landed families were still seen as natural rulers of society.[85] Property and entitlement in the long run, exemplified by the countryside estates made possible by heroic and scandalous careers in the colonies, rendered the results of trade and colonial expansion admissible in a society reluctant to accept newfound wealth.

Property rights thus in manifold ways made the colonial extension of rule both legal and natural. They validated possession through conquest, marked the native society as lacking in the obvious criteria of civilization, and legitimized the patrimonial domain of state power. The legitimacy of property, however, was not without its ambiguities. There was in general a great deal of anxiety about what rightfully belonged to an individual and what belonged to the state. Possessions of the East India Company as the monopoly of a chartered corporation, according to some political commentators, were in essence public property and reverted to the state either in the case of a national crisis or need, or naturally with the legal termination of the Company's charter.[86] Such contradictions were apparent in parliamentary debates and in the lobbying for and against the Company's monopoly. On the fine point of constitutional law, at any rate, the precise question of sovereignty and the constitutional relationship between the state, Company, and possessions in India was never settled in the eighteenth century.[87]

The rights of the Company were extended not only to an exclusive trade but to the *bona fide* property of a corporate body politic: territory and revenue. A prominent British historian of political economy, Adam Anderson, addressed the issue in the latter half of the eighteenth century, emphatically conflating dominion with property. He went on to assert:

Public property excludes communion amongst nations; private property communion amongst persons. For, as particular persons, which they possess privately of other persons: so countries and territories, like greater manors, divided each from the other by limits and borders, are the public properties of nations, which they possess exclusively of one another.[88]

One can detect in this formulation how the relations between the nation, household, and property rights were being constructed in the late eighteenth century. The administrative understanding of landed society in Bengal, particularly during measures undertaken by Governor Cornwallis, was deeply influenced by some of the principal tenets of the French *philosophes,* particularly the idea of Voltaire that inheritance and good society presupposed private property. Also, apart from the wrangling between advocates of physiocracy and mercantilism, as E. P. Thompson asserts, an unquestioned faith in the creation of landed settlements in India derived in the long run from the Whiggish obsession with hereditary estates.[89]

A genuine, private, individuated sense of property, however, was not to be easily found in India; neither were the foundations of true public property of the state secure. An established procedure of collecting revenue, in particular, was seen to have had no firm ground on Indian soil. The long Mughal yoke in India, to paraphrase Dalrymple, had stripped the tiller of the land of his rights by giving too much power to farmers and collectors of revenue, reducing him to the state of a meager laborer working for daily subsistence. The prince had thus raised a number of petty tyrants held in thrall by an overarching despotic power. He was entitled to a share in all the produce of the earth and whatever was nourished by it, mounting imposts on inland trade, houses, markets, and shops, and extracting great profits from the dispensation of justice, fines, and amercement. Nothing was exempt from some form of tax or tribute. Thomas Law, member of the Board of Revenue in Bengal and later a committee member of the Association for the Preservation of Liberty and Property in London, asserted in his treatises that after having studied the books of the Mughals, the "capricious edicts of pleased tyrants," and having realized the "terrible bigotry and violence" that produced them, he had come to the firm conclusion that the Mughals had destroyed the possibility of a regular system of revenue.[90] No mode of indigenous authority was above suspicion, which is not without its irony, as the most commonly accepted definition of property rights in this era was summed up by William Blackstone as "that sole and *despotic* dominion which one man claims and exercises over the external things of the world, in total exclusion of the right of any other individual in the universe."[91]

Given this perception of native society, it is not difficult to see why there was such a drive in the closing years of the eighteenth century for a permanent settlement of revenues from land and marketplaces. Revenue as public property of the state was a predominant concern for the East India Company, especially as land revenue from Bengal was seen as a vital source of bullion to pay for investments in Asia, which included the China trade. A regular collection from land, in the traditions of Whiggish gentrification, could best be secured through a settled husbandry and a consolidation of landed interests. Estates in land, resembling enclosures back at home, were seen as being indispensable to the unhindered collection of revenue, and further, to the creation of a viable landed gentry. At the same time, fiscal measures were undertaken to overhaul and regulate the whole sphere of market exchange, abolishing most existing tolls, claims, privileges, and dues of local rulers, subordinate chiefs, and religious institutions.[92]

Some contemporary observers, such as T. H. Colebrooke regarded the ending of such exactions as a mixed blessing. They had been taken off by the Company to promote commerce, and yet the removal of local restrictions and regulations, and of the retinue of officers who protected small markets in the countryside, had led to an overall decline in the number of markets.[93] Markets that survived this inquisition had also suffered. Peasants and traders now had to travel far longer distances than before. Although such reforms were carried out with a firm belief that they would bring about the freedom of trade, the state's share of revenue from internal trade was not sacrificed toward this aim, and by the turn of the century there had grown a far-flung and elaborate network of customhouses. There was no fundamental contradiction in this, given the prevalent tenets of political economy, where the direct regulation of commerce by the state would not have seemed improper or unnatural.

THE ANXIETY OF MEDIATION

The dominant framework of Georgian political economy that served as the direct, functional, and ideological archive for the rise of the company-state in India was also responsible for some of the historic contradictions and reformulations of legitimate rule in the face of a colonial society. The resilience and adaptability of the English state as a political formation, Derek Sayer has argued, were significantly derived from its antiquity and from the fact that the state apparatus was thoroughly invested with symbols of the nation.[94] Such formations were also consonant with a certain experience of class, society, and patriarchal order. The first travesty of exerted hegemony in the Indian context was clearly the absence of this entire social and cultural space. Much more detailed research would have to be conducted in order to see how the nuances of class relationship were reinscribed in the colony or fashioned over time out of the inequalities borne in indigenous society. The contingency of conquest in all possibility wrought a gulf between agents of the state and wider society, especially as martial nationalism with its most powerful imperial and racial inflections became integral to the pursuit of colonial domination.

And yet most attempts at hegemony in this age of burgeoning capitalism sought consensus, if not a preconceived public sphere, through which a new civil society could be envisioned. The early colonial state in India was thus obliged to rehearse the idea of a shared commonwealth and a fictive realm of consent, although racial, linguistic, societal, sexual, and administrative practices show that this covenant could hardly be realized. What endured through the opening decades of British rule in India, and was carried over onto the period of authoritarian rule and utilitarian reform in the nineteenth century, was a resolute vision of moral and societal improvement undaunted by the dubious acquiescence of its beneficiaries. This was the hard-earned lesson of the Georgian gentry, a product of what E. P. Thompson has called the "long ascent of the ideology of the patrician Whigs."[95]

At its loftiest, this benevolent and enlightened purpose of rule could be translated into a grand colonizing mission, a moral responsibility that England held first for Great(er) Britain and then on behalf of Europe towards the lesser civilized world. Thus Abbe Raynal urged the administrators of the East India Company to end all tyranny and despotism through their laws and to restore to the rest of mankind their rights. Reminding the English of their obligation to bring happiness to the people of India, he advised:

> Make your new subjects enjoy the sweets of property. Portion out to them the fields on which they were born: they will learn to cultivate it for themselves. Attached to you by these favors, more than ever they were by fear, they will pay you with joy the tribute you impose with moderation. They will instruct the children to adore and admire your government; and the successive generations will transmit, with their inheritance, the sentiments of their happiness mixed with that of their gratitude.[96]

The creation of a progressive colonial subject population, however, framed within the bounds of property and liberty was not by any means an easy or straightforward process. Although Burke, among others, had enjoined the administrators of India: "you will teach the people that live under you, that it is their interest to be your subjects," there was always the fear that lack of covenant between the ruler and the ruled would always undermine the liberal foundations of legitimate authority.[97]

One arena for the exercise of state power particularly fraught with a crisis of consent was criminal justice, where the criminal offender was supposed to be tried, following Blackstone, by law made by his own consent. This very necessity that punishment be made meaningful to the offender prompted above all other considerations the decision to codify, regulate, and reform what was chosen as a body of indigenous legal texts. Law and punishment urged the application of high orientalist scholarship, particularly during the time of Governor-General Warren Hastings, who asserted that Indians should be governed by their own laws. Nevertheless, contemporary Islamic tenets of criminal law and prosecution continued to be seen with great degree of mistrust and suspicion by Company administrators. A contemporary observation stated: "whoever reads the Koran, must be obliged to confess, that it conveys no notions, either of the relative duties of mankind in society, or the formation of the body politic, or of the principles of governing; nothing, in a word, which constitutes a legislative code."[98]

The bulk of colonial subjects, the Hindus, could not be brought within the writs of this arrangement as they were deemed totally ignorant of the Islamic languages, thus not fully knowledgeable of their own criminal behavior. Even during the period when indigenous criminal courts and establishments were maintained in principle by the Company, officials such as Thomas Law insisted that trials for treason and sedition against the government should be taken away from the direct hands of the native Islamic establishment. Even a brief survey of the administration of the criminal justice system at this period will show how elusive the idea of a generic colonial subject was, especially with the ethnographic stereotype of the Hindu as a natural slave and the Moor as a former conqueror, dispossessed, vengeful, and seditious. Such ideas, ingrained in colonial administrative policy, would create lasting contradictions in the juridical configuration of Indian society.

Although the philosophy and ambition of "indirect rule," could not be easily translated, the East India Company's regime from the perspective of Indian subjects appeared equally arbitrary and despotic. Traditional rulers of native society had been either stripped of their power or made uneasily complicit in the workings of the state. A profound sense of unease during the early part of the Company's rule in Bengal was felt by many observers. Gholam Hossein Khan, a nobleman writing during the closing decades of the century who had served both under the Mughal and the British, captured this alienation in his account.[99] Measures introduced by foreign rulers, in his eyes, were neither beneficial nor effective, as a general aversion of the English to the company of native subordinates made it impossible for any accord to grow between the conquerors and the conquered. The new rulers were alien to the manners, customs, and the languages of the country, and did not understand how tribute (including land revenue) was raised from various rulers and chieftains. They were in the habit of giving salaries in money to the servants of the government, rather than grants in produce from land. Hossein had never seen or heard of some of the British customs, such as counting the inhabitants of every town and city, and examining how much they had earned and spent or how many had died. Differences in the mode of governance were irreconcilable, yet the English were introducing their customs and usage without adequate deliberation. He felt, moreover, that whatever the colonial rulers had learnt about the institutions of India came from their own servants, whose opinions were neither impartial nor independent.

Hossein's views sharply disrupt a progressive course or a singular or linear history for the East India Company's rule in Bengal; they also give us a clue to reimagine the coherence of the colonial state in terms of the *effect* of its power. This paradox of domination and legitimacy, although not specific to a colonial experience, was nevertheless evident to contemporary observers.

Thomas Pownall, writing during the same period, noticed similar ambiguities in the conception of statehood on the part of the British:

> Although the sovereignty of the native Government of the country within the bounds of the dominion of the East India Company is abolished and annihilated, yet the forms and orders, the offices, and ostensible officers of Government remain—the tenure of the lands remains as it did; the rents and revenues as they did; —the state of rights personal and political, the rule of government, such as they were; the sovereign power and direction however, the absolute military command, the absolute perpetuity of right in the revenues . . . is held under a very jealous and exclusive power in the hands of the Company: although it suffers the government to be exercised by the nominal officers of the state—yet it is the holder of the state in its own hands. . . .[100]

Such a formulation reflects a crisis of legitimacy and an admission of despotic rule. Pownall asserted that the Company should "act as what it is"— live up to the political and moral responsibilities that accompany the establishment of state power—whether power be delegated to the Company or retained by the Crown. These observations, then, may enable us to rethink the history of the colonial state forged through the commercial expansion of Georgian England, a process that presupposed the dictates of empire. Formation of this state was not merely incidental to the contingency of commerce but possible through direct ideological intervention. Its external frontiers, pushed forward by the military, saw as much reversal and advance as its internal frontiers of law, taxation, and punishment.

Military commitment for imperial expansionism, especially the need to command indigenous troops who made up the rank and file, constantly called for the sacrifice of Britons in a cause that bore the contradictions of both nation and profit. By the turn of the century, critical observers like William Cobbett did not hesitate to condemn the loss of great numbers of English officers and soldiers in at least thirty years of "constant, never-ceasing war in India," the butcheries without glory, the "sheer love" of gain and plunder, and aggressions "completely unjustifiable and inexcusable."[101] In fact the accusation that the Company had conducted unjust wars in India, especially during the period of expansion under Wellesley, had gained an ever wider currency. During parliamentary debates on the state of affairs in India in 1805, Charles James Fox himself charged that the Company seemed to seek every pretence to declare war, and that there seemed to be no clear indication when this propensity would cease. "We in fact, seemed in India, to be like Macbeth," Charles James Fox exclaimed, " 'so steeped in blood' that we thought it vain to get back."[102]

Legal and moral prescriptions, and the instruments of regulation and coercion that sustained the ruling ideology of the expanding fiscal-military state in India, despite such condemnation, remained in many ways reminiscent of Georgian England, although put on indefinite trial in an alien culture. In England the workings of tradition, precedent, and law brought political stability to the gentry at the expense of the agrarian poor and urban plebians. In the conception of early colonial rule in India, one can perhaps detect similar lessons of class and authority that may have provided valuable and necessary means of violence and order. How far the Indian experience affected in actual substance the workings of the state back in England is a question that remains to be answered more fully. It is possible that the fiscal militarism of the English state had already developed in some distinct directions in the seventeenth and early eighteenth century, before the Company in India began to wage its wars of expansion. One indication of this was the rising demand for the orderly collection of taxes and maintenance of the instruments of public security.[103] A very important function of the fiscal-military state was war, which, as Michael Braddick has demonstrated recently, employed an increasingly large number of recruits to replenish the fields of battle, and engaged parliamentary taxation to meet fiscal deficits during periods of exigency.[104] These very abilities made possible the extension of the Seven Years War in India to the advantage of England and the British Empire. In this regard, at any rate, the colonial state in India was nothing but an adaptation of the English state itself.

2

History as Imperial Lesson

Sir James Mackintosh sailed back home from Bombay on November 6, 1811.[1] He found himself in the ship a "spacious apartment" of nine square feet with one side port, two windows to the deck, sitting at a desk placed on an old library-steps table alongside a large camphor trunk full of books and papers. "My happiness at present," he wrote at the time, "depends on a few simple circumstances . . . a cool breeze and a quiet quarter deck."[2] On board he began composing the introduction to his illustrious history of the 1688 Revolution. Writing amid the bustle, he likened his circumstances to those of Julius Caesar trying to draw up plans for the next battle. The situation for the conception of a history of England, he reflected, could not have been more curious; these were circumstances decidedly more "inauspicious and vulgar" than what Gibbon found as he lingered by the ruins of the Capitol, listening to vespers that stirred the conception of his magnum opus. The setting was apt, nonetheless: "But a cabin nine feet square in a merchant ship, manned by Mahommedan sailors, on the coast of Malabar, is, if not a convenient, at least a characteristic place, for the beginning of the history of a maritime and commercial empire."[3]

Mackintosh lived in India for about seven years. He arrived as a recorder (judge with criminal jurisdiction in the city) of Bombay and in two years received a commission as judge in the vice-admiral's court.[4] He would often compare himself to Cicero banished from Rome: he had brought with him a large library and looked with great anticipation in his self-conscious exile to the cases of books and reviews sent from England.[5] Consigned to "the most obscure corner of India" in 1804, from where nothing English was "trifling, or little, or dull," he wrote to his friend Richard Sharp that he would have gladly welcomed the very refuse of Debrett the bookseller.[6] India did not suit either his health or his temperament; his wife had to return to England early in the year 1810 for the sake of their younger children,[7] and he intended to remain for a few more years to secure his pension, though was not to be, on account of the climate and his worsening health.

Mackintosh wrote to Lord Wellesley in 1805 that he wanted to compile *The History and Present State of the British Dominions in India,* a task he never accomplished.[8] But Colonel Mark Wilks took up the *History of Mysore* at his insistence, and he urged John Malcolm to write the *Political History of India.*[9] In his inaugural address to the Literary Society of Bombay, which he founded and presided over till his death, he urged that as Europeans detached from the "main body of civilised men," sent out to remote countries, they should "levy contributions of knowledge" as well as "gain victories over barbarism."[10] India provided yet another field for the "beneficent progress" of knowledge to "illuminate and humanize the whole race of man." The conquest of India was the first step to the revelation of its history: "When a large portion of a country so interesting as India fell into the hands of one of the most intelligent and inquisitive nations of the world, it was natural to expect that its ancient and present state should at least be fully disclosed."[11] Events of India suggested to him the immense vista of empire: the war against the Marathas, he wrote to George Moore, "has ended in establishing the direct authority, or the uncontrollable influence, of England, from Lahore to Cape Comorin. Your map will help your memory to form some idea of the immensity of this Empire."[12] This was a dominion that reigned over a "monstrous detail of evil," and such was the "infernal character of Asiatic governments" that the English power seemed to be "a blessing to the inhabitants of India." True, this government did not share with the governed a community of interests or feelings and left much to be desired, but compared with an Indian regime, it was "angelic."[13]

India for Mackintosh was a half-acknowledged backdrop for the staging of an edifying history of England. The conquest of India, he wrote on the voyage back to England, displayed the power of European knowledge "to subject all other parts of the earth."[14] England was one nation among many in Europe, and thus a history of England and the causes of its present eminence was "not interesting or even intelligible" without the history of other nations. Only a history of truly accomplished nations taken together could show why England constituted a realm of "free people—perfectly exempt from all deeds of anarchy, of tyranny, and of conquest" and a people "strengthened and not enervated" after the glorious war of 1688 by the blessings of a long peace. It is fair to say that images of India must have crossed his mind as he penned his history's opening lines on the general state of affairs in England at the accession of James II: "Though a struggle with calamity strengthens and elevates the mind, the necessity of passive submission to long adversity is rather likely to weaken and subdue it. . . ."[15]

India became a possession of the British during roughly the same age in which the history and the destiny of the British imperial nation-state became intertwined. This chapter traces the emergence of a colonial historical account of the Indian conquest and explores the way in which Indian events and characters were assimilated into the history of an imperial nation-state.

THE CONSENT OF MANKIND

Mackintosh and his contemporaries, educated in the last decades of the eighteenth century, shared an Olympian vision of the study of human past. History was preeminently the examination of the form and substance of governments and institutions across time. Mackintosh himself—author of the *Vindiciae Gallicae* and Whig defender of the fruits of the French Revolution—noted in 1797 in his lectures on history delivered at the Lincoln's Inn that only the historian could penetrate "the same fundamental, comprehensive truths, the sacred master-principles which are the guardians of human society," a sentiment we shall encounter at length below.[16]

India provided for the British an appropriate context for a classical-historical exegesis on the moral and temporal lessons of imperial conquest. Rehearsal of the past as a guide for manly action, commerce, and war was essential to the East India Company stalwarts in the age of European rivalry and colonial expansion. Histories in the eighteenth century were supposed to be both patriotic and exemplary. More importantly, history was tied to a deep antiquarianism that instructed that the precepts of sovereignty, state, and the body politic of the United Kingdom ultimately derived from imperial and republican Rome and the immemorial democracy of the Greek islands. The history of Britain in India, and thus also the possibility of an *Indian* history, became clear as the conquest of India unfolded before the very eyes of British and Company historians. In his history of England, David Hume had already outlined what would become a commonplace with Victorian antiquarians, archeologists, and guardians of the British racial heritage such as John Beddoe—that Roman conquest unified the people of the islands for the first time and brought Britain into the circle of history. Early histories of the English conquest of India suggested a similar pattern.

Robert Orme, entreated by Lord Clive to write a first official account of the East India Company's triumph, attempted a comprehensive history of Mughal and early British India, with "ideas, plan, style and arrangement" based on Thucydides, whom he considered his "master."[17] Orme wrote his first book on the history of the loss and recovery of Fort William, Calcutta, the defeat of the Bengal nawab, and the British possession of eastern India. His second book was a detailed study of the military transactions leading to the entrenchment of British rule in India. The designated task, to be sure, was not only a retrospective study of events outlining the British advantage over India, but also the moral edification of his fellow countrymen.

Such a rendition carried the deep imprint of history as a grand cautionary exercise, a mirror to the ambitions and pitfalls of national and imperial desire. History in the Ciceronian exemplar had found a new and commanding dignity in eighteenth-century Britain[18] ever since Bolingbroke popularized the Dionysian notion of history as the teaching of philosophy by example. Sheridan's dictionary defined history as a narrative of events and facts rendered with dignity.[19] And Mackintosh put the value of history in eliciting the "consent of mankind in first principles."[20] William Jones himself, in his account of the life of Nadir Shah, would find in Cicero as the historian of Rome the closest figure of the "perfect historian" who "must know many languages, many arts, many sciences; and, that he may not be reduced to borrow his materials wholly from other men, he must have acquired the height of political wisdom, by long experience in the great affairs of his country, both in peace and war."[21] Such were the standards of scholarship and statesmanship on which the history of the Orient could properly be judged.

Following Jones and Orme, the historical record of Indian civilization, especially during the centuries during which it supposedly lay eclipsed under the yoke of a conquering Islam, was thus to be measured against the august and magisterial narratives of European history and antiquity. History upheld the value of liberty against the folly of tyranny and despotism and seemed to explain why Indians were unfree and what their extent of servitude should be as subjects governed by the British. In this chapter I contend that there was an emerging contradiction in the study of India between the natural-historical classificatory impulse of the Enlightenment and the moral-sentimental historical narration described above. It was the historical mode, however, that in the end suffused the style and technique of representation of India. Clio was the first handmaiden of colonial conquest. Other forms of knowledge followed.

What I am about to suggest must ring familiar to students of Edward Said, in that history was but one of the several disciplines that shaped orientalism and its attending imperialist worldview. Clearly a great deal of historiographical labor went into what Said calls the "veridic discourse about the Orient" as part of its "sheer knitted-together strength."[22] India was very much at the early center of this accretion of knowledge, aided by the presumption of political dominance. And yet I view the purpose of history in the self-awareness of an emergent colonialism as not always clear—sometimes an assertive, sometimes an anxious exercise that entailed a protracted reexamination of the English and occidental pasts in the light of imperial expansion. And thus, rather than the question of identity posed in terms of similarity and difference, I proceed with an emphasis on the opposition between intimacy and distance, between the idea that all human history is essentially the same and the idea that the Indian history ought to be considered as the past of an alien and separate civilization. The accent on the centrality of the historiographical method here follows the brief but strikingly insightful suggestion made by Bernard S. Cohn that for the

English in India, history provided the ontological foundation for their inquiry into how the natural and social worlds were constituted.[23]

It is clear that the prospect of military conquest in India did not precipitate a sudden interest or an unprecedented revelation of the Indian past. India—variously described as the East Indies, Indostan, or Hindostan—was already an established subject of curiosity in England and Europe at large, and this was quickly and further encouraged by the diffusion of knowledge gained by the first administrators of the East India Company into the learned communities of England.[24] The age of Enlightenment had already apprehended the Orient as a serious object of study in the comparative progress of the humankind, and the growing British presence in India provided a ready access to an ancient eastern civilization.

The first histories of India that sprung from serious administrative and academic exercise—relying on knowledge that made its way from the coasts of India all the way to the heart of England—were subject to two fundamental impulses and their inevitable tensions. One was the continuing legacy of the Scottish moral enlightenment, which had laid out the four stages of human progress in which India occupied the position of neither a fundamentally rude nor a particularly polished nation. The second guiding sentiment can perhaps be roughly termed as a Burkean tradition that spoke for the history not of all mankind but of the particular and instructive progression of the British polity, its laws, liberties, and its ancient constitution. In this second consideration, India was truly an unfamiliar place, and the history of the British in India was less about Indians and more about the moral consequences of imperial rule on the character of Englishmen.[25] History was the long shadow of time-honored manners and the mould of deep tradition that had shaped the essence of the British nation.[26] In the first instance, India was a visible reminder of a state of society left behind in Europe or the repository of a flawed political development that European nations did not experience, such as oriental despotism. In the second, India was simply a context that put the best of the British liberal tradition on trial.

The historiography of British India that emerged during the later eighteenth and early nineteenth century was an heir to both these frames of explanation. Even patently utilitarian explanations of the Indian past, such as arrangements of revenue, nature of land rights, and the succeeding institutions of governance, implied these fundamental strands. The received historiography of the company Raj in India, as we shall see below, came to maturation in an era in which the very history of Britain as an imperial nation-state was in contention. In this, as I shall suggest later, the history of India in a peculiar sense necessitated at least a partial resolution of some significant and controversial questions of national and civilizational importance. An important cornerstone of this historiography was the idea of an imperial civilizing and expansionist crusade in which the monarchy of the United Kingdom of Great Britain and the English Parliament represented the providential purpose of a new *imperium.*[27] In this burgeoning conception the glorious and cautionary tale of imperial Rome had already taken center stage.

IMPERIAL MIMESIS

The idea that an imperial spirit was ingrained in the manifest history of the British nation, as Richard Koebner pointed out some decades ago, was clearly an assertion that developed in the eighteenth century, when not only had the islands come together under the writ of one kingdom, but dependencies had been firmly secured overseas.[28] However, the notion of an *imperio populi Romani* had begun to animate the patriotic and national imagination of the English in the age of Gibbon. The historical analogy with Rome had not yet led to the much more familiar claim of the subsequent century—that the institutions of the English derive in seed from the Roman empire—much as Hilaire Belloc put it plainly in the 1920s: "the Roman civilization was that of England from her origins."[29] But Rome as a political and a poetic idea, fortified during the Augustan era, was clearly bequeathed to the later centuries.[30] The comparison between ancient Rome and modern Britain was rife in the eighteenth century, and the similarity of their mixed constitutions was noted in the works of Walter Moyle and Edward Montagu.[31] Many feared that, just like Rome, Britain was in the danger of lapsing from the state of liberty to that of despotism through luxury and political corruption.[32]

The Roman inheritance of England and Britain was, of course, part of a larger perspective that Gibbon's work represented. An entire century of scholarship had been captured by the idea that the study of Rome in decline was also a study of the beginnings of modern Europe.[33] Just a few years before the publication of the first volume of Gibbon's *Decline and Fall* (1776), William Robertson had published his magisterial *History of the Reign of the Emperor Charles V*, subtitled *A View of the Progress of Society in Europe from the Subversion of the Roman Empire to the Beginning of the Sixteenth Century* (1769). According to Robertson, the destruction of Rome by the barbarians revolutionized the political state and manners of the European nations and molded the powers of Europe "into one great political system."[34] In an age marked by increasing conflict and bloodshed over the possibility of overseas empires, especially evident in the far flung theater of the Seven Years War, it is not difficult to see why the fate of imperial Rome should be used as a lesson in prudence and restraint in the instruction of patriotism.

Edward Gibbon, one should remember, seldom drew an obvious comparison between Britain and Rome in his historical writings,[35] but it is clear from his correspondence that he was eager to keep abreast of the East India Company's exploits in India and like many of his illustrious contemporaries, witnessed the epic trial of Warren Hastings.[36] Richard Sheridan, in his lengthy parliamentary diatribe against Hastings in 1788, invoked at length Gibbon's history of Rome, claiming that the wrongdoings of the Company in India were indeed far worse than anything the Romans had ever done.[37]

In 1778, it seems that Gibbon had been following the news of British military exercises in India and America and rejoiced at the French threat having been defused for a while in western India with an apparent change of policy among the warlike Marathas.[38] In 1779 he wrote that it was essential that the "French have not any place of arms in the East Indies."[39] In the same year, he observed lightheartedly to Georges Deyverdun that the declines of the two empires, Roman and British, were comparable, and that he had contributed much to that of the former.[40] The question of imperial decadence for him was crucial to the understanding of modern history. The British were, of course, much more powerful than the Romans, and he seemed to think that their fall would be much more gradual.[41]

Narratives of European antiquity in Georgian England recast empires of the past allegorically for a politically alive, wider reading public. The very style with which the historical judgment of events and facts was rendered at this period made it possible to attach moral idioms to current happenings. Classical historical learning had become the essential ingredient of a late Enlightenment and a refined sensibility towards the human predicament,[42] and thus questions of imperial decline, tyranny, despotism, and liberty were seen as relevant to the Britain of the time as to the Greece or Rome of yore. History was the prime tool of pedagogy to impart both patriotic virtues and obedience to legitimate authority. As Rev. George Thompson set forth in his *Spirit of General History* (1791): "history should teach men to endeavor to remove the evils which are pernicious to society; to correct the faults of government, and establish public good upon a rightful foundation."[43]

The exemplary mode of historical writing in the eighteenth century had been a central concern of Robert Henry's influential *History of Great Britain . . . on a New Plan* (1771–1703). The chief design of the work was:

> To give the reader a concise account of the most important events which have happened in Great Britain . . . with a distinct view of the religion, laws, learning, arts, commerce, and manners of its inhabitants, in every age . . . intended to draw a faithful picture of the characters and circumstances of our ancestors . . . to describe . . . the great actions which they performed, and the disgraces they sustained; the liberties they enjoyed, and the thralldom to which they were subjected; the knowledge natural, moral, and religious, with which they were illuminated, and the darkness in which they were involved . . . the virtues with which they were adorned, and the vice with which they were infected.[44]

William Russell's widely regarded *History of Modern Europe . . . [from] the Fall of the Roman Empire . . . [to] 1763* was written for young students as a series of letters from a nobleman to his son. Russell explained in the preface:

> And the character of a nobleman and a father was assumed, in order to give more weight the moral and political maxims, and to entitle the author to offer, without

seeming to dictate to the world, such reflections on life and manners as are supposed more immediately to belong to the higher orders in society.[45]

Russell's paternal and aristocratic instructor considered the downfall of Rome vital to the understanding of the elements of modern history and the founding of modern European nations such as England; history was not just meant for the "disquisitions of a mere scholar" but contained the very "origins of our laws, manners, and customs; the progress of society, of arts, and of letters."[46] Alexander Tytler's popular lectures in universal history in Edinburgh, published later as *Elements of General History* (1801), proclaimed that it was an "indispensable duty of every man of liberal birth" to be acquainted with the science of politics and history as "the school of politics."[47] History enabled mankind to verify all the "precepts of morality and of prudence." It explained the "springs of human action" and the causes of the "rise, grandeur, revolutions, and fall of empires."[48] It removed prejudices, nourished the love of one's country, and directed to the "best means of its improvement."[49] The Tory historian William Mitford's *History of Greece* (1784–1810), written at the instance of Gibbon, a fellow militia officer in his youth, was designed to refute the principles of the French and American revolutions and to defend the sanctity of the British constitution.[50] "The oldest traditional memorials of Greece" wrote Mitford, "relate, not to war and conquest, the only materials for the annals of barbarous ages, but to the invention or introduction of institutions the most indispensable to political society."[51]

These examples of the purported utility of historical edification help elucidate the political and intellectual context in which the early histories of India and of the British Empire were about to be received. The imperial moment mediated between the history of England *sui generis* and its writ over the British islands, between the autonomous progress of its political constitution and the expansive, universal histories of humankind. The mirror of history that had been handed down by antiquarian scholarship offered the present and future of empire in the glimpse of empires past. This was perhaps the most essential mimetic function of imperial history, directed at a convoluted knowledge of the self. But there was another surface of the mirror, which became more and more apparent as the frontiers of empire expanded beyond common expectations. Here the particular historical identity of the nation had to be extricated from the prospect of a multitudinous history of mankind that was beginning to unfold in the wake of imperial expansion.

INDIA OF THE MORAL ENLIGHTENMENT

The incursion of British arms in India occurred at a time in which the Enlightenment sense of a common human past had taken hold of the current historical imagination. Through the course of the eighteenth century the principles underlying the idea of a Great Chain of Being—a plenteous and continuous natural order with discernible shades of progress—had found wide acceptance among most thinkers in Western Europe. Historians were hardly immune to such a conception. The record of civilization seemed to strengthen the assertion that the temporal course of humanity followed a natural order of things. History could now yield to what Arthur Lovejoy would call the Baconian spirit, the triumphant march of "patient empirical inquiry."[52]

Both Montesquieu and Gibbon were exponents of an idea of a universal history of mankind, although in dissimilar ways. Human societies exhibited a bewildering diversity of forms, but the pattern and direction of history could be clearly identified: from backwardness to progress, from barbarism and irrationality to the rule of reason.[53] There was one rather simple explanation of climate and geography as the mainspring of human character, of human history as the history of natural causes, accounting for the difference between different nations and cultures; the other, perhaps more profound explication of the course of human history was the struggle between reason and unreason. Nature and reason had by now emerged as the two significant touchstones of historical writing. For Hume, history afforded a glimpse into the salient aspects of human nature evident in not only the "convulsions of the civilized state" but also the "revolutions incident to barbarians."[54] Gibbon's Rome fell, on the contrary, not by some immutable law of nature, but through the sheer follies of irrationality, barbarism, and religious fervor, demonstrating the constancy of history as an endless "*tableau des crimes et des malheurs*"—a lesson Gibbon took to heart from Voltaire.

Natural explanations would soon take a front seat. Much of known and unknown human history could now be studied together as what Kames put forthrightly as "a History of the Species, in its progress from the savage state to its highest civilization and improvement."[55] The history of the crowd of mankind, wrote Adam Ferguson in his *Essay on the History of Civil Society,* published in 1767, was driven not by divine providence nor by the active agency of man, but "by the circumstances in which they are placed."[56] The forms of society, like the very winds that blow, derived from origins "obscure and distant" and made their way forward "with equal blindness to the future."[57] Modern as well as ancient history, and the study of the "practice of nations in every quarter of the world, and in every condition, whether that of the barbarian or the polished," all bore out the validity of the assertion that the "seeds of every form are lodged in human nature."[58]

The moral enlightenment had laid the ground for a burgeoning confidence in historical naturalism that eventually found its way into a much wider public domain. In his *Spirit of General History,* compiled from lectures delivered to a general audience and invoking Hume and Voltaire, the Reverend George Thompson declared that the "history of mankind from the beginning of the world to the present time, is a chain consisting of many links; and to strike off one, would be to decompose the whole."[59] It seems evident that India was very much part of this extended concatenation of human conditions, and towards the end of the eighteenth century it appeared intermittently as an ancient civilization in the writing of major philosophers of the moral enlightenment.

These images, I would urge, are crucial to an appreciation of the first serious historical treatments of India that followed the early stages of British ascendancy. The Enlightenment view of oriental societies provides an essential context for the early Company histories, especially the work of Robert Orme, official historiographer of the East India Company, whom we shall discuss at greater length later in this chapter. Here one finds the narrative of British conquest of India and triumph over the French interspersed with the study of Indian manners, customs, and character as essential and unchanging attributes. This duality appears in the very title of the posthumous dedication of Orme's *Historical Fragments* (1782), presented to the Court of Directors of the East India Company in 1806 with the following inscription: "The world is indebted for those discoveries in the history and sciences of the East which have given to the English name in India a reputation for learning not less exalted than its fame in arms and legislation. . . ."[60]

Orme's fame rested on not only his fine knowledge of Indian historical events but what William Jones described as his "accurate knowledge of Asiatic manners."[61] Such manners consisted of a series of observations on the climate, luxuries, abundant produce, indolence of the people, fecundity of women, and effeminacy of men in India, observations more reminiscent of the quirks of James Burnett, Lord Monboddo than his professed exemplar, Thucydides. Jones himself, in his preliminary discourse delivered to the Asiatic Society, which was inaugurated in 1784, defined history as a branch of learning that was "either an account of natural productions, or the genuine records of empires and states."[62] Indeed, natural history seemed to provide ready explanations for the state of development of oriental societies.

The assertion that nature in warmer climates is overflowing and keeps the inhabitants from the vigorous exercise of body and mind and thus from social advancement can be found readily in John Millar's *Origin of the Distinction of Ranks,* a work published in 1771, within a few years of Orme's *Transactions.* Millar considered climate to be one of the most important circumstances that dictated the improvement of societies:

> In warm countries the earth is often extremely fertile, and with little culture is capable of producing whatever is necessary for substance. To labour under the extreme heat of the sun is, at the same time, exceedingly troublesome and oppressive. The inhabitants, therefore, of such countries, while they enjoy a degree of affluence, and, while by mildness of climate they are exempted from many inconveniences and wants, are seldom disposed to any laborious exertion, and thus, acquiring the habits of indolence, become addicted to sensual pleasure, and liable to all those infirmities which are nourished by idleness and sloth.[63]

Rank and obedience derived in principle from this basic character of "feudal dependence" nourished by the same conditions that led to despotism.[64] The

extensive kingdoms of the East Indies were based on this ideal; the hereditary warriors, once subject to the independent rajahs, had eventually come
to constitute the extensive nobility of the "Great Mogul."

Lord Kames, in his *Sketches,* wondered similarly "how such swarms of
people can find bread" in countries of the East.[65] He was convinced that the
people of India were not fully and fruitfully employed; their manufactures
were simply the product of a "country where hand-labour is a drug for the
want of employment."[66] William Robertson, generally sympathetic in his
judgments, still held that Indians were destined from birth to become habituated to the employment of hands, a condition that easily explained the
"high degree of perfection" in the realm of manufactures, accompanied by
the lack of any spirit of invention.[67]

Despite a dependency on the bounty of nature, the India of the Enlightenment was endowed with attributes of a true civilization and accorded a certain stage in the history of human advancement. Polished or civilized nations
were commercial nations, while a "people regardless of commercial arts" characterized rude or barbarian nations, as Adam Ferguson would have it.[68] Robertson was undoubtedly struck by the "early and high civilization of the people of
India"[69] regarding its political constitution and form of government, spirit of
the laws, useful and elegant arts, and cultivation of the sciences. The cultivation of land and the recognition of permanent tenure in land marked a stage
of social progress prior to commerce and industry.[70] Indian society, however,
was marred by the pervasive influence of despotism, which robbed the people
of their ancient rights and freedoms, in contrast to the rude nations of America, who represented the "human race in the infancy of society."[71]

To capture the essence of oriental despotism in India, Ferguson
sketched an elaborate portrait of the Mughal emperor Aurangzeb, who had
"aimed at the summit of human greatness."[72] Although he sought imperial fortune, Aurangzeb rose above the "enjoyment of ease" and the "grati-
fications of animal appetite." Unlike the barbarian, he was immune to
sensual pleasure as well as the feelings of human nature, and could thus
strike a pose of "that awful majesty" in the presence of admiring crowds
"overwhelmed with the sense of his greatness, and with that of their own
debasement."[73] And so, declared Ferguson, "the chains of perpetual slavery . . . appear to be riveted in the East."

And yet, in the West, too, men were perfectly capable of bowing to "splendid equipage" and regarded with awe the "pomp of a princely estate."[74] In the
East, servility was inherited from ancestors, while in the West people became
corrupt and weak through their "own arts and contrivances." Despotism and
corruption were thus equally incident to polished and advanced nations.

A TEST OF HISTORICAL FAMILIARITY

One legacy of the Enlightenment view was the realization that the malaise of
corruption, tyranny, and despotism was simply not a preserve of oriental

countries such as India but perilously close to affairs of the contemporary state. The mirror of the East was then something of a ruse and had been used with great effect to reduce ambitious statesmen, the most defamatory case in point being Montesquieu's *Persian Letters,* often considered as thinly veiled barbs aimed at the regency of Phillipe d'Orléans. As Montesquieu's protagonist Usbek remarked to Ibben: "Monarchy is a state of tension, which always degenerates into despotism or republicanism."[75] Although this is a wry aside, despotism appears here as an enduring flaw of the human character as much as an oriental flagrancy.

A discussion of despotism as a trope for British conduct in India can be found most famously, no doubt, in Burke's condemnation of the affairs of the East India Company. In his speech on the opening of the impeachment of Warren Hastings in 1788, Burke accused the governor-general of having sought refuge in "geographical morality," an assertion that when Europeans traverse certain latitudes and longitudes, their innate virtues become irrelevant.[76] He refused to grant Hastings what he suspected was his outstanding plea, that he had governed in India according to "arbitrary and despotic powers" that were in keeping with "Oriental principles." In his speeches, Burke, unlike many of his contemporaries, rejected for the most part the notion of an endemic tyranny of the Orient.[77] There are only a few exceptions where he admitted Indians to be servile, most notably, perhaps, in his description of Hastings and his "black agents," who are "secret and mysterious," capable of concealing the dark deeds of Europeans done through them.[78]

Despite the thrust of Burke's sentiments, India was liable to be seen as a civilization distant in both space and time. The image of a despotic society— a repository of arbitrary rulers and helpless subjects, timeless and immune to advancement—had come to dominate the familiar view. The mildness of the Eastern climate and the quiescent nature of the natives could "assuage the rigours of despotical government," wrote Ferguson.[79] Transferred without struggle "from one master to another," the natives of India continued to pursue their industry and to "acquiesce in the enjoyments of life, and the hopes of animal pleasure"; the "modern description of India" was nothing but a "repetition of the ancient."[80] In Robertson's account, India is lost to history until the arrival of Alexander. The Greeks provide the "first authentic information" of India in regards to her climate, soil, productions, and inhabitants, demonstrating in their accounts its unchanging history:

> In a country where the manners, the customs, and even the dress of the people, are almost as permanent and invariable as the face of nature itself, it is wonderful how exactly the description given by Alexander's officers delineate what we now behold in India, at the distance of two thousand years.[81]

Elsewhere, Robertson had commented on how Rome itself had been run down by an addiction to Eastern luxuries that led to the jealously of despotism and an extinction of the martial spirit.[82] India was by now a familiar oriental territory, a conspicuous part of Burke's "great map of mankind" where every state of barbarism and refinement was in plain sight at the same instant, and the knowledge of human nature, manners, and characters of diverse peoples did not have to rely simply on the meager records of history.[83]

This vexed question of temporality in the passages between the historicist and the ahistorical representation of India and Indians is particularly relevant to the argument in this chapter. There was a growing divergence between India as a *context* for a history of the British nation and empire, and India as a *subject* of historical and ethnological inquiry. This contradiction is nowhere more apparent than in Robert Orme, the designated historian of British national exploits in India. The first volume of the *History of the Military Transactions* (1763) was conceived as account of the Company in India, ending in the war between the British and the French in 1756, and the second volume as an account of the rise of English commerce in eastern India, the loss of Calcutta, and the subsequent vindication of the Company's military strength in 1763. This general history of Britain's military achievements in India was written for the wider public especially, as there was no other place in the world where the British arms had "acquired more honor."[84] Two hundred copies were sold in three years, and among its admirers were William Jones and William Robertson.

Orme's narrative, however, is interrupted in places by observations on the geography, climate, manners, customs, and peculiar modes of governance in India. In Book VI of the second volume, for example, Orme sets out to provide "some portion of the history of the Mahomedan government" as a background to his investigation of the progress of English commerce in the province of Bengal.[85] After having described in detail the topography of the region and the course of the river Ganges, Orme turns to a climatic explanation of the character of the natives. The "luxuriance of the soil supplies the subsistence of the inhabitants with less labour than any other country in the world," he writes, and thus "in spite of despotism the province is extremely populous."[86] What is the source of such "abundance of advantages peculiar to this country"? They have accrued, thought Orme, through generations and are in keeping with:

> the languor peculiar to the unelastic atmosphere of the climate, to debase the essential qualities of the human race, and notwithstanding the general effeminacy of character which is visible in all the Indians throughout the empire, the natives of Bengal are still of weaker frame and more enervated disposition that those of any other province: bodily strength, courage, and fortitude are unknown: even the labour of common people is totally void of energy. . . .[87]

Such a passage, seemingly at odds with the main flow of the narrative, is but a variation on a theme of the moral enlightenment that we have seen above, reminiscent of Ferguson, Millar, and Kames. The difference, however, is that

Orme spent fourteen years of his life in India and was able to observe it first-hand. He had left England in 1742 at the age of fourteen to join the services of the Company, first a writer and then a factor, a member of the Madras Council, and one of the main architects of the campaign in southern India against the French.[88] He would have succeeded as the governor of Madras, but it was the very climate of India that affected his health, and he had to leave for England in 1758. While a writer in Calcutta, Orme had started to write in 1752 a treatise on native manners and customs, which would later be published posthumously with his *Fragments,* entitled "A General Idea of the Government and People of Indostan." Orme justified his observations as the result of an attention given to this subject during a residence of several years in India; and yet, his understanding of Indian society was severely compromised by his ignorance of Indian languages except for colloquial Hindustani.[89]

In this tract, the natives of India are reduced to near-caricature as part of the human race "struggling through such mighty ills as render its condition scarcely superior to that of the brutes of the field."[90] Such unfortunate inhabitants had been long subject to the "iron sway of despotism" and yet continued to be populous, even capable of turning out finer articles of manufacture. The key to this sordid forbearance was the effect of the climate itself, which not only enervated their spirits but also turned them into the most effeminate inhabitants of the globe. Orme thus presented Indians as ageless and, despite numerous external conquests, as having "lost very little of their original character."[91] The original inhabitants, the Hindus, were beyond historical reckoning, as they had "all memory of the ages" in which their mythology and religion took shape.[92]

Robertson, who was, as we have seen, much more charitable towards Indians and their civilization, did not find a reliable written record among the ancient Hindus, and considered them prior to written history, much like the rest of antiquity before the account of the Greeks, relegated to the "region of conjecture, of fable, and of uncertainty."[93] The first authentic accounts were of the writers who came with Alexander, most importantly Megasthenes, corroborated by Arrian, Strabo, and also the eyewitness accounts of travelers such as Tavernier and Bernier.[94] Robertson matched these with more recent eyewitness accounts of Forster and Orme. This chronological gulf did not seem to matter as far as the fundamental facts of Indian society were concerned, such as the system of caste, which, above all, was a "striking peculiarity" of the state of the country, a living proof of the "permanence of its institutions, and the immutability in the manners of its inhabitants."[95] Robertson, following the ancient heathen chroniclers, deemed Indians to be *Autochthones,* true natives of the soil whose origin could not be further traced. This view became quickly entrenched among a wider public. The *Asiatic Annual Register* of 1799, in a précis of the history of British India debating the origin of the primeval inhabitants, declared, citing Orme: "We therefore concur in the received opinion, that the Hindu race were the original inhabitants of Hindustan."[96]

THE HISTORY OF A CONQUERED NATION

Orme was one of the earliest commentators to have divided the natives of India into two distinct races or nations, the Gentoos and the Moors. The Moors, who had conquered the country with "little difficulty,"[97] had subjugated the meek and effeminate Gentoos, "the original people of the country."[98] The yoke of despotism had taught them the "necessity of patience," while slavery had sharpened their finesse in trade and manufacture. According to Orme, slavery of the subject population is key to an appreciation of Indian despotism. He remarks in the *Fragments:* "I must apologize for reminding the reader so often, of the gradation of slavery which subsists throughout Indostan; without carrying this idea continually with us, it is impossible to form any idea of these people."[99]

The conquering Moors, endowed by nature with the martial spirit, had also been corrupted by India: her climate and habits had "enervated the strong fibres with which the Tartars conquered it."[100] Moors in India, within the space of two generations, had acquired "the indolence and pusillanimity of the original inhabitants."[101] This, however, was a peculiar affliction, that made them not as timid and effeminate as the Gentoos, but inhuman, cruel, avaricious, and vile.[102]

The history of India also implied the incommensurable history of the two races. Orme's first publication began with a history of the Mohammedan conquests, followed by those of the British. Hindus had been deemed as unfit for a serious study of the historical record. Edmund Burke, who gathered much of his historical knowledge from a reading of Jonathan Zephania Holwell's work,[103] seemed to concur with the idea that there were indeed "two distinct people in India, totally distinct to each other in characters, lives and manners."[104] He too took the Gentoos to be the original people of India, now subjects of the British Empire, but spoke characteristically in defense of their mild, feminine (not effeminate) manners, their principles, their "green old age," and their reverence for antiquity.[105]

The origin of the natives of India represented for Burke "the first era in which we are to view the history of the East."[106] The next was the dominion of Islam, the "era of the Arabs," attended by despotism and "great misfortune." After the ferocity of conquest and conversion died down, the Arabs, not having had much success against the "constancy of the sufferers," allowed their subjects, although robbed of their ancient sovereignty, to subsist in relative quiet. The next era was the era of Tamerlane, or the Tartars, who left the Hindus with a degree of independency, followed by the era of Akbar (Burke mistakenly uses Khouli Khan) where, despite a despotic frame of rule, they were protected. The last era before the arrival of the British on the political scene was the era of the independent provinces of the country after the demise of the empire built by the successors of Tamerlane. The last and present unfortunate era began, according to Burke, with the year 1756, marking the ascendancy of the British.

Note that Burke's historical account relegates the native Hindus clearly to antiquity, while history begins to move squarely with subsequent Arab and Mughal conquering regimes. Unlike Orme, Burke had refrained from vilifying the Muslim dynasties, in part, perhaps, to accentuate the villainy of Hastings. Other contemporaries were not as kind. Holwell himself painted a ghastly picture of Aurangzeb and his successors who copied his "bloody example," leaving a record of the "miserable effects of this fatal passion for rule."[107] The very rapacity of the native regimes in the eighteenth century seemed to invite the ultimate intervention and protection of the British. Luke Scrafton in his *Reflections* (1763) also assumed the religion, customs, and the government of native Indians to have been resilient to the Mohammedan conquerors.[108] His Gentoos, like Orme's, are also a meek, unfeeling, and ravaged people, lacking in ambition and vigor. The enervating heat of the climate stifles the virtuous passions, leaving only avarice that leads to an oppressive government, inspiring no loyalty or patriotic feeling.

By all accounts, then, the British in India seemed to have found a body of subjects who had been repeatedly violated in the past. Even critics of Company rule, such as Nathaniel Brassy Halhed, scholar of Persian, grammarian, and advisor to Warren Hastings, describing the "moral and political state" of India and its inhabitants, saw their condition as inextricably linked to the causes that have generally held Asia "in slavery from the very first epoch of history."[109] Alexander Dow, one of the leading explicators of oriental despotism, saw in the history of India "a striking picture of the deplorable condition of a people subjected to arbitrary sway."[110] India had always been subject to the whims of conquerors, an "ample field for private ambition, and for public tyranny." The rise of Islamic empires in India could be explained very easily as the maturity and "perfect growth" of the "seeds of despotism, which the nature of the climate and fertility of the soil had sown in India."[111] Slavery had thus been blended with human nature among an "indolent and ignorant race of men." The Muslim conquest, according to Dow, had also precluded the possibility of a genuine, indigenous chronicle of India. Introducing the translation of Ferishta's history to the public, he implied that the task for British historians of India was to discover and understand the "internal history of India." Rather than a history of Hindustan or a description of the "affairs of the Hindoos," Ferishta's account, compiled during the time of the Mughal emperor Jahangir, was rather a history of the "Mahommedan Empire in India." The prejudice of the Muslim conquerors had blinded them to the historical record of the ancient Indians, which lay entangled in the fabulous and untrustworthy chronology of the Brahmins.[112]

Yet Dow did not simply dismiss the Hindu annals. They had to be deciphered, translated, and brought to light; it could be demonstrated that they "carry their authentic history farther back into antiquity than any other nation now existing."[113] This, after all, was the inspiration of orientalist scholars such as William Jones and Halhed. Robertson set out to describe the civil policy, the arts, the sciences, and the religious institutions of the ancient Indians, to establish the "wonderful progress" they had once made. A proper knowledge of the civilization and antiquity of Indians mattered to Robertson, who like Burke, hoped that it might have an ameliorating influence upon the behavior of the Europeans towards them. It was unfortunate "for the human species" that the Europeans found people in inferior states of society and progress wherever they staked their dominion; in Africa they had enslaved, and in America they had exterminated the natives.[114] And even in India, which, according to Robertson, was much further advanced than the above, the "colour of the inhabitants, their effeminate appearance, their unwarlike spirit, the wild extravagance of their religious tenets and ceremonies" had convinced the Europeans of their "own pre-eminence" in that they treated these subjects "as an inferior race of men." It was important to try and cultivate among those who had most recently subjugated India a "proper sentiment" toward their "natural rights" as men. Robertson brings his disquisition to a close by reflecting on the regard paid by the Mughal emperor Akbar to his Hindu subjects, who were given equal protection and favor. Akbar had that "liberality of mind" which opened him to their virtues and attainments. Robertson seemed to suggest tacitly that the British would do well to emulate such an embracing attitude, exemplified by the likes of Warren Hastings, who had tried to imitate and surpass "two centuries afterwards, the illustrious example of Akber."[115]

The historical representation of India as a nation long subjugated and languishing under the burden of despotism now connoted the dominant position of the British as the most recent custodians of this ancient civilization. The East India Company had acquired, as Orme saw it, the miserable subjects of the despotic rulers of Hindustan, whose condition had been further worsened by the fact that no indigenous regime had obtained the "power to control the vast extent of its dominion."[116] It would be not too difficult to see all this as rhetoric that merely justified territorial acquisitions in India. But the emerging historical image of a dependent India conveyed a different dimension altogether to the larger narrative of imperial expansion. The Enlightenment, as we have seen, had opened up the possibility of a comparative and objective study of mankind, and even faith in the linearity of human progress. The incontestable fact of empire had added a magisterial impartiality and aloofness to this view. As Mackintosh, in his lectures on the "Law of Nature and Nations" (1797), put it plainly, it was now possible to "bring before us man in a lower state and more abject condition that any in which he was ever seen" and also to "make human society pass in review before our mind."[117] The mighty empires of Asia had now been opened to reveal the "tame, but ancient and immovable" civilization of China as well as the "meek and servile natives of Hindostan, who preserve their ingenuity, their skill, and their science, through a long series of ages, under the yoke of foreign tyrants."

The early colonial histories of India *pace* Orme would begin to treat the history of India with a more studied detachment. Both geographically and temporally, India seemed to have become a more distant acquisition. Orme, commenting on the general dissimulation and impenetrability of the Indian character, was moved to expound upon how noble the sentiments of Christian morality appeared when compared to the perverted instincts of the people of Hindustan, and how grateful seemed the "cause of liberty" in a country whose political record was replete with violence and bloodshed without moral restraint.[118] At the same time, however, such dissimulation, urged to the contrary a most serious adherence to the historical character of Britons entrusted with the administration of India. The following section is a study of how such an émigré sense of history came to be.

HISTORY AND THE IMPERIAL CHARACTER

By the turn of the century, while British rule was being consolidated in various parts of the Indian subcontinent, the need for a regular, trustworthy, and permanently established civil service became apparent.[119] The seeds of this had been established during reform of the revenue collection initiated by Lord Cornwallis, who tried to extract young company administrators from the clutches of their Indian intermediaries in the internal government of the provinces of Bengal. There had also emerged the problem of an elaborate and staid system of patronage, based often on family and income, whereby a director of the Company would nominate members of his immediate and larger family; this was true especially for families who had produced civil servants over more than one generation, such as the Plowdens and the Thackerays.[120] Thus between 1762 and 1781 more than thirty-six sons or nephews of civil servants joined the Bengal Civil Service, and about thirty-four between 1790–1800; in the latter period almost one in seven appointments took place through such family patronage.[121]

The Committee of Patronage, established in 1798, was particularly concerned about writers' positions being sold. Corruption at home and abroad impelled Marquis Wellesley to begin reforming the entire administrative system soon after his arrival in Bengal (1798). In January 1800 he wrote confidentially to Henry Dundas of the Board of Control that no servant of the Company that he had met in India was fit to be a member of the executive government in the presidencies, as their "education, habits, and manners, all tend to disqualify them from a situation in which general knowledge, and extended views of policy, as well as dignity of character and conduct, are required."[122]

In his Minute in Council at Fort William, Calcutta, in August 1804, Wellesley proposed to extend his reform through the establishment of a college to train servants of the Company, declaring that the "duty and policy of the British Government in India therefore require . . . the system of confiding the immediate exercise of every branch of and department of the Government to Europeans educated in its own service, and subject to its own direct control."[123] It was not an easy matter to mete out justice to "millions of people of various languages, manners, usages, and religions," nor to "administer a vast and complicated system of revenue," nor indeed to maintain "civil order."[124] This was a charge that demanded a noble and public calling on the part of young India-bound Britons, for no more "arduous or complicated duties of magistracy" could exist in the world. Their future roles as judges, governors, magistrates, and ambassadors in India required that their education, habits of life, manners, and morals should be strictly regulated. And thus not only should their knowledge of the various branches of science and literature be sound, but also their acquaintance with the history, languages, customs, and manners of the people of India, native codes of law and religion, and the political and commercial connection of Great Britain to India. In essence, the governor-general was asking for a blend of classical education and practical knowledge of the Orient. This could be a new breed of public servants, skillful statesmen "sufficiently grounded in the general principles of ethics, civil jurisprudence, the laws of nations, and general history."[125] Wellesley wanted to establish Fort William as the premier institution, modeled on the colleges of Oxford and Cambridge, where such a system of disciplined learning could take place by sequestering young men for the length of at least three years before they joined the Indian service.

Wellesley's proposed curriculum provides a quick glimpse into the kind of classical and liberal education that had become indispensable in public service: the harvest of both civic humanism and the Enlightenment.[126] Along with Indian and oriental languages, students at Fort William were expected to gain an insight into ethics, civil jurisprudence, law of nations and of England, political economy, Greek, Latin, and English classics. They had to acquire proficiency in botany, chemistry, and astronomy. They also had to study general history, ancient and modern, the history and antiquities of Hindustan (which included that of the Deccan, or southern India), and natural history. History was very much at the heart of the roster, a guide to virtuous and moral conduct, a bulwark against the corrupt and beguiling society of Indians and against the "peculiar depravities incident to the climate, and to the characters of the natives."[127]

Wellesley had established the college in Calcutta without the consent of the Court of Directors, which was in favor of the principles behind its foundation, but wanted instead to set up the college in England.[128] The directors proposed to retain Fort William, as it would further the instruction of graduates from England, especially in the oriental languages. A committee was formed under Charles Grant, whose emendation of Wellesley's plan, requiring much less money, was accepted in 1803, and the East-India College was founded in Haileybury, Hertford. The objective behind its establishment was to provide a steady "supply of persons duly qualified to discharge the various and important duties required from the civil servants of the Company administering the government of India."[129] The college was expected to receive students at the age of fifteen who would continue till eighteen, and instruct them in the history, customs, and manners of the "different nations of the East," law, and political economy as part of a "general system of education."[130] It was equally incumbent on them to acquire the proper "moral and religious conduct" and the "principles of ethics and natural theology and in the evidences doctrines and the duties of revealed religion."[131] The directors felt that young Britons "should be imbued with reverence and love" for the religion, constitution, and laws of their own country before they left for many years of life among people in every way dissimilar to their own."[132] Thomas Malthus, who took a position as a professor of general history, politics, and finance in 1805, vindicated the usefulness of restricting prospective servants of India at Haileybury. He believed that it was an arduous task to begin a course of law, history, political economy, and natural philosophy in India at the age of sixteen, where the "enfeebling effects of the climate" discouraged any strenuous efforts.[133] The foundation of general knowledge was "best laid in the West."[134] Malthus defended the college against the charge that its students lacked discipline and asserted that they "are formed in their morals, prepared in their character, and qualified in their education" for the stations they were to occupy in India.

The foregoing agenda suggests a signal transformation that had taken place in the proposed education of men were who to rule India. Writers who were once required to have what was known simply as "commercial knowledge"— intended, as an irate proprietor of the Company stock put it, to "weigh tea, count bales, and measure muslins"[135]—were now urged to take up classical and general literature, including the tracts of orators and historians of Greece and Rome, and attend dutifully to lectures on the arts of reasoning and composition.[136] They were to familiarize themselves with the general course of human history and the history of modern European nations. They were to penetrate the new branches of statistics and political economy and were examined on the laws of England and the foundations of the British constitution.

British rule in India was thus being vindicated by what we have already seen as a popular classical-historical outlook: the replication of institutions that upheld moral conduct. As Lord Minto, another governor-general of India, remarked in his public disputation of 1813, without "classical instruction" no English gentleman was "on level with his fellows."[137] All candidates for admission into the college were required to furnish a testimonial from their schoolmasters and pass an examination in Greek, Latin, and arithmetic. Testimonials of this period (1806–1810) show that masters emphasized their pupils' accomplishments in classical learning, along with French, mathematics, geography, bookkeeping, and the like, to present them as suitable for a coveted career in India.[138] C. J. Heathcote, master of the Hackney School, wrote of his pupil Henry Blundell that he had been "in the habit of reading the Greek and Latin classics" and that he had read Homer, Xenophon, Cicero, Virgil, and Horace.[139] James Gregory, a private tutor in the family of the lord bishop of Kildare, wrote of young Philip Lindsay that he had acquired a "literary and regular education" with proficiency in Latin and Greek and tolerable grasp of French and geography.[140] One Mr. John Master had read a good part of Xenonphon's *Works,* the seventeen first books of the *Iliad* along with Virgil and Horace, and had been "in the constant habit of composing on moral and religious subjects, both in Latin and English, in verse and prose"; another Henry Gardiner of Harrow impressed his tutors with his "moral conduct and classical attainments."[141] William Cole, master of the Royal Grammar School of Guilford, Surrey, wrote of Benjamin Taylor that he had read Virgil and Caesar and could "construe with facility" the Greek Testaments.[142] Such qualifications continued to be valuable through at least the next two decades of the nineteenth century, as testimonials from both English and Scottish academies suggest.[143]

To what purpose was such education to be realized in India? The East India Company, as we have seen in the preceding chapter, had regenerated itself as a surrogate and expatriate English state in India. Wellesley had urged that in the line of duty, policy, and honor, it was incumbent on the English that they not administer India "as a temporary and precarious acquisition"; the stability of the Indian empire required "durable principles of internal order," a mild and enlightened government, and an entire system of administration that required "a succession of able Magistrates, wise and honest Judges, and skilful Statesmen."[144] Such a plan vindicated what Burke had argued almost two decades before—that it was not enough to let the Court of Directors remain in sole charge of the Company servants, a large body "possessed of high and extensive Powers, and exercising them at a very great Distance from the Source and Seat of Government."[145] The British government in India should be "preserved in the strictest Obedience to the Government at Home," in the interests of both Great Britain and the natives of India.[146] In his speech on Fox's India Bill, Burke charged that the English youth in India were intoxicated with authority and amassed fortunes before they were "ripe in principle."[147]

The education thus prescribed to students at both the College of Fort William as well as the East-India College at Haileybury illustrates a turn to history as a public undertaking that both Burke and Mackintosh might have endorsed. Haileybury itself was built by the young architect William Wilkins on classical proportions. Its building became a future landmark for the architectural style known as the Greek revival. The crest of the college, bearing the motto *Auspicio Regis et Senatus Anglia,* signified the legacy of the Roman republic.[148] This was in the spirit of a long history of Roman heroic figures employed in the self-styling of eminent Englishmen in India. In 1764 Clive had been carved in marble as a Roman emperor. John Bacon was commissioned to make a statue of the Marquis of Cornwallis in Roman military uniform in the Town Hall of Calcutta. In 1830 Sir Richard Westmacott would finish the marble statue of Hastings as a Roman senator, now displayed in the Victoria Memorial Museum, Calcutta.[149]

History as icon, much like pedagogy, was seen as an essential ingredient of public virtue, and historical reasoning was considered much more than simply administrative expedience. Burke had argued fervently in his *Reflections on the Revolution in France* that the laws, opinions, and "inveterate usages of our country" that had been handed down by the "prejudice of ages" were indeed privileges that distinguished the English temper and secured individuals against the injustice and despotism inherent in the human nature.[150] History for Burke was one great volume "unrolled for our instruction," namely miseries brought upon the world by the long "train of disorderly appetites"— ambition, avarice, revenge, sedition, and the like—a repository for future wisdom drawn from the past errors and weaknesses of mankind.[151] The examples of history might be remote and not always clear, he cautioned to the fallen aristocracy of Europe, but the cultivation of history was a necessary habit, "an exercise to strengthen the mind."[152] Discerning public men should not be misled in this regard by historians, who were not only prejudiced and ignorant but also more attached to "system than [to] truth."

Burke was hopeful that the history of the next century, better grasped and utilized, would teach a "civilized posterity" to shun the wrongs of his own barbarous times. Such a sentiment, one could argue, pervades Burke's view of India in general, a vision of history that was passed on to Wellesley and the subsequent patrons of the education of civil servants in England and in India. Students at the Fort William College in Calcutta were asked before obtaining their qualifying degree to hold four public disputations in Persian or Bengali, as both opponents and respondents, on propositions submitted by themselves on a moral, historical, or literary subject or regarding oriental manners and customs.[153] Haileybury College, judging by the essays published in the *Haileybury Observer*—whose editorial board between 1839 and 1842 boasted figures such as C. J. Erskine, James Frazer, Sir Monier Williams, John Strachey, and W. S. Seton-Karr—continued through the first half of the nineteenth century to cultivate the ideals of a classical education.[154] Among subjects covered[155] were literature, politics, history, biography, romance, poetry, and satire, and the pages of the *Observer* abound in Greek and Latin pseudonyms and translations of Homer, Horace, and Anacreon.

It is essential to keep this education in mind in order to understand the attitude of company historians who succeeded Orme and Mill. Raised in the civil service, trained in the languages and the colonial administration, with a firsthand knowledge of the country and its inhabitants, they seemed to confirm much of what Dundas had feared: the "danger attending the collection of literary and philosophical men" that would lead to Jacobinism in

India.[156] The prevalent standpoint, however, turned out to be a more conservative one, distinguishing clearly between the historical foundations of the nation at home and the history of the Company's Indian subjects.

OFFICIAL HISTORIOGRAPHIES

Historical sketches became routine in the administrative circles of British India with the progress of the nineteenth century. Wellesley's territorial expansion had led to a never-ending series of revenue settlements and had also augmented the need for constant political intelligence to keep hostile powers—especially the French—at bay. Such policies resulted in a new welter of treaties and negotiations with native Indian powers. There was a demand for variegated, immediate, and functional studies of the Indian past. In this pursuit, the broad and reflective judgment of the manners, customs, habits, character, and civilization of Indians became less important, while at the same time sediments of censure and deprecation of the country as a degenerate body politic became more deeply imbedded.

The publication of James Mill's *History* was, by all counts, a most significant gesture towards such a common view of the role of the British on the subcontinent. Mill dispensed with the empathy that Jones and Robertson had shown towards the natives of India, raising a serious doubt whether such a "rude and credulous people" could ever have had proper laws, forms of government, or a genuine sense of history.[157] India, according to Mill, had always been at the mercy of the invader's sword and thus deprived of an autonomous historical record, and awaited a modern European civilization to decipher her accurate past.[158]

Mill's view, no doubt, would become characteristic of the official attitude of Britons in charge of India and in many ways sums up the critical distance predictive of a confident and expansive imperialism. What I would like to explore here, however, is not so much this hardening of attitude but rather the widespread practice of history-writing as integral to the colonial administrative regimen, a habit reflected in statistical accounts, gazetteers, reports, journals, and travelogues, in other words, the entire corpus of bureaucratic rule. Some of the pioneers of this sort of history-writing, unlike Mill, were men who rode with the army or made their mark as committed and active civil servants. They became figures of imperial legend; a hardy, robust "race of public servants unsurpassed in the history of the world," to quote historian and biographer John Kaye—those who looked to India as a home and to the Indian services as their life's work, representing the best of Britain in India.[159] Thus it was the scholar-administrator on horseback who advanced the historical knowledge of the interior of the subcontinent in the era of the largest territorial expansion: the likes of Mark Wilks, John Malcolm, and Mountstuart Elphinstone.

One of the earliest instances of historical writing conceived in the midst of the struggle against the French and the ruling house of Mysore in southern India is William Hollingbery's *History,* published in 1805, of the Nizam of Hyderabad, a ruling house that became allied by treaty to the Company. Hollingbery dedicated his work to the two most distinguished men in the military and diplomatic service at the time, Col. William Kirkpatrick and Lt. Col. John Malcolm. In many ways his was a "firsthand" account, Hollingbery having served at the British Residency of Hyderabad and also in the embassy led by Malcolm to the kingdom of Persia.[160] The main premise of the work should be familiar by now, and although it predates Mill, the sentiments are comparable. In the section listed as "geographical and historical observations," the author provides a summary sketch of the inhabitants of southern India, noting their internal differences. People of the woods and the littoral are "very barbarous" while the inhabitants of the interior are "more polished."[161] Both descend from the original Hindus, whose system of caste account for this "strange mixture of polity and barbarity." Superstition, misery, and ignorance reign among the peasants, whose faculties are stunted, hardly surpassing "the level of the monkeys that inhabit the woods, and the cattle that assist [their] labours."[162] There are also the descendants of the "original Mohummedan invaders," who hold a degree of dominion over the rest; many were former Hindus partially relieved of their "mental ignorance" through conversion and thus had acquired some capacity for judgment. Such assertions, however, have little to do with the subsequent narrative history of the kingdom of Hyderabad and its position vis-à-vis the East India Company.

Hollingbery's *History* is a compilation of several accounts, including the Persian chronicle of Ferishta and the works of Orme and Henry Vansittart, as well as original documents, but the main purpose of the narrative is to provide the context and explanation for the British military campaigns: Mughal power wanes in the south because of the "fatal error" of emperor Aurangzeb's destruction of the smaller Muslim kingdoms in his failed attempt at military conquest, leading to the rise of the Marathas and other predatory regimes such as Hyder in Mysore, which not only employ European soldiers in their armies but seek the assistance of the French as rivals of the British.[163] The prominent points of the history are the English alliance with the Nizam (once provincial governors of the Mughals) against the threat of Tipu Sultan, war against the Marathas, the eventual destruction of the French subsidiary force and thus the Jacobin threat in southern India, and the great subsidiary treaty with Hyderabad, a cornerstone of Wellesley's new *pax Britannica.*[164]

Mark Wilks, who rose to the position of lieutenant in the Madras army at Fort St. George, was companion to Col. James Stuart in 1793 during the war against Tipu Sultan, and served between 1803 and 1808 as the political resident at the court of Mysore, was a more prominent example of a historian close to the front. His widely admired *Historical Sketches of the South of India in an Attempt to Trace the History of Mysoor* was a work that was based on his access to state records, especially those of Fort St. George, his participation in the very campaigns he describes, and his official knowledge of political and diplomatic transactions. Wilks was also able to see the official records of Mysore that had been taken from Seringapatam to Calcutta after the destruction of Tipu's regime.[165]

Wilks begins his account with the idea that conquest, revolution, and the eventual decay of the polity were usual in uncivilized nations such as India and were forces that afflicted the Muslim dynasties equally.[166] The despotic fiber of Indian society was impervious to both outside conquest and internal rebellion: "the whole scheme of polity, whether of the victors or the vanquished, the very idea of civil liberty had absolutely never entered into the contemplation. . . ."[167] Significantly, Wilks discounted the exclusive effect of climate on the despotic character of the "two great classes of mankind," the Muslims and the Hindus of India; one underlying moral cause was the "shackles imposed on the human mind by the union of the divine and human code" of laws and institutions.

Despite such distinctions at the outset, the depiction of Hyder Ali's rapacious character and the tyranny of the ruling house of Mysore, a terrible scourge that threatened the very "extinction of the British power in India,"[168] reads like an object lesson in despotic practice. Not only does Wilks portray Hyder as unremitting in duplicity and vengeance, but he endows him with an inordinate carnal appetite: "Hyder observed neither limit in the extent, nor principle in the means of gratification; and on the capture of a place, a department charged with the scrutiny of female beauty, discharged their functions with as much vigilance as that which searched for treasure."[169] And yet, in the very same passage, while describing him as an animal "sunk in sensuality," Wilks portrays a man with a mind "never permitted to wander from the most rigid attention to public business," in whose kingdom nothing was delayed because of the "indolence or self-indulgence of the sovereign."[170] Tipu appears even worse in comparison, consumed by "a dark and intolerant bigotry," vainglorious and easily intoxicated by success, perverted by "the meanest passions."[171]

Wilks's narrative ends in 1799 with Tipu slain, the English victory having put an end to the "uncontrolled exercise of the right of conquest"[172] among native powers, and with the ancient Hindu kingdom of Mysore restored as a subsidiary of the English government—an act applauded in the "remotest parts of India" and acknowledged with unlimited gratitude by the people to be governed."[173] Mackintosh, with whom Wilks had corresponded, hailed this work as the "first example of a book on Indian history founded on a critical examination of testimony and probability, and from which the absurdities of fable and etymology are banished."[174] He found the story of the rise, progress, and decline of a Hindu principality and the rise of a "Mahometan usurper, who founded a conquering monarchy," compelling and instructive, for without the English stand, Islam might have brought the whole of southern India under the sway of one empire. While he considered this to be a faithful account, he found Wilks excessively polite and diffident, reluctant to state his opinions boldly. He had strayed far too close to Indians and thus had "too favorable a testimony to the state of society" that in reality amounted to little more than a collection of "robbers and imposters."[175]

A certain measure of paternalistic concern for the inhabitants of India is evident in the new breed of history that emerged in the era of the greatest triumph of the East India Company's military standards. Prevalent attitudes to British rule in India foreshadowed the coming age of romantic historiography that would find all aspects of antiquity precious. There seemed to be new hope for the improvement of that portion of the humankind that had not ever tasted the fruit of liberty. John Malcolm, as soldier, civil servant, and scholar, was, I would argue, the first historian to assume this sentiment, signaling a certain maturity in the imperial vision of India's past, evident in the way in which he "applied himself to the investigation of Indian history, and endeavoured to master the principles by the observance of which our great Indian Empire had been founded, and on which alone it could be maintained."[176]

Malcolm began his career in the army as hostilities were unfolding between the British and Mysore, and served in the army of the Nizam as an interpreter. He had taught himself Persian with the help of scribes (native *munshis*) in the retinue of Graeme Mercer, a diplomatic officer, and had also learned several of the native languages. Wellesley sent him as an envoy to the Persian court in 1799, a journey that he would make two more times. He was encouraged by Mackintosh to write histories of Persia and India,[177] and during his third mission to Persia in 1810, while sailing to the Gulf he was already busy writing the *Political Sketches of India* (1811) and would soon put together the history of Persia that made him famous in Europe.

Malcolm depicted the ancient kingdoms of Persia as equally magnificent and barbaric: "the polished fragments of vast palaces, and the remains of flattering sculpture, prove only that they were rich and powerful monarchs, not that they had happy or civilized subjects."[178] Like all Eastern kings, they sought grandeur and fame through conquest; the very same passions animated Khushrau, Ardashir, Naushirwan, Chenghiz, Tamerlane, and Nadir Shah. No matter what their personal characters were, all were absolute, and their subjects were "strangers to freedom," condemned from the earliest to the present day to despotism.[179] Such a disposition towards Islamic rulers is hardly surprising on the part of a loyal public servant of the East India Company; Malcolm simply stated what was deemed a truism: "It would be a waste of time to discuss the principles on which orthodox Mahommedans believe the right of governing others to be founded. Since the death of Mahomed, the right of every race of potentates that professed his religion, has rested chiefly on the sword. . . ."

Later in his life, discussing the history of central India, Malcolm would judge the Mughal Empire in India in the same manner, arguing that the policy of "toleration and liberal indulgence which Akber extended to his Hindu subjects" was nonetheless doomed to failure under his successors, in particular Aurangzeb, for it was in the end intolerable to the "spirit of a religion established by the sword" whose tenets included conversion, death, or heavy tribute from infidels.[180]

Nonetheless, though despotism did frame his prose, the main body of Malcolm's history, culled from various indigenous authorities, is remarkably free of casual asides such as the above. It is also often brilliant in details, owing principally to his command of the Persian language, an ability that endeared him to orientalists such William Erskine and Alexander Hamilton of Haileybury in Hertford. Language and the ability to translate and scrutinize the inchoate historical record of oriental societies inspired Malcolm: "The best key to primitive history of a people is the history of its language; no witness is so cogent or so faithful; for, however those who have used it may have debased it into the instrument of falsehood, the language itself can never lie."[181]

Yet the very scheme of the *History of Persia* points to the lack of distinction between the past and the present of a despotic society. Just as his historical description ends in 1808, the year of Fateh Ali Khan's alliance with the English, a narrative of the religion, government, climate, manners, usages, and kingship of the Persians ensues. While the historical account shows a rigorous examination of sources, the ethnographic description is full of generalities and assertions. There is thus a striking continuity here between the past and present: no political or military revolution in all of twenty centuries has changed the essential condition of the Persians; they "are not at present a very different people from what they were in the time of Darius. . . ."[182]

Contrast this with the changes that mark the administration of India under British rule in the *Political History of India* (an enlarged edition of *The Political Sketches of India*), a tract he completed around the same time. The protagonists in this story are clearly the British; the chronological progression is marked by the successive rule of the governors general, followed by a study of British administration and the British community in India. Statesmen such as Wellesley, under whose watch Malcolm rose as a political agent, thus wielded an entirely unprecedented and unique power to change the fabric of Indian society:

> The general result of his administration changed the face of India: and a course of events, extraordinary as they were important, gave, in that quarter of the globe, an entire new character to the British power; which, at the close of this nobleman's government, was completely paramount to that of all the states of India, and at the liberty to choose, as its wisdom should dictate, the course of policy best suited to its condition.[183]

Although openly critical of some of the policies undertaken by the British administration in India, a habit that arguably affected his public career, Malcolm lays out in no uncertain terms the achievements of "that extraordinary empire which the British nation has founded in the East," held by the "respect and awe with which the comparative superiority of our knowledge, justice, and system of rule, have inspired the inhabitants of our own territories."[184] Such feelings of gratitude were largely a result of "that wretched and oppressive rule, from which the introduction of our power relieved our present subjects; and to the comparative tranquility and happiness which they enjoy under our dominion."[185] British rule had replaced the "indolent and declining" Mohammedan governments that did not protect the people of India from the depredation of freebooters. It was also a relief from the "principles of falsehood and treachery" that marked the relationship of the native states with each other, which was the principal reason they sought the mediation and friendship of the English. Although they were an alien power, the English in India had succeeded in maintaining an unwavering standard of fidelity.

HISTORIES IMPERIAL AND NATIONAL

Malcolm's remarks bring the subject of our present inquiry to a provisional close—the trajectory of an imperial historiography from the uncertainty of conquest to the quotidian rituals of colonial administration. It should be clear by now that this progression was registered in a new temporal sequence: Hindu antiquity followed by the invasion of Islam and the eventual intercession of the British. Such a scheme dovetailed with the idea that Muslim usurpers, who were more warlike, had overcome the native Hindus by virtue of climate, religion, or morality. Most British historians of India in the nineteenth century would come to accept a certain version of this story of despotism and racial degeneration, most characteristically expressed by Malcolm's compatriot, Mountstuart Elphinstone, governor of Bombay, in his *History of India: The Hindu and Mahometan Periods;* written in the 1830s after his departure from India, it was a book that would become very popular.[186]

More than the characterization of India, the distillation of such a view opens up an intriguing and remarkable question about the nature of national and imperial uses of history and their mutual constitution. I have already suggested that early historical accounts of India had to breach the anxiety of intimacy, and that later histories of the postconquest period cultivated a distance from the society of the ruled. Yet the question remains as to the true subjective limits of such histories. Where would be the lines drawn between Indian history and the history of what Malcolm called the "British nation in India"?[187] Empires do not always resemble nations in the symbols of territory and sovereignty, and it is likely that imperial history could be in a sense truly homeless, a nomadic subject at best. The men who went out to fight and rule in India represented what the historian John William Kaye called the "three great national divisions of the British empire": the English, the Scotch, and the Irish, men who were not "strangers and sojourners in the land" but who "looked to India as their Home, and to Indian services as their Career."[188]

I would like to argue however, in light of what I have discussed so far that the history of India *and* the history of Britons in India were assimilated into a wider, amorphous, and undefined imperial nationalism that sublimated the particular national sentiments that had sprung from the Indian encounter while reinforcing at the same time the deeper racial and prejudicial divisions. The recurrence of moral censure in the themes of despotism and degeneracy merely denote these very assertions of contiguity and difference. It is also important to point out that it took a long period of time before the history of India assumed a meaningful part of a selective national-historical memory, in the sense of the collective anamnesis that has recently been characterized in the context of English history by Raphael Samuel.[189]

Leading journals of the day, such as the *Annual Register,* Cobbett's *Political Register,* and the *Edinburgh Review* did from time to time carry discussions of the Indian empire and even excited a degree of public opinion, but it is difficult to elicit from these tracts an unambiguous expression of national sentiment around the Indian empire alone.[190] The *Annual Register* for 1758, which carried portions of Hollwell's famous account of the Black Hole incident in Calcutta, considered the events as having the effect of an instructive Aristotelian tragedy rather than being a national outrage, which it would come to be known as in the next century. Excerpts of Orme's *Military Transactions* appeared in the 1764 *Annual Register,* introduced as an account of the people who inhabit the "great empire of Indostan," their manners and customs, and the "astonishing events" that have made the history of the Indian wars "an object of general curiosity."[191] But it also praised Orme for his "air of disinterestedness, and of freedom from all passion and prejudice, public or private," especially in his treatment of England's principle enemy, the French in India, which was free of national bigotry. What captured a degree of national press and attention were the Mysore wars, in which, as Peter Marshall has suggested, the reading public became acquainted with Tipu Sultan as a national enemy.[192] Even so, realistic descriptions of the scale and logistics of the actual battles fought were overridden by the images and epithets of what Kate Teltscher has rightly labeled as the fantasy of "oriental contamination" menacing the prospects of a British pacification of southern India.[193]

A distinction must be made here between patriotic nationalism and the articulation of a collective national identity. Stefan Collini reminds us that it has been "for a long time an unspoken premiss of much of English historiography that nationalism was something that happened to other people."[194] Imperial historiography in India bears out much of this insight. Unlike most straightforward histories of national self-determination—where historical writing constitutes what Etienne Balibar has described as a retrospective and conscious "self-manifestation of the national personality"[195]—imperial histories of India strenuously denied any such resolution. While scrupulously distancing their society from the company of Indians, the British also sought to disassociate their own history from the Indian past. In this regard, it seems quite fitting that Sir James Mackintosh's Indian encounter left few visible traces on his august history of the islands. By Malcolm's time the disjuncture between historical experience and historical knowledge had come full circle.

I have attempted thus to trace the fabrication of a new genealogy of the imperial state in India, the form of which, as I argue in Chapter 1, was intimately tied to the state at home. This genealogy was rooted in notions of superiority derived from the naturalism of the Enlightenment as well as the ancient heritage of imperial Rome. The peculiarly elusive nationalism of imperial histories of British India lurks in the purported invincibility of a new imperial Britain and its ability to withstand the physical, moral, and cultural threat posed by India. All the attention on the defects of Indian society— lack of national unity, moral degeneracy, and despotism—can then be read as an appeal for assurance in the invention of an imperial tradition fraught with contradictory idioms.

3

Invasive Prospects

"SPACES OF WHITE PAPER"

Joseph Conrad, recounting his boyhood fascination with the Age of Discovery in Europe, described maps of the still-uncharted Africa and the Orient as "dull imaginary wonders of the dark ages . . . replaced by exciting spaces of white paper."[1] This chapter is an exploration of the gradual extinction of such uninscribed spaces in India. It might seem on the surface that mapping and travel occupied opposite extremes of visual experience for Britons as they began to spread their interests through the inner reaches of the Indian subcontinent. Maps guided travelers, planners of battles, and assessors of revenue and made discernible the strategic value of territory and the economic value of land and its produce. But the reverse was also true: without some prior knowledge of the country and access to its interior, maps could not be drawn or filled in. Between these two impulses emerged the cartographic replica of political territory. The mapping of India permitted a certain play of visual imagination that belied the episodic nature of the Indian conquest and the indefinite frontiers of the new state. In this sense it was an indispensable exercise of authority, re-ordering the country on paper.

In the century before that of Conrad's childhood, when Britain was rapidly expanding her territorial possessions, the survey of land was analogous to the ordering of language and perhaps knowledge in general. In his plan for a dictionary of the English language in 1747, Samuel Johnson styled himself as an explorer as much as a lexicographer. Bringing the English language to order for Johnson was akin to an invasion in which he could not be sure whether he would be able to complete the conquest but could "at least discover the coast, civilize part of the inhabitants, and make it easy for some other adventurer to proceed farther, to reduce them wholly to subjection, and settle them under laws."[2] Between the commanding exercise of cartographic surveys and the eventual visual conformity of the map, this chapter will propose, there is a significant discrepancy that contributes immensely to the value of the map as a sign. During the British occupation of India, the visual realism of the map became indispensable. With maps emerged the geopolitical viscera of British India, enabling other modes of survey and reinforcing their scientific integrity. To state the obvious, the first maps of the subcontinent were drawn mostly for the purposes of British rulers by British surveyors and their Indian assistants. For the majority of India's inhabitants, there was no such imperative to visualize their country in such precise physical and mathematical detail on a selective grid. The British asserted what no other political entity in the past had been able to in claiming to have woven together a newly acquired territory into a continuous and conclusive image. Whatever the nature of political conquest, however ingenuous the political compromises worked out with indigenous rulers, kings, and chieftains, the Indian map became synonymous with an imperial view of political space.

It would be fair to say that it is only recently that colonial cartography has become the subject of sustained historical interest or debate. In his now-distinguished *Imagined Communities,* Benedict Anderson pointed out how indebted nationalism in the colonized world has been to the imperial imagination of dominion, represented by the census, map, and museum.[3] More recently we have a comprehensive monograph on the British mapping of India in Matthew Edney's *Mapping and Empire,*[4] which invites us to denaturalize the colonial map of India, proposing that it is a "construction" that should be located in the changing context of political developments and scientific ideology. Thanks to Edney's work and also that of Thongchai Winichakul on Thailand[5] we can locate the modern map as a historical signifier across very different political and cultural contexts.

The map, it may be contended, is a sign that masks its field of signification in distinct and selective ways. First, it subsumes the contingencies, incompleteness, and inconsistencies of military occupation. The geographical knowledge of India grew out of an invasive agenda. The earliest surveys in northern India took place in the event of large-scale operations against native rulers and chieftains lodged in forts across the countryside, where expertise in topographical draftsmanship was highly valued for the building of emergency bridges, raising batteries, digging saps and parallels for mining, and preparing roads and routes over hostile terrain. These ventures carried with them a clear writ of conquest, and maps were proof that remote parts of the country had become accessible, and that routes had opened up through what James Rennell, pioneer of the first atlas of India, would describe as a "number of barbarous nations . . . extremely jealous of Europeans."[6] The reason why the East India Company's troops prevailed relatively easily over military resistance of local rulers in India, it was believed, was this ability to gather topographical details, strategic posts, and routes through quick military surveys and the redeployment of such knowledge in further campaigns. Every successful military confrontation led the way for a team of surveyors, pushing the political penumbra of the Company from its riverside and coastal trading outposts to the interior. In this context, Britain's contemporary political experience in the expedition against the Scottish Highlanders, long-term rivalry with the French for strategic control of territory in North America, and military efforts during the war of American independence all played instructive roles.

Second, imperial cartography brought with it to India a whole ensemble of political and economic relationships that had developed in England between the understanding and depiction of private property, landscape, and topography. Such ideas resonated with the new colonial state in India and its imperatives of securing military dominance and fiscal sufficiency. Third, I suggest that the circulation and consumption of maps were aspects of a new materialism that produced the garden, landscape, and enclosure, but with dissimilar political consequences, a signifier sharing what Baudrillard calls the "triumphant democracy of all artificial signs."[7] But subject to acts of reproduction, reprint, and referral through the artifice of the state, it also succeeded in shedding the exclusivity of its signature. Universally consumed, maps acquired a visual currency where the mapmaker's virtuosity and expertise would lie buried in the abundance of geographical images. The map could be then locked into its own signification of reality: country, territory, power. Comparing maps to other representative artifacts of modernity, which may include both colonialism and capitalism, we can begin to assess their impact: unlike money it would not generate within itself the potential to assume the shape of any other object of value, but like money it was a demiurgic force that would mediate the very experiential reality of space.[8]

The history of the British in India falls within that geopolitical parameter within which the map emerged as an *aide memoire* of the modern era. This is a question of enormous interest to the revision of the history of the core and periphery of imperial historiography. By looking more closely at both the technology and the narrative content of the cartographic image, we can rethink the relationship between the overlapping images of the state, nation, and the empire that made possible a sustained image of British India over the course of two centuries. The new atlas of India portended a surprising omniscience on the part of a fledgling colonial state; however, I suggest below that before endowing the British Empire in India with the panoptic gaze of modern, disciplinary institutions, we examine the history of the map as the signature and imprimatur of contending visions of territory. Rather than indicating the sufficiency of power, the new atlas of India may be represented as a site for the struggle for both the authenticity and the authority of the cartographic state, one that was able to impose its own technology of representation on political territory that had been wrested from the Mughals and their successors. The art of modern landscape and the brave new science of geography were important weapons of that struggle.

FIELDS OF OBSERVATION

All this is not to suggest that the cartographic knowledge that Europeans, particularly the British, brought with them to India marked an unprecedented revolution in the description of space. After all, medieval Arab geographers had evolved sophisticated methods of charting, the use of quadrants, and a body of knowledge that was well known throughout the Islamic world, including that of Mughal India. Mughal emperors frequently the used charts and sketches known as *naqsha*. A conventional view would be that the scientific progress in eighteenth-century Europe was marked by great "advances" in the quantitative capacities of instruments of measurement and the ability to bring the surface of the earth under unified and "accurate" mathematical scrutiny. The quadrant had been adapted to new findings by John Hadley (1730) with the help of reflecting mirrors, and by the 1770s a portable chronometer had been devised that could accurately measure longitudes, enabling the reduction of the earth's curved surface to a fixed geometrical grid. Around the same period Jesse Ramsden came up with the design of the early theodolite, which enabled the reading of angles to the second.

But this straightforward narrative of scientific improvement distracts from the crucial ideological shift in the instrumentality of mapping; the capacity for precision in cartographic representation can be viewed as secondary to major shifts in the nature and understanding of mapping itself. When maps became public artifacts and the stamps of authentic territory, they not only implied an universal observer but actually displaced other narrative and pictorial signs that once mediated the labor and signature of artists. Why and when the mathematical precision of observation replaced other features of general cosmography and chorography are questions that cannot detain us here, but the dominance of cartographic survey can be indeed located in the *longue durée* of a certain epistemology. Foucault contended that, in the case of natural history, the idea of scientific observation was premised upon a liberation of visibility from all empirical (sensory) burdens and "restricted to black and white"—thus the great importance attached to what he calls "the appearance of screened objects: lines, surfaces, forms, reliefs."[9] Most important, it revolutionized the position of the subject by rendering the eye of the observer invisible. We can apprehend the immensity of this displacement in Wittgenstein's *Tractatus Logico-Philosophicus,* where he finally dispensed with the Cartesian constraints of the thinking subject. This absence is akin to the relationship between the eye and the visual field (*Gesichtsfeld*); "nothing in the visual field allows you to infer that it is seen by an eye."[10] In the realm of travel and exploration, argues Barbara Stafford, a distinctively scientific visualism emerged in the eighteenth century that was clearly different from other prevalent modes of seeing.[11] This was marked by an intensity of observation and an "aggressive identity of a particular object" in relation to the beholder.[12]

Cartography in eighteenth- and nineteenth-century Europe as objectification of landscape belongs clearly to this domain of natural history. André Miquel's classic study *La Géographie Humaine du Monde Musulman Jusqu'au Milieu du IIe Siècle* advances the argument that during the Middle Ages, and even until the nineteenth century, a general history and perception of the discipline of geodesy was shared by both the European and the Islamic worlds. As he puts it:

> Jusque là en effet, la géographie, musulmane ou européenne trouve son trait commun dans un rapport étroit avec le voyage, la "peinture" du monde, la "description" des pays, toutes expressions qui soulignent bien que cette géographie se définit par la représentation d'un monde extérieur, qu'elle est donc illustrative et explicative d'un donné qui lui préexiste . . . en leurs domaines respectifs, un art synonyme de figuration ou une histoire soucieuse de leçons et d'examples."[13]

According to Miquel, man in Islamic geography was the moral and logical center, or indeed a microcosm, of the entire creation of which the map or chart is just an image. Cartography, then, was the *conscious illustration* of an entity preexistent and given.[14]

Insofar as the notion of monocular vision and methods of linear perspective were developed through the work of Ramus and figures such as Brunelleschi and Alberti during the Renaissance, as Pierre Francastel has demonstrated, this was no sudden decisive departure in pictorial representation of space.[15] Although the techniques were known and deployed, the so-called "realism" (a rigorous application of Euclidean optical principles) was lodged within conventional signs that were peculiar to the Renaissance style of depicting space, existing along with parallel modes within an identifiable topology.[16] In fact, diagrammatic representation of natural objects (including certain techniques of landscape) and the absolute validity of a visual interpretation that is geometrically and mathematically sound are peculiar to the recent past of European science. Lindberg and Steneck have asserted that "all medieval and Renaissance philosophers, of course, would have agreed that sight alone does not suffice for knowledge. . . . Moreover, all would have acknowledged that the senses, including sight, sometimes deceive."[17] Recent explorations of the relationship between the history of painting and mapping in Europe, particularly among Dutch artists, suggest that the two are closely tied in their development; the proximity of the cross-staff, compass, pencil, pen, palette, and brush belie conventional distinctions drawn between cartography as a scientific and painting as an artistic activity.[18] Andrew Hemingway, commenting on Constable's well-known assertion that painting was indeed a science and should be pursued along the lines of inquiry into the laws of nature, points out that science was distinguished not so much by impartial observation as by the knowledge of theoretical principles.[19]

It can be also be advanced that medieval cartography both in Europe and Asia had a pedagogic and narrative content. Stories, lessons, metaphors, and analogies were all part of a rich topology based on notions of "contiguity and separation, succession, surroundings and continuity."[20] This, to my knowledge, is certainly true for Mughal *naqshas:* formalized layout of gardens, landscape, and idealized town plans that relate very closely to the artistic tradition of calligraphy and miniatures.[21] What can be seen as distinguishing mapmaking in British India is thus a struggle between a search for scientific accuracy, on the one hand, and an exigency of visual representation, on the other. Although imperial geography was unquestionably based on the science of observation and projection, the early maps of British India bore the sensory, aesthetic, and historical legacy of the map as an artifact, with their own webs of signification. In fact it was only around the period of the Great Trigonometrical Survey of India that the new cartography attempted to part company with such previous depiction of territory.

TOPOLOGIES: UNITED KINGDOM AND MUGHAL INDIA

Cartography of England as a coherent territory appeared roughly during the age of Elizabethan consolidation through coastal and overseas navigation, military surveys, and estate surveys for the sale and mortgage of landed property.[22] Between the first county surveys of Christopher Saxton and editions of his maps published in 1611 by John Speed in the *Theatre of the Empire of Great Britain,* an atlas of England was produced that predominated until the major resurveys of the eighteenth and nineteenth centuries.[23] However, this cartography was an illustration of the dynastic realm, with coats of arms and other dynastic insignia. In Michael Drayton's *Poly-Olbion,* which was composed with Camden's *Britannia* and Saxton's maps in view, natural features were personified by images of nymphs and shepherds. Even more interestingly, the frontispiece depicts Albion sitting under the triumphant arch in "power and plenty," actually draped in a map of England.[24] In other words, cartography and chorography in the late medieval world belonged to an ensemble of signs and depiction that embodied the idea of a commonwealth or kingdom in the person of the ruler (Queen Elizabeth) or an idealized representation (Albion or Britannia). Much of this kind of depiction of the parts and the whole of the country presupposed an older Ptolemaic vision, where geography was seen as the description of the whole and chorography as that of the parts or, from the standpoint of the artist, the head of a portrait as compared to individual features such as the ear or the eye.[25] This was part of the repertoire of significations out of which the nation could be fashioned retrospectively.

Mughal charts depicting the splendor of imperial rule illustrate that although they were produced under a very different political culture, they shared some of these general conventions of pictorial authority whereby maps were subsumed under a larger conception of an imperial body politic. In a part of the world still without the blessings of print-capitalism, with sacred and literary manuscripts delegated to the province of the calligrapher, the draftsman, the scribe, and the painter, the image of the empire was perhaps much less reified and more experiential. Thus the very presentation of the Mughal cavalry, the peripatetic royal camp with its huge train, the layout and hierarchy of the imperial *darbar* (court), and entreaty and supplication face-to-face with the emperor (*nazar*) were aspects of relating empirically to the realm. More specifically, imperial banners and *nishans* provided lasting icons for the Mughal throne. The *shamsa,* or the image of the sun, was hung on the royal gates and in the palace. During festivals the imperial umbrella (*chatr*) was unfurled, and the standard (*'alam*) was raised from which was hung the *qur,* or a scarlet bag of flags, seals, and other insignia to be unfolded in public view.[26] Marks of distinction were conferred upon independent princes, such as the *nalki* (the palanquin in which they traveled so that their feet did not touch the ground), the *mahi maratib* (literally: rank of the Pisces) and the *kaukaba* (polished iron balls suspended from the standard as an ensign, and by extension as a royal train). These were signs that could be used only by princes whose ancestors had been so honored.[27] Even more important, it is doubtful that the idea of a bounded territorial unit with a fixed center of rule was relevant to the understanding of meaningful political authority during the Mughal era. Much like the household in Elizabethan England, the "capital" (as distinct from royal cities or forts) was often a royal camp in motion, and the *pa-i-takht,* or the foot of the throne, was an idealized emplacement that held the realm together.

Geography as "description of the inhabited world" (*surat jami' al-arz*) was a very different sort of enterprise, cosmological in scope and founded on medieval Persian notions of the contiguous and contrasting seven climes (*aqalim*).[28] Arab geographers did indeed venture far beyond Ptolemy in astronomical and mathematical observations of the earth and the celestial spheres. They studied the earth's spherical qualities, eclipse and equinox, the azimuth, and the heavenly bodies to locate points on the earth's surface, latitudes and longitudes, and to navigate the oceans.[29] Terrestrial coordinates were important for accurate projections in astrology, and the widespread search for the direction of prayer in the Muslim world inspired many lists of latitudes and longitudes. Geography as part of the enveloping knowledge of an expanding Islam was entrusted with a value that was beyond simply the military, fiscal, or statistical. The well-known Persian geographical cyclopedia compiled at the end of the tenth century, *Hudud al-Alam* (*The Regions of the World*), which was very popular in India, claims to have brought to light not only the properties of the earth and its disposition, but also the climatic and edaphic attributes of the various regions, the extent of cultivation, the state of various peoples of distant lands, the customs of the kings, deficiencies and amenities of kingdoms, the description of mountains, rivers, seas, and deserts, and their various products.[30] Irfan Habib locates the use of such world maps in Mughal India as early as the fourteenth century with Hamdullah Mustaufi's *Tarikh-i Guzida* and also later in the seventeenth century with Sadiq Isfahani's *Shahid-i Sadiq*.[31] But here, again, description of the "seven climes" the marking of divisions according to the varying length of the longest days along parallels, and a refusal to locate the exact position of cities (following the usual set of practices in Arab mapmaking) demonstrate that such geographies were not quite subservient to the needs of the empire under whose very auspices they were conceived.

Topographical charts commissioned by Mughal rulers that have survived are very much in the realm of graphic composition. Route maps of the royal camp are often long, bird's-eye-view strips of landscape that faithfully inscribe the journey with stations where the imperial entourage halted.[32] Examples of town plans give a sense of layout and aerial perspective, but they are not much concerned with scale or with perspectival or projectional accuracy. Much more emphasis is placed on the details of domes, palaces, and major gateways. More crucially perhaps, Mughal cartography remained uninterested in the linear demarcation of political boundaries for both external and internal frontiers, in keeping with the wider tradition of Arabo-Islamic mapping practices.[33] Frontiers were usually considered natural, and the edges of countries, according to treatises such as the *Hudud al-Alam,* were separated by mountains, rivers, and deserts.[34] It is true that European techniques of linear perspective in painting were not unknown to the Mughals. Abu al-Fazl's account testifies that Akbar patronized, among other styles of painting, the *ahl-i farang* or the "magic making of the Europeans," regarded as a particular kind of artistic virtuosity.[35] By the seventeenth century, European globes and maps were being introduced to the Mughal nobility through the factors of the trading companies. Yet such techniques were not assimilated. Emperor Jahangir returned Sir Thomas Roe's gift of Mercator's *Atlas* because scholars and theologians at the court could not make sense of it.[36] In the cosmography of medieval India, the figure of the emperor was visually inseparable from the body of the polity.

Even a quick perusal of miniatures sponsored by the Mughal court reveals how overwhelming was the desire for an idealized representation of the emperor. Globes and maritime charts imported by European traders thus slipped easily into the portraiture of the emperor. Take for example Abu'l Hasan's famous portrait of Jahangir and the Safavid emperor Shah 'Abbas. Jahangir stands on a tame lion, dwarfing the frail Shah, who is borne by a sheep. All the figures rest on a terrestrial globe.[37] Jahangir's lion is spread across all of central Asia, while the Shah's sheep is pushed as far back as the Mediterranean.[38]

MAPS AND THE MILITARY TERRAIN

Eighteenth-century European cartography, on the contrary, indebted to the centralization of the fiscal-military state, was becoming increasingly utilitarian. Military geography surveys, surveys of encampments and fortifications, and documentary maps of military campaigns dominated the attention of countries that were competing for trade overseas. Maps were central to the planning, construction, and defense of fortified coastal settlements in overseas territories. Reconnaissance charts and siege cartography in various terrain were objects of serious study in military academies.[39] So were the plans, elevations, and sections of forts and buildings.

Topographical survey in the service of the military began in England under the guidance of the Board of Ordnance, a defunct organ of the state reconstituted in 1683 to deal with questions of national defense, ordnance supplies, and the deployment of engineering corps and artillery regiments. Among other responsibilities, the board was to act as the custodian of lands, depots, and forts and all overseas possessions.[40] Most of the early surveys done in England and Scotland were sanctioned by the Board of Ordnance, which is probably the reason the phrase "ordnance survey" was used to denote all surveying activity in England.[41] The Royal Military Academy at Woolich was set up in 1741 to train, along with the cadet officers of artillery and engineering, a contingent of surveyors and draftsmen. Engineers and gunners of the British Army had to learn both military and architectural drawing.[42] Among other subjects taught were fortification and artillery, mathematics and geography, drawing, classics, writing and arithmetic, and the art of surveying and leveling.

To emphasize the point that the graphic and military arts were indeed closely related, one only has to look at the career of Paul Sandby, a young artist, twenty-one years of age, who was appointed as a draftsman on the survey of the Highlands under Colonel Watson after the Jacobite uprising of 1745.[43] In 1768, Paul Sandby was appointed chief drawing master at the academy, and he emphasized the mapping of terrain in relation to the logistics of troop movement. By this period, surveyors were receiving a comprehensive and standardized education that consisted of specialized subjects such as trigonometry, topographical mapping, and theories of mathematical perspective.[44] Such training was subsequently also available at the Military College in High Wycombe and also at Great Marlow, where illustrious painters such as William Alexander and W. S. Gilpin were to serve as instructors of drawing.[45]

The unquestionably military nature of survey operations in the eighteenth century is important to bear in mind, for the two most extensive surveys undertaken by the British Army during the period—William Roy's mapping of Scotland and James Rennell's survey of Bengal—closely followed military operations. In fact, the survey of the Highlands provided the opportunity for the forcible assimilation of a land and people into the political sway of kingdom, and informed surveys conducted in the colonies. The careers of

Roy and Rennell were similar. Both were engineering officers, elected Fellows of the Royal Society, and both took part in military campaigns against the French. Both shared an interest in the subjects of history and archeology. Roy was the author of *Military Antiquities of the Romans in North Britain* (1793), and Rennell, the *Geographical System of Herodotus* (1800). Antiquarian imagination and classicist historicism played an important role in geography and the planning of military operations of the army away from home. This was a period in which a substantive correspondence had been established between the living present of geography and the grand chronology of classical history.[46]

Scotland was surveyed after the English Army suppressed the Jacobite rebellion against the Act of Union, which brought the country under a unified Parliament. The survey marked the political appropriation of the entire region along with the banning of the Highlander dress and other signs of the clans and the passing of the Abolition of Heritable Jurisdiction Act in 1747. One of the manifest reasons for the route surveys in Scotland was the fact that Lt. Col. David Watson, deputy quartermaster general of North Britain, whose primary task was to set up army posts and build roads in the newly "pacified" territories, found military operations handicapped for the want of accurate maps. The nature and objectives of this survey were described by Roy in the following manner:

> The rise and progress of the rebellion which broke out in the Highlands of Scotland in 1745, and which was finally suppressed by His Royal Highness the Duke of Cumberland at the battle of Culloden in the following year, convinced the Government of what infinite importance it would be to the state that a country, so very inaccessible by nature, should be so *thoroughly explored and laid open,* by establishing military posts in its inmost recesses, and carrying roads of communication to its remotest parts.[47]

Thus the first mapping of the Scotland was achieved through a series of military route surveys locating landmarks in the countryside (woodland, grassland, moor, or fermtoun) and noting the houses and estates of notables. In the same vein, early cartography in India was also launched to lay open the country and defend British possessions against neighboring regimes. Military establishments at Fort William in Calcutta or Fort St. George in Madras, set up merely for the defense of trading practices, were insufficient after the conquests of Coromandel and Bengal, in view of large operations into the interior and campaigns against native rulers lodged in forts across the countryside. Around this time there was a need for soldiers who were engineers by profession and had the technical expertise in building bridges, raising batteries, digging saps and parallels for mining, and preparing roads over hostile terrain. The rise of field operations in India saw the proliferation of engineering soldiers, known in the early period as pioneers and later as members of the corps of Sappers and Miners. The engineer, as a practitioner of military art, was supposed to be:

An able, expert man, who by a perfect knowledge in mathematics, delineates upon a paper or marks on the ground, all sorts of forts and other works proper for offence and defence. He should understand the art of fortification, so as to be able not only to discover the defects of a plan, but to find a remedy proper for them, as also how to make an attack upon, as well as to defend the place. Engineers are extremely necessary for these purposes . . . When at a siege the engineers have narrowly surveyed the place, they are to make the report to the General, by acquainting him which part they adjudge the weakest, and where approaches may be made with most success. Their business is also to delineate the lines of circumvallation and contravallation, taking all the advantages to the ground; to mark out the trenches, places of arms, batteries and lodgements.[48]

Geographical surveys in India started primarily with members of the Engineering Corps. The Bengal Engineers, for instance, were famous not so much for their valor in the battlefield but for producing heroic surveyors such as Rennell, Mark and Thomas Wood, Francis Wilford, John Macdonald, Charles and James Mouat, and Thomas Robertson.[49] One can suggest, perhaps, that before the consolidation of an educated civil service, academic military training was a privileged mode of knowledge in the exploration of India, and geographical knowledge in particular was generated during the progress of an army in campaign.

During the latter half of the eighteenth century, the education of the military officers of the Company was conducted partly at the Royal Military College at Marlow, and partly at Woolwich. However, in the face of a mounting demand for experts in artillery and field engineers on the colonial front in Hindustan, the East India Company established its own Military Seminary at Addiscombe Place, near Croydon, in 1809.[50] Cadets at the seminary were eligible to join the Engineering, Artillery, or Infantry corps. Of these, the most "distinguished" were chosen to serve as engineers. Courses at the seminary were designed to promote the general aim of the directors of the Company—that liberal learning and sciences were key to the military art and therefore to rule in the colonies. Thus students also had to learn the elements of native languages. Subjects taught were mathematics, fortification, military drawing, surveying, Hindustani, civil and lithographic drawing, French, and Latin.[51] The list of texts used at the seminary is illuminating if one wishes to reconstruct the military-geographic perspective of early prospectors of trade, warfare, and settlement in India: Hindustani and Latin dictionaries, Woodhouse's *Spherical Trigonometry,* Inman's *Nautical Astronomy* and *Nautical Tables,* Cape's *Mathematics,* Straith's *Treatise on Fortification,* Fielding's *Perspective,* Shakespear's *Hindusthani Grammar,* de la Voye's *French Instructions* and Julius Caesar's *Commentaries.*

Such a curriculum suggests that the so-called "amateur artist" and the gentleman-soldier were both schooled in similar techniques of the landscape, and that during the period in question the art of sketching was considered as a necessary tool in the art of warfare. Mapmaking had undoubtedly impacted the world of academic art, most of all in landscape painting. In *The Art of*

Describing, Svetlana Alpers writes that cartography influenced Dutch art of the early modern era significantly when maps started to become a commonplace household item among members of the mercantile class. Alpers discusses the "geographic world view" of the Dutch landscape paintings of Bruegel, Goltzius, Van Goyen, and Ruisdael, as well as the cartographic vistas of Koninck.[52] We know that Paul Sandby was much influenced by the Dutch masters. Specimens of his early work submitted to the Board of Ordnance at the time he applied for the post of draftsman were copies of Abraham Bloemart's engravings.[53] Among Sanby's landscapes most inspired by the Dutch tradition were two watercolor-and-pencil views of Leith, one which was published (1751) among a series of views from Scotland. Sandby, principal drawing master at Woolwich between 1768 and 1797, produced students such as Michael Rooker and Thomas Hearne, the latter appointed early in his career as a draftsman in the Leeward Islands.[54]

It can be argued that the aesthetic principles of the picturesque eventually overshadowed the more explicitly topographical aspects of landscape painting and appreciation at the turn of the century. However, the shared experiences of drawing and draftsmanship indicate that the map and the landscape developed as complementary habits of naturalist perception. As Jonathan Richardson reasoned in his *Essay on the Theory of Painting* (1773), drawing entailed a "just representation of nature."[55] In order to follow nature exactly, a man must not only be well acquainted with it but must have "a reasonable knowledge of geometry, proportion . . . anatomy, osteology, and perspective," for, as the ancients knew only too well, one could not see what things were if one knew not "what they ought to be."[56] Techniques of mapping and survey, particularly as enshrined in the practices of the Ordnance Survey draftsmen, continued to inform nineteenth century English painting of the countryside, including the work of Constable and Turner. Constable's work on Stour Valley employed elevated views from differing angles and military-style landmarks, and it has been suggested that both Matremont's recommendations for military sketches and Samuel Adams's *Geometrical and Graphic Essays* (1792) were among his references.[57] At the same time, military academies routinely taught both civil and architectural drawing. Placing cartography as a product of such military and artistic concerns should help us identify what sort of aesthetic and sanguinary labor lurks behind its superficies.

INSCRIPTIONS OF OWNERSHIP

As I suggest in Chapter 1, in the period of British expansion in India the vision of a dominion or annexed territory was directly linked to the interests of commerce and the idea of defensible property. The British historian of political economy, Adam Anderson, addressed the issue in the latter half of the eighteenth century by explaining that dominion was best understood as property, or a right of possessing and using anything as one's own.[58] Anderson distinguished private property as the limitation of communion between two persons, analogous to public property, which delimited the common ground among nations. Countries and territories, like estates separated from each other by precisely drawn limits and borders, were nothing but the public property of nations.[59] National commerce, especially when based on mercantilism, entailed a search for material resources and territorial expansion based on ideas of acquisition similar to that of a commercial body. In fact such distinctions tended to blur in the case of overseas chartered companies such as the East India Company.

Such expressions of political and economic geography were tied to the widening reach of the fiscal-military state and its systems of centralization, computation, and control of resources. State formation and nation-building in Europe, secured through territorial wars, had already put a high premium on the accuracy of geographical knowledge. Chandra Mukherjee argues that political centralization of European states was achieved not only through control over land, mobilization of taxation, and military planning, but through a profoundly affecting cultural integration via the cartographic image.[60] Yet, in many ways, it was the colonial world that provided an early and apposite site for the grand objectives of European geographical science. Maps quickly became the easiest means to depict, control, and circulate information on physical and human resources in newly conquered colonies. Geographical knowledge and military expedience had already been tied together, and as Foucault suggests in passing, geographical terms such as *territory, domain, field,* and *region* are implicated with the discourse of power and, more pointedly, military designation.[61]

In the period under consideration, there emerged in Britain a clearly discernible relationship between the idea of landed property and national political economy. All land was potentially alienable property, a realization that affected the idyllic conceptions of landscape in the era of the picturesque just as it did the older geographical images of the nation itself. This transition of the nation from the commonweal to a public estate, liable to cadastral measurement, is perhaps analogous to the passage from the medieval commons to the later enclosures. Rendered in such a context, the symbolic function of the map becomes even more intriguing. The relationship between maps, landscapes, cadastral surveys, national boundaries, and the rise of geographical science is beyond the argument of this chapter. However, the following propositions are in order before the cartographic imperatives of the early British Empire in India can be located within the context of English history itself.

The assertion is now commonplace that landscape painting emerged as a dominant genre in the age of enclosure and the changing class composition of agrarian landownership. Drawing on the work of Ann Birmingham, one could say that during the second half of the eighteenth century the middle classes of Britain discovered and acknowledged the aesthetic worth of the English countryside and at the same time invested the idea of nature with transcendental value.[62] While the countryside was being enclosed, surveyed, and brought within the rule of property, the aesthetic ideology of the picturesque was being developed and debated vigorously following the directions laid down by Reverend Gilpin.[63] In the late eighteenth century, the English countryside was rapidly becoming the object of tourism among the middle classes, with private estates and residences being open for display to the public.[64] Such activities of viewing and displaying chosen sites, explains Elizabeth Helsinger, "created for those who could participate in it a claim of England as their national aesthetic property."[65] In order to be truly English, the proponents of the picturesque enjoined, one had to be a keen student of the rustic landscape.

Artists from England who visited and painted Indian landscapes during the era of the political ascendancy of the East India Company, among them Thomas and William Daniells and William Hodges, appropriated the natural scenery and common geography of India and set them to ideals of the picturesque.[66] Hodges, who had been an official draftsman on Captain Cook's South Pacific expedition (1772–1775), traveled tirelessly up the Ganges between cities of northern India between 1780 and 1783, sketching the Indian countryside, monuments, and ruins.[67] The Daniells were topographic artists by training who toured extensively in India during the 1780s, traveling through north India to the foothills of the Himalayas. They used the camera obscura in India with accurate results, evident in their voluminous sketches of India that are drawn to reliable perspective and scale.[68]

Such dedication to the accurate and picturesque representation of India seems to belie the fact that the East India Company and its commercial policymakers did not view India as the place for a settler colony. By the turn of the century, covenanted servants of the Company, ensigns, and cadets of the fleet and inland garrisons were being firmly discouraged from obtaining private fortunes in India, let alone establishing estates in the Indian countryside. How, then, did the Indian picturesque purport to project the ownership of India? Indian ruins and rugged Indian nature, brought to public view, indicate a custodial responsibility in the era of parliamentary reform and review of the East India Company's charter. India was to be held for the greater purposes of empire. The geography of the Indian subcontinent was thus opening up a space for national and public imaginings where the domestic antagonisms of class and the constraints of joining the rank of elites and aristocrats might be overlooked. While the landscape provided the expressive imagery of imperial discourse, as pointed out by W. J. T. Mitchell,[69] the painted image and its reception were bound by aesthetic conventions. In a crucial manner, the map helped reify a concurrently national and imperial vista, particularly as it mediated between graphic description and accurate observation.

In a larger and somewhat different sense, the emerging discipline of geography provided the ripe context for such a reception of the map. Here was a reinscription of spatial meanings that brought astronomy, geodesy, climatology, natural history, the study of languages, and human institutions together in a grand encyclopedic panorama.[70] Akin to Johnson's explorations of the English language, geographers such as Bohun in the seventeenth and Guthrie in the eighteenth century reassembled Europe's expeditions into territories unknown or little known, and thus named and rendered into common public knowledge the particularities of the distant continents of Asia, America, and Africa. The major difference between such compendia and the explorers' travelogues lies in the act of naming and renaming. Rather than planting names in passing as signposts of the journey, which has been studied so suggestively by Paul Carter in his book *The Road to Botany Bay,* seventeenth- and eighteenth-century geographers were busy assimilating such original signs into regular geographical grammars and "dictionaries." Bohun's *Geographical Dictionary,* based avowedly on the work of Stephanus Byzantius (ca. A.D. 400), is thus concerned with not only geographical details but grammatical and historical derivations so that all the ancient, Latin, and "vulgar" names of remote places can be usefully reduced to common public perusal.[71] Geography as a useful art undertook to fix the "knowledge of times and places" for both history and travel and to excite the imagination of the "English nobility and gentry."[72] Jeremy Black has aptly employed the phrase "carto-literacy" to capture this widespread phenomenon. Thus maps were becoming indispensable not only in the signing of treaties, depiction of frontiers, and wartime crises, but also as accompaniments to historical descriptions.[73] Cadets, midshipmen, and writers proceeding to India in the early nineteenth century for civil, military, or naval service all carried with them from England maps of India that were listed by warehouses such as H. Herbert of the Strand, A. D. Welch of Leadenhall Street, Maynard and Pyne, and Silver Co. as part of the necessary articles for the voyage to and use in India.[74]

EMPIRE AND THE DESCRIPTION OF CONQUEST

When the East India Company acquired settlements on the eastern seaboard of India, geographical information about the country was limited to coastal charts and plans of fortifications. The only available European map of detail was the *Carte de l'Inde* of D'Anvile, drawn at the request of the French East India Company in 1752 and based on observations made by the Jesuits. Around 1760, the Local Council of Bengal ordered a preliminary survey and assessment of the new possessions to ascertain the extent of cultivatable land and revenue. There was also the need to explore the coastal, riparian, and other routes of communication and to find strategic passes on the western frontier, which were threatened by roving Maratha horsemen.[75] Early surveys were keen to determine access to the country through waterways. Thus the charts of the Bay of Bengal drawn by Bartholemew Plaisted and de Gloss's survey of routes between the River Hooghly and the deltaic creeks of the inhospitable Sunderbans towards Dacca were all concerned with the passage of boats and navigability of rivers. In the eighteenth century, when most major sea-lanes to the East Indies through the Bay of Bengal were commanded by the East-Indiamen, hydrography, marine survey, and the measurement of coastlines were much more important than the charting of routes inland. This littoral vantage persisted. Alexander Dalrymple, who produced coastal and marine charts, warned navigators that these did not quite fit the description of true surveys, "where *everything* is *minutely* and *accurately* laid down, so that there is no room for *additions* or *corrections*"[76]

When in 1765 the Company emerged as a territorial power and assumed the responsibility of collecting revenue on behalf of the Mughal emperor, the directors realized the immediate necessity of maps and plans for "a full and satisfactory information of all . . . possessions, their value, and the importance they are to the Company . . . [and] a plan of the Bengal frontier towards Orixa [*sic*], with . . . opinions for the best means of preventing invasion on that side."[77] Robert Orme, historian of the East India Company, requested during this time a map of Bengal that would show not only the outlines of the provinces but their respective subdivisions. Orme's *Essay on the Art of War,* written for readership Robert Clive and Richard Smith, emphasized the military value of cartography:

> We have in general very few good charts in India—our Generals have not paid much attention to the subject. . . . If those in the administration are sensible of the advantages resulting from it, they would never scruple the expense. . . . I would have a plan for your whole frontier, with the engineer's observations from league to league.[78]

According to Orme, the Company should not confine its inquiry merely to roads and waterways, but should cover the "very site of the country."[79] Clive promised Orme that an "exact chart" of Bengal, Bihar, Orissa, and the whole of Mughal Empire stretching to Delhi, and a map of Ganges and other major rivers would be commissioned. Such a map would enable a thorough perspective of the strategic position of the Company vis-à-vis native ruling groups such as the Jats, Rohillas, Bhumihar Rajputs, and the Marathas. Clive wrote to the directors in 1767 appointing the young Captain Rennell for the difficult task of acquiring an accurate general survey of the whole country: "So much depends upon accurate surveys, both in military operations and in coming at a true knowledge of the value of your possessions, that we have employed everybody on this service who could be spared and were capable. . . ."[80]

James Rennell had been trained as a surveyor in the Royal Navy, volunteered for service in Borneo in the East Indies, and finally joined the East India Company's forces for employment in survey operations.[81] With a detachment of *sepoys* or foot soldiers at his disposal, Rennell scoured the plains and forests of north India for seven years, fixing latitudes, marking the productivity of land, charting the course of rivers, and studying the details of the terrain. Stories of his encounter with snakes, tigers, and leopards are legion in the annals of the survey of India. Rennell's survey demonstrated that upper India had been chastised by the Company's army to the extent that the survey team could traverse a hostile territory without encountering serious and sustained resistance. Where discrepancies arose between the boundaries drafted by the surveyors and the indigenous markers of small districts, peasants most often refused to cooperate and provide information. Sometimes they even deserted their huts at the arrival of the survey team.[82] Local opposition to the survey was not tolerated. The evidence on this seems to be scattered; but just a few examples should suffice here. During the survey near the River Teesta, Rennell was unable to procure coolies and bearers, and local inhabitants refused to supply provisions. The diwan of Olyapour had threatened to punish any person willing to serve the survey, as he was vehemently opposed to the idea of the survey taking coolies forcibly in his dominions.[83] Rennell wrote to the diwan warning him that he would be taken prisoner unless he complied immediately, and after the British Resident in nearby Rungpore assisted him with bearers and coolies, the diwan's residence was set on fire by the surveyors.[84]

The survey, thus, from time to time had to request the escort of large battalions, especially in disturbed areas. At the end of 1770, during the survey of roads toward the north of the Ganges near Pulsah, Rennell was involved in a serious altercation with the local people and Zamindar Kader Beg. In his own account:

> A few minutes after our arrival the villagers came arm'd, & threatened to fall upon us. I asked them if they had any Complaint to make. They abused me, told me no, & insisted that I should go away. We soon dispersed them without making use of any Weapons, as I never suffer a Sepoy to fire till matters come to an Extremity.[85]

Later, the chief confronted his party, and a skirmish followed. Rennell himself took a shot at the zamindar, which missed him but killed an assistant; the incident succeeded in driving the protestors away. And in another fateful encounter with ascetic militants during operations in the upper reaches of Rungpore, Rennell was severely wounded and almost lost his life. The Sanyasis, one of the first groups to have rebelled against the British in the Company's dominions in the late eighteenth century, took grave exception to the survey and evidently failed to appreciate the distinction between soldiers and surveyors. It is indeed curious, though, that apart from these few passing mentions, Rennell's memoir and journals do not give much indication of the nature of day-to-day confrontations the survey team had with various local rulers and villages on the way. These accounts are written as routine inventories, with great details of place names, topography, latitudes, and longitudes. People, as a general rule, do not obtrude on the pure geographical relief.

Rennell's atlas succeeded in bringing British possessions in eastern India under the purview of a coherent and uniform set of maps and generated for the first time an active interest in London in the geography of India.[86] These first prints allowed for an exceptional imaginary of empire. He wrote in the first preface to his atlas:

> Whilst the theater of the British wars in Hindoostan was limited to a particular province . . . little curiosity was excited towards the general geography of the country: but now that we are engaged either in wars, alliances, or negociations with all the principle powers of the Empire, and have displayed British standards from one extreme of it to the other; a map of Hindoostan, such as will explain the local circumstances of our political connections, and the marches of our armies, cannot but be highly interesting to every person whose imagination has been struck by the splendour of our victories.[87]

It is clear that the new imperial geography of British rule in India exemplified by Rennell's achievement signified much more than measurement of territory. The title page of the manuscript atlas, *Essay Towards an Improvement in Geography,* published in 1782, displays two officers of the East India Company's army carrying the Union Jack, with smoking pieces of artillery at their feet. Another collection of Rennell's maps, published in 1792, is entitled *The Marches of the British Armies in the Peninsula of India.* Rennell's map was a monument to British victory, "by means of which the British Nation obtained, and has hitherto upheld, its Influence in India,"[88] as is evident from the famous title cartouche which appeared in the first edition in 1782, where the Roman figure of Britannia receives the sacred Hindu law books from tonsured Brahmins. In the dedicative engraving Britannia seems intent on the texts being handed to her or perhaps the bale of cotton on the foreground, while the eyes of the Brahmins are downcast and avert her gaze. This image bears a resemblance to the ceiling painting by Spiridione Roma in the East India House (Company headquarters, Leadenhall Street), entitled *Britannia Receiving the Riches of the East,* and the chimneypiece sculpture by Michael Rysbrack on the same theme. In both works, Britannia appears to look beyond India or the "East" (a feminine figure whose torso is uncovered) and her offerings, and so does Father Thames.[89]

While Archer opines that such compositions sought to capture the lure of India, John Berger suggests that they show the circularity of relationship between the colonizer and the colonized, and the purpose is that the British should appear both distant and powerful.[90] Rennell's cartouche resembles most of all, however, a lesser known-drawing by the artist Arthur William Devis, who was in India between 1785 and 1795.[91] Here, once again, Britannia receives the sacred book from a tonsured Brahmin who bends his torso reverentially. But they are both atop a geographical globe showing the Indian peninsula and the Bay of Bengal, while smoke emerges from deltaic Bengal and fills the firmament (Figure 1, Devis, *An Allegory of British Rule in India*). Presiding over both figures is the majestic apparition of what seems to be an Indian holy man who curiously resembles the solemn Father Thames in Roma's and Rysbrack's work.

Figure 1 Arthur Devis, *Allegory of British Rule in India.* Courtesy of the Harris Museum and Art Gallery.

Invocation of a Britain of Roman heritage and antiquity in these particular motifs—striking, as it was, in the context of the possibility of British supremacy over India—was hardly novel. Such views had already been summoned to lend dignity to the empire by the mid-eighteenth century. George Bickham Senior and Junior, calligraphers, engravers, cartographers, and chorographers, in their *British Monarchy,* which had been published by an act of Parliament in October, 1747, dedicated a grandiose frontispiece to Britannia seated on a pedestal, with the following inscription:

> Fair Britannia in stately Pomp appears
> Her Might and Majesty the World reveres
> From Pole to Pole She hears her Acts resound
> And rules an Empire by no Ocean bound.[92]

Such dominions were comprised of the British Isles, the Electoral States, the American colonies and the African and Indian settlements (Figure 2, George Bickham, *The British Monarchy*). Bickham's engravings also included a map showing the king of Britain's dominions in Europe, Africa, and America and a conical projection of the globe dominated by a dedication to George II (Figure 3, George Bickham, *The British Monarchy*).

Calligraphic virtuosity and penmanship had been a hallmark of cartographers in England ever since mapmaker Jodocus Hondius engraved the early English copybook *Theatrum Artis Scribendi* in 1594 and William Hole engraved the *Pen's Excellence* in 1618. Rennell's cartouche may be seen as the continuation of an older form of artistry belonging to a genre of mapmaking as an extension of a graphic, descriptive tradition of geography. Bickham offers a vignette of such a tradition in his introduction to the *British Monarchy* when he proclaims that geography is among the "first and most necessary" of the liberal arts, "without some tincture of which, all our Ideas of remote Transactions, Events, Productions, or whatever falls not under the cognizance of our Senses, must be ever confused and imperfect."[93] Along with maps, the use of archaic icons complemented a growing tradition of historical illustration. Later in the century, Clarendon's *Historical Narrative of the Rebellion and Civil Wars in England* had been published with lavish portraits, Robert Adam had brought out the richly illustrated *Ruins of the Palace of the Emperor Diocletian* (1764), and Joseph Strutt had engraved memorable historical images for his *Chronicle of England* (1777–1778). This visibility and rising popularity of the historical image provides a clearer context for the early cartography of empire. Francis Haskell maintains that such engraved images were intended to present a rather limited interpretation where the artist did not aim at presenting what the onlooker was not already familiar with.[94]

Matthew Edney suggests that Rennell failed to identify the Company as the legitimate ruler of Bengal; not only do his maps acknowledge the Mughal emperor as a viable font of authority but they adopt the names and borders

The African and Indian Settlements.

These Forts and Factories are under the Protection of y Crown, but the Property of the *African* and *Indian* Companies, who garison them in their own Names.

The *African* Company have *James Fort* on *Gambia* River. Most of their other Forts, of which the chief is *Cape-Coast Castle*, lie from West to East on the Coast of *Guinea*, in about 5 Degrees N. Lat. This Company is at present so low, that it annually applies to Parliament for Money to maintain these Places: But the Trade of Negroes is notwithstanding as great as ever, being chiefly carried on by private Adventurers.

The *East India* Company, whose Trade is in a very flourishing Condition, have the Island of *St. Helena*, betwixt *Africa* & *South America*, for their Ships to call at in their Passage. In *India* their chief Settlements are *Bombay* on the *Malabar*, and Fort *St. George*, or *Madras*, on the *Coromandel* Coast. A great Number of small Factories depend on these. They have also Fort *William* upon *Hugly* River, a
Branch

Figure 2 George Bickham, *Indian Settlements*. Courtesy of Frank Graham.

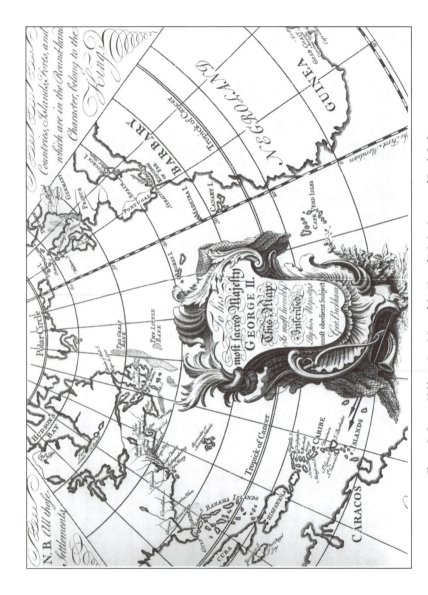

Figure 3 George Bickham, *Dominions of the King of Britain*. Courtesy of Frank Graham.

of many former Mughal provinces within India.[95] This can be explained partly by the fact that the Company derived its right to collect the revenue of the eastern provinces as the diwan of the Mughal Empire, a favor it had won in 1765. Yet, although such a title placed the English nominally under the aegis of the Mughals, they nevertheless had succeeded in obtaining the diwani because their army, as we have already seen in a preceding chapter, had in fact prevailed against the joint forces of the former nawab of Bengal, the nawab of Awadh, and the Mughal Emperor himself. In return the British simply paid a regular annual tribute into the Mughal treasury. Moreover, the Indian settlements, forts, and factories were also under the protection of the Crown and ratified by act of Parliament; they were the property of the Company and garrisoned in their own name.[96] During this period the Mughal Empire had already entered its twilight years. Rennell's acknowledgment of Mughal India thus indicates deeper ambiguities of conquest and possession that move beneath the surface of geographical images. Apart from one important painting of the presentation of the diwani to Clive (which can be interpreted as the British acceptance of Mughal authority as much as the *de facto* capitulation of Emperor Shah Alam), there is little in the description or depiction of British India that invokes the sovereignty of the Mughals or the marking of the passage between a Mughal and a British India.

Rennell's atlas plainly marks this unseen struggle over the assertion of sovereignty. British possessions are charted in great detail and appear in blocks of red. The use of red or pink for territorial hold, and of distinct colors to demarcate internal frontiers, seems to foreshadow practices that would become standard only in the nineteenth century. Adjoining countries are inscribed not merely as old provinces of the Mughal empire but in the names of the principal enemies of the Company: Seiks [*sic*], the Mogul, Mahrattas [*sic*], Tipoo, and the Nizam. "Country powers" also appear as colored segments: Maratha country and Berar are green, Hyderabad blue, Awadh and Mysore yellow. With further military inroads and survey teams on the heels of the army, such segments would give way to detailed features and place-names.

After Rennell, the two major military-cartographic fronts were against Marathas in the west and Tipu in the south. Caldwell and Duncan, following General Goddard's army to Gujarat, extended a baseline for the measurement of distances, and after the defeat of the Maratha chiefs, Turner and Reynolds completed the map of the Bombay presidency.[97] In the war against Tipu Sultan, Governor-General Cornwallis appointed Alexander Kyd, a military engineer, as surveyor-general. Robert Colebrooke, a member of the survey team, following the Grand Army to Seringapatam, had already drafted a skeleton map of Mysore. During the final campaign, Alexander Beatson accompanied the army as surveyor-general, and a commission was appointed after the death of Tipu Sultan (the independent ruler of Mysore) to settle the geographical details of his country.[98] No dedicative cartouche, to my knowledge, celebrates the fall of this dreaded enemy in the maps that were drawn. But we know that the artists Arthur W. Devis and Robert Home were present when Lord Cornwallis received the sons of Tipu Sultan as hostages.[99] Devis made some sketches and composed, as we have seen, the scene of the discovery of Tipu's death at the fall of Seringapatnam, while Home was moved to paint a panoramic scene of the surrender in 1794. Here the fable of conquest diverges from the exactitude of the map. But Rennell, having painted the coasts of India red where British exploits had taken place, laid open the prospects of imperial geography. Committed to paper and ink, war, territorial expansion, annexation, and diplomatic subterfuge had now become inseparable from cartography.

ANATOMY OF AN EMPIRE

Within just a few decades of the publication of Rennell's map, the instrumental rationality of the cartographic exercise would tend to exceed the authority of the cartographic image. William Lambton, founder of the Great Trigonometrical Survey of India and veteran of the American Revolutionary War, commenting on the feasibility of a comprehensive atlas of the whole subcontinent in view of the unquestioned hegemony of British arms, remarked that:

> a great advantage to general geography would be derived from extending a survey across the Peninsula of India, for the purpose of determining the positions of the principal geographical points; and seeing that, by the success of the British arms during the late glorious campaign, district or country is acquired, which not only opens a free communication with the Malabar Coast but affords a most admirable means of connecting that with the cost of Coromandel by *an uninterrupted series of triangles, and of continuing that series to an almost unlimited extent in every direction.*[100]

Lambton's survey was based upon mathematical first principles: first, to determine the value in terms of linear measure of a degrees of latitudes and longitudes; second, to measure an accurate distance between two points fixed on a longitude, called a *base line,* and to plot a third point by calculating angles by the optical instrument of measurement known as the theodolite. Thus would be established a "triangle station." Lambton began his triangulation with a base line measured near Madras, and his first series of triangles ran from east to west toward the two flanks of the peninsula.[101] By 1818 he had succeeded in carrying a progression of triangles to the southern tip of India and from there proceeded up by the seventy-eighth meridian towards the north, when the government of India officially recognized the work as the Great Trigonometrical Survey. Between 1802 and 1815 the whole of the southern peninsula south of the river Krishna had been covered by a network of triangles, with the geographical location of several thousand prominent points charted in order to compile a general map of the southern peninsula.[102] Lambton's work would be carried on by surveyors-general Mackenzie and Everest in order to include the whole of India.

The trigonometric survey in India was recognized widely by contemporaries as a remarkable feat of geographical calculation and as the establishment of ideal scientific principles of measuring the land. With the Great Trigonometrical Survey coming into full operation, a gradual divergence took place between the pursuit of geographical knowledge and military contingency. By the time Everest was extending Lambton's mission to the upper reaches of the northern plains, British dominance had been established over most native rulers, whether their territories were actually annexed or not. In 1822, the directors of the Company decided to compile an atlas of India on a scale of a quarter-inch to a mile, attempting to incorporate all the recent survey work. Sheets were engraved in London as the information gradually became available, producing a standard map of India for the next eighty years of rule.[103] By this time papermaking had become fully mechanized and the printing press powered by steam, accelerating the reproduction of printed maps.[104]

An "uninterrupted series of triangles" carried with it the promise of mathematical perfectibility in the representation of both geodetic space and geographical place. Edney's work reminds us that this remained an illusive ideal and that economic and political constraints continued to compromise its comprehensive scope throughout the nineteenth century.[105] The 1820's *Atlas of India,* he argues, provided an archival structure to which additions and corrections could be made retrospectively. The steady onward progress of scientific cartography was thus an indispensable myth that sustained the image of a lasting empire. The beginning of triangulation in India thus marks the consolidation of the geopolitical reality known as the British Raj. With the end of military uncertainty and dissociation of the company-state from its oriental and despotic past, the political space of British India could earn a neutral, measured stature.

The colonial map of India, however, was still quite distinct from the usual map of a continuous nation-state. The Raj was a variegated "body politic" with shifting political boundaries of indigenous rules, often marked by colors, where internal borders continued to imply stories of conquest and submission. While Rennell's maps of the late eighteenth century depict colored segments of "enemy" territory, maps of India after the trigonometrical survey shade regions according to their political status in relation to British forces. Captain J. Sutherland in 1833, preparing a note on the political relations of the British government in India, was asked by the surveyor-general to "obtain in a rough way the area, or contents in square miles, of each state, without the labor of elaborate calculation," a measure that could not be obtained from existing maps.[106] In this scheme, the boundary of each state was marked off on a skeleton map drawn on paper, cut out, and carefully weighed both individually and collectively. The estimate was that the area of native states who had signed a treaty of alliance with the Company amounted to 449,845 square miles, and territory under direct British rule, including small quasi-autonomous states, made up 626,746 square miles. Sutherland classified native states under the following heads: Foreign (e.g., Persia and Kabul), External (e.g., Nepal on the frontier), and Internal (those that had been forced to relinquish independent political relations). Internal native states were further split into six classes according to the nature of their diplomatic relations with the British. Here was a list of regions in the subcontinent, subjugated through wars of conquest and unequal treaties, that were actually cut out from the physical map and weighed in relation to it:[107]

> First Class: treaties offensive and defensive; right on their part to claim protection, external and internal, from the British government: right on its part to interfere in their internal affairs.
> Second Class: treaties offensive and defensive; right on their part to claim protection, external and internal, from the British government, and the aid of its troops to realize their just claims from their own subjects: no right on its part to interfere in their internal affairs.
> Third Class: treaties offensive and defensive; states mostly tributary, acknowledging the supremacy of, and promising subordinate cooperation to, the British government; but supreme rulers in their own dominions.
> Fourth Class: guarantee and protection, subordinate cooperation, but supremacy in their own territory.
> Fifth Class: amity and friendship.
> Sixth Class: protection, with right on the part of the British government to control internal affairs.

Such states, moreover, were divided according to predominance of region and religion; for instance, four were "Mohammedan states," nineteen were Rajput, six belonged to "other Hindu tribes," and there were other "inferior Rajaships" and "Jagirdaris (land revenue assignments)." Demonstrably, the diplomatic chessboard of the Raj was physically actualized through the map which now could be cut, pasted, and manipulated at will. Sectarian and regional segmentation of the geo-body, as exemplified above, would have a telling impact on the imagination of the nation within the parameters of the colonial state. Such operations further testify to the objective quality of space acquired by the map of the Indian subcontinent.

But what can be discerned of the point of view of the people whose land was brought thus under imperial scrutiny and who were hardly privy to its scientific mission? Such histories of mapping from the ground remain to be excavated. Operations of a large survey must have resembled the movement of a peculiar and cumbrous army. From contemporary accounts, it appears that the survey camp, complete with the rituals and regalia of the Raj, was an elaborate affair.[108] Twelve sets of long metal bars averaging 750 feet were laid on tripods under a movable tent. There were large masonry towers built at the site to set the accuracy of base lines. The entire operation of a triangulation base could last more than two months. W. H. Sleeman, during his extensive tours, recorded how people in Central India were attributing the failure of crops and blight to the frequent measurement of land by surveyors and the operations of the trigonometrical survey.[109] Brahmin priests were requisitioned to exorcise the peaks and masonry pillars from which the engineers had taken their angles, and the landmarks left by the survey teams were destroyed during short intervals of absence, much to their frustration. The peasants believed that men of the survey who "required to do their work by the aid of fires lighted in the dead of the night in high places, which no one but themselves seemed able to comprehend, must hold communion with supernatural beings, a communion which they thought would be displeasing to the Deity."[110] Marches of surveying teams thus left a powerful impression on the countryside. Whole villages sometimes had to be moved to set up landmarks and clear the field of vision for the theodolite, and on a few occasions, desecration of temples could not be avoided when putting up visible markers.

Cartographic images of British India thus point to the visual history of both soldiering and surveying, a history of the use of lenses and other instruments of objectification wielded with unprecedented impunity in the colonial territory. It is the eventual hypostasis of the map as basic visual currency that sustained a complex colonial imagery of India and thus an obverse image of the British themselves. Here, then, is the radical divergence between the military survey as a contingent and uneven exercise in power and the relative immutability of the cartographic symbol. While it may be suggestive to treat this as the interlocking of the picturesque and the scientific gaze of the British in India, we have to be careful in distinguishing the act of mapping and its outcome. This is not the place to dispute the Foucaultian premise of the gaze and the particular institutional histories of the all-seeing, impersonal panopticon. The gaze in this eminently modern sense is predisposed not only toward the ultimate primacy of the seen, but very much toward the intimate relationship between the act and the object of observation under specific regimes of surveillance.[111]

British-India did not readily achieve such a homogeneity in its conception of power. It is this sense that the colonial map can be seen as part of the historical diversity that attended the experience of imperial modernity in India. While we cannot privilege the map as the *summa* of colonial knowledge, we can hardly deny its interposition between the observer and the observed. Unlike, perhaps, in nationalistic imagination, where the map becomes coextensive with other mnemonics of living territory, the colonial map instantiates an outline of a state from without that can only be replicated, adjusted, and reinforced. One could argue plausibly that with the map of India in place, validity of rule could be further sought through surveys more carnal, stratified, and vital, that is, roughly corresponding with the geological, archaeological, and anthropological. The map in and of itself then became much less prominent in the ensemble of dominant images of India under colonial rule. In the years during which the sovereignty of England remained in question, the cartographic imagery of India provided a crucial semblance of autonomy and sufficiency for the colonial state.

4

Domesticity and Dominion

Dominion is acquired two ways, by generation and by conquest.
The right of dominion by generation, is that which the parent hath over his children.
——Thomas Hobbes, *Leviathan*

Breathing in the softest of climates; having so few real wants; and receiving
even the luxuries of other nations with little labor, from the fertility of their
own soil; the Indian must become the most effeminate inhabitant of the
globe; and this is the very point at which we now see him.
——Robert Orme, *Historical Fragments,* 1782

In his denunciation of the Bengalis written in 1840, Thomas Babington Macaulay, found Eastern India to be populated by a class of subjects who were "enervated by a soft climate and accustomed to peaceful employments, [and] bore the same relation to other Asiatics which the Asiatics generally bear to the bold and energetic children of Europe."[1] He observed further that:

> Castillians have a proverb, that in Valencia the earth is water and the men women; and the description is at least equally applicable to the vast plain of the Lower Ganges. Whatever the Bengali does he does languidly. His favorite pursuits are sedentary. He shrinks from bodily exertion; and, though, voluble in dispute, and singularly pertinacious in the war of chicane, he seldom engages in a personal conflict, and scarcely even enlists as a soldier.

Many decades later, in 1899, G. W. Stevens, one time special correspondent of the Daily Mail, expressed the same opinion:

> By his legs you shall know the Bengali. The leg of a free man is straight or a little bandy, so that he can stand on it solidly: his calf is taper and his thigh flat. The

Bengali's leg is either skin and bone, and the same size all the way down, with knocking knobs for knees, or else it is very flat and globular, also turning at the knees, with round thighs like a woman's. The Bengali's leg is the leg of a slave.[2]

These two observations, though egregious at first sight, would not have been considered novel or insidious during the advent of British rule in India. The discursive twists through which the Bengalis became the prototype of enfeebled, enslaved, and engendered imperial subjects were much more than products of overt racism or simply of the need for an assertive, self-validating, masculine identity for Englishmen in India. From its very inception, the colonial political economy was burdened with the ideological work of sorting out its relations to various unequal colonial subjects in accordance with dominant ideas of sexuality, gender, domesticity, and the division of labor.

I argue in this chapter that colonial rule was consonant with intimate forms of inequality that can be traced back to the depths of European history. In the process of imperial expansion, Britain created a multitude of subjects arranged in various degrees of difference from and inferiority to its own native subjects. Such diverse peoples, wrote the Reverend William Tennant, a keen observer of indigenous life in India, had been entrusted to Britannia as the predominant "Ruler of Nations" in the world; providence had cast many millions "into her arms, for their protection and welfare."[3] And as Britain commanded territories in Asia, Africa, and America more extensive than "ever fell under the dominion of any ancient or modern nation," it had become her duty to "controul the destinies of so large a portion of the human race."[4] Administrators of mercantilist corporations, Parliaments, and missionaries of spiritual and civilizational improvement would arrange and rearrange these subjects into various, often contradictory, hierarchies. The latitudes of encounter between Britons and the original inhabitants of their far-flung empire were exceptionally wide and their very scale tended to threaten the fundamental liberal impulse of the civilizing mission as well as normative conceptions of society.

Some of these attitudes were directly influenced by Enlightenment ideas of natural history, but specific prejudices were products of particular histories of imperial expansion. Sir James Mackintosh, in his lectures on the "Law of Nature and Nations," reflecting on the sudden explosion of the knowledge of hitherto unknown regions of the globe in England, described some of these newly discovered people thus:

We can pass human society in review before our mind, from the brutal and helpless barbarism of Terra del Fuego, and the mild and voluptuous savages of Otaheite, to the tame, but ancient and immovable, civilization of China, which bestows its own arts on every successive race of conquerors, to the meek and servile natives of Hindostan, who preserve their ingenuity, their skill and their science, through a long series of ages, under the yoke of foreign tyrants—to the gross and incorrigible rudeness of the

Ottomans, incapable of improvement, and extinguishing the remains of civilization among their unhappy subjects. . . .[5]

This passage, delivered in London in 1797, is remarkable not only in the astonishing confidence of tone but also in the pairing of attributes. The adjectives—"mild and voluptuous," "tame but ancient," "meek and servile," "gross and incorrigible"—prefigure both a degree of intimacy and the standpoint of an observer of extraordinary privilege. A testimony to the emerging natural-historical classification of mankind, this was also a tribute to the growing confidence in the perpetuity of British possessions worldwide. The new imperial typology of subject populations thus remained imprecise, a muddle of ethnocentric prejudice and attempts at impartial observation brought upon by unexpected increase in territory, adding new and unfortunate specimens to the list of people already assigned to the lowest places in the natural hierarchy of subjects in the island empire—the Highland Scots, and the Lower Irish.

The arguments in this chapter are specific to the case of British India, but it is implied that the social and sexual ordering of Britain's imperial subjects could be followed back to similar subjects closer at home in England. The incipient paternalism of the colonial state and its shifting hierarchy of gender, I argue, hark back to the Hanoverian household and its devolution of authority within the family, and more generally to the idea of the state as an extended domestic arena. As Judith Butler would suggest, the excavation of the historic strata of authority and privilege in any given society may not reveal their true referent, for the deepest categories lay buried in the very crevices of dominant discourse. This is an inherent limitation of the questions we ask of the formation of any identity. Butler suggests that it is tricky to study agency in itself, as it is mired in an entire concatenation of political significations. Agency, according to Butler, "can never be understood as a controlling or original authorship over that signifying chain, and it cannot *be the power,* once installed, and constituted in and by that chain, to set a course for its own future."[6]

Insofar as this chapter examines forms of colonial domesticity, I have tried not to posit a simple and straightforward history of men and their relationship to institutions of imperial rule. For one thing, such histories have already been written.[7] I turn here, in a somewhat different view, to some recent studies of the Victorian middle class that have raised new and important questions on the relationship between self-respect and public behavior of men and the values invested in a properly regulated domestic household.[8] This unwritten compact between domesticity and manliness among influential sections of the nineteenth century English middle class seems to have had its origins in a much earlier period.[9] This chapter explores similar questions within the microcosm of British colonial society in India, especially those aspects of the patriarchal household that subtended foundations of the colonial state. What seems to be particularly intriguing are the unintended consequences of the imposition of a largely alien polity on India, a state whose domestic ideology ran into ambiguity and contradiction due in part to the difficulties of the British in sorting out the gendered and sexual aspects of their relationship with Indians as subjects. It is in this context that the history of colonial domesticity becomes relevant as a clue to the less visible and thus most entrenched idioms of British rule. The British-Indian political economy was based on an evolving taxonomy of the subject population, particularly along the lines of their effeminacy and masculinity. Such classification is also to be found in early ethnographic descriptions of the domestic life, work, and bodies of the inhabitants of the Indian countryside in the period in which the company-state established its sway over the Indian countryside.

STATE AND THE PATRIARCHAL HOUSEHOLD

There is little doubt that the political discourse of Enlightenment produced an overt, even excessive reference to patriarchal authority in the conception of statehood. Kant is the obvious source here, when he tries to expose the despotism inherent in the medievalist concept of the *imperium paternale,* arguing for a *patriotic* government defined as *imperium non paternale.* In the despotic state, subjects are likened to immature children who do not have the means to judge their own good or bad and look up to the head of the state for guidance, whereas in the patriotic state, everyone "regards the common-wealth as the maternal womb, or the land as the paternal ground from which he himself sprang and which he must leave to his descendants as a treasured pledge."[10] Note the specificity of gender here. In this and various other ren-ditions, the eighteenth century, it might be argued, interrogated and received the Aristotelian relationships between *oikia, oikos,* and the *polis.* An impor-tant instance in this debate in the context of England was Locke's rebuttal of Robert Filmer's *Patriarcha,* where he repudiated the biblical injunction of filial submission to the figure of the king and suggested a much wider arena of relationships in society in the conception of a meaningful polity: man and wife, parents and children, master and servant.

Yet, as Linda Kerber's investigation of the discourse of the Enlighten-ment has shown, arguments against the tyranny of the authoritarian state invoked a partial political role for women, and then only to revalue the posi-tion of the family; thus they effectively foreclosed the question of participa-tion and reduced the problem of autonomy for women as individuals to their *relations* within the purview of the family.[11] Such political exclusion tended to generate negative markers of civilization: nonmale, nonadult, nonwhite, nongentrified, and so on. While older symbols of paternal authority were being repudiated, through both the idea of regicide and egalitarian (especially in the works of the *philosophes*) attacks against medieval notions of the king's representative bodies constituting the body politic, an equally grave empha-sis was being placed on the idea of family, inheritance, and indeed the *repro-duction* of civil society, inhering most visibly in the changing notions of property. The various negotiations that political philosophy of the Enlightenment conducted with its medieval legacy in regard to paternal notions of legitimate authority cannot be discussed in any detail here. Yet, with specific reference to Hanoverian England, this chapter underlines the vital importance of the household in the legitimation of the benevolent, protective, and punishing powers of the state.

Keith Tribe's analysis of the eighteenth century discourse of political economy and political arithmetic shows *inter alia* how central the notion of the household (*oeconomy*), was to debates over the limits of state authority in the creation and measurement of wealth in society.[12] A concept of the household had been reified in the course of the formation of the English state, particularly through the Georgian period. Philip Corrigan and Derek Sayer, a couple of decades ago, stressed the dearth of historical approaches to this phenomenon, calling for the need to relate the so-called private realms of the household to the "public sphere" of rule and arguing that across the eighteenth and nineteenth century, "the centerpiece of the social fabric was the family, its patriarchal order and society reflecting that of society as a whole."[13] Their questions are being addressed in recent research, discussed below, which are of value to the present argument.

The family was certainly a strong organizing metaphor for the state in the eighteenth century. Sir James Steuart, in his *Inquiry into the Principles of Political Economy,* published in 1767, contended that the economy of the family was directly analogous to the political economy of a state, except that in a state "there are no servants, all are children."[14] John Bennet, in his treatise on the importance of commercial expansion of Britain to the colonies, advising on how to improve and regulate the trading settlements and plantations, stressed that polity was the father of the state, and trade and agriculture, respectively, its nurse and mother.[15] Such examples can be multiplied. A certain vision of economic and political order, indebted to the competing and interrelated formations of individual gain, profit of corporations, public finance, and revenue administration, was being organized around ideas of domesticity. The need for order could not proceed without this ultimate faith in a paternalist conception of statehood, however loud may be the claims to liberty and individualist choice in the running of political institutions.

Authority granted in the domestic household was being reinscribed in the nation-state. In the realms of both family and the polity in early modern England, there was a growing need for stability and tradition, for society was being reshaped by rapidly changing class fortunes, attended by the confusion of station and rank.[16] Towards the end of the eighteenth century, certain distinctive habits of middle-class domesticity had taken shape, where the wife and children now assisted the male head of the household, especially in family-run business enterprises.[17] Overall, the gentrified family acquired a sharper definition, with the decline of clientage constituted by retainers, servants and tenants and a tightening of the reins of inheritable property. By the time Blackstone's *Commentaries on the Laws of England* had been compiled, the right of property had already been defined as a possession obtaining only during the lifetime of the individual and ceasing upon death, a rule which would secure the idea of inheritance and succession firmly to bourgeois patrimony.[18] "All the power a man hath over his own subject," claimed Lord Kames in his legal treatise, *Principle of Equity,* "are included in his right of property."[19] Blackstone, defining the absolute nature of this right, called it: "that sole and despotic dominion which one man claims and exercises over the external things in the world, in total exclusion of the right of any other individual in the universe."[20] Through forms of property and propriety, the gentrified household was emerging as analogous to the political order. It is worth recounting here that pastoral, churchly marriage was the only communion between man and woman recognized by the state, at least till the 1830s, inhering in the mediation of God the Father, the Holy Father, and the prince bishop.[21] Once this process of identification of the household and the state was completed, private, individuated, manly forms of property would be understood only in opposition to the public property of the state, founded along the genealogy of the commonwealth.

Much of this process was certainly a function of class. The family estate was indeed the bastion of the aristocracy, inasmuch as it constituted itself as a privileged class fragment. As Habakkuk pointed out, the landed estate ensured a sense of continuity in ownership as no other forms of property could provide.[22] The estate was the essential fruit of the Whiggish struggle for ascendancy, a physical emblem of social status *par excellance,* and a repository of carefully accumulated family tradition. In this sense, the household precisely anticipated the nation. Defoe captured the idea in a flash of insightful prose in *Atlantis Major,* at the beginning of the eighteenth century, in the context of Tory-Whigg rivalry over Scotland:

> It is true, that Estate is not any just Addition to the Character of a Person; but it will for ever remain a Truth; And all Nations will shew a regard to it, *viz.,* that those may be supposed to be the most proper Persons to be trusted with the Conservation of the Liberties of their Country, who have by their Birth and Inheritance the largest Shares in the Possession of it.[23]

In the survey and settlement of outlying parts of the British Isles, as we have seen in the last chapter, cadastral and military techniques of observation were indeed the foundations of a certain kind of knowledge that presupposed a language of possession on the part of the English state. Between Roy's survey of Scotland and John Sinclair's statistical account we can detect the rising compatibility between notions of mapping, private and public property, sovereignty of the state, and the measurement of the productive capacity of subjects. These will be taken up later in this chapter.

What we have here for now is a curious dissociation. The household, as the model for the commonwealth as well as the nation-state, assumed the dominant locus of patriarchy precisely as it was about to shed its traditional lodgments of kinship and patronage. The middle class home began to be endowed with attributes of morality and progress that seemed to point at the older aristocratic households as dens of venality, opulence, and habitual excesses of wealth. Virtue, frugality, and order, as both Susan Amussen and Margaret Hunt have pointed out, would soon become the touchstones of the middle class family.[24] Thus Goldsmith in *The Vicar of Wakefield* admonishes the superfluity of fortune and the luxury of dependants, whereby a rich man such as Mr. Thornhill surrounds himself with the "rabble of mankind."[25] Such excess, indicating declining standards of the aristocratic oligarchy, was seen by Goldsmith and his contemporaries as directly responsible for the moral deterioration of the state, where the honest voice of the "middle orders of mankind," who should be the true custodians of freedom and liberty, goes unheeded.[26]

The family and household provided the essential, formative, and legitimizing domain of the exercise and apprenticeship in power for younger men in society. Where else would the nation-state recruit its patriarchal ideals? In his *Sketches of the History of Man,* Lord Kames demonstrated how the head of the household personified all other dependents in the passage between family and nation: "The master of a family is immediately connected with his country: his wife, his children, his servants, are immediately connected with him, and with his country, through him *only.*"[27]

Empirical work on the formation of the English middle class, particularly that of Leonore Davidoff and Catherine Hall, confirms the assertion that the growth of large extrafamilial institutions and the widening and diverse fields of occupation in commerce, finance, and industry accelerated the divides between the family and the world, home and the workplace, and the private and public spheres of operation and identification.[28] Both the landed estate and the commercial firm contributed, it has been argued, to a distinctive sense of masculine agency—normative, paternalist, and above all endowed with the security of property. Indeed, the mutually reinforcing ideas of liberty and property, qualities that appeared to be the natural endowments of every true-born Englishman, can certainly be related to the gradual sequestration of the immediate family and home from external domains defined by manly pursuits. Yet divisions felt in the material world that could and did effectively fragment the core communitarian aspects of identity must have yielded other, perhaps more reified forms of association.

Here, I would argue, the notion of a domestic economy that could ensure the reproduction of society in its entirety played a signal role in creating a new belonging, a renewed sense of regulative order and discipline. This was certainly the case, as I have pointed out, in the conception of political economy. Domesticity thus relieved from the concrete materiality of the family, could provide a valuable space where men could identify, even patriotically, with their place in the nation-state. A deeply invested and empowered criterion of order, it played a singular role in the manner in which Englishmen and other Britons saw their place in India and in the hierarchy of Indians in the new society within British-Indian territories that was taking shape. Colonial society thus created a vast new theater for generations of English and other men from the islands, and their terms of dominance over women and within their families contributed to the organizing principles of a British-Indian society that was overwhelmingly male and often homosocial in character. The history of these formations lies scattered in the barrack rooms, gymnasiums, and clubs as much as within the confines of the bungalow.

THE QUEST FOR DOMINION

Dominion in the eighteenth century was inextricably tied to the idea of a political-economic order and the fundamental value of property as a social institution. The new subject of political economy, much like political arithmetic before it, addressed a broad set of concerns about the nature and limits of private and corporate gain and the consequences of unbridled passion for economic profit, measured in terms of their impact on the well-being of the political order. As Albert Hirschman has argued so persuasively, the idea of political economy for thinkers of the moral enlightenment such as Sir James Steuart, John Millar, and even Adam Smith was intimately related to state and statecraft.[29] Enduring economic interests in society had long been regarded as a bulwark against natural and baser instincts of mankind, and in the eighteenth century the idea of an organized realm of exchange and commerce increasingly came to be seen as the moral and ideological basis for the improvement of the political order.[30] In the context of colonial expansion, there seems to have been even less discrepancy between the objectives of political economy and the role of the state. This was particularly true in instances where the state was obliged to bend and transform indigenous societies and nurture ideas and institutions supporting private property.

Adam Anderson, in his voluminous history of commerce, addressed this issue in the latter half of the century by associating dominion squarely with the institution of public property. He had argued, as we have already seen, that public property divided nations, just as private property divided and delimited people. Countries and territories, according to Anderson, were like greater manors, alienated from each the other through limits and borders; they were the "public properties of nations" possessed "exclusively of one another."[31] This could well be one of the clearest articulations of dominion during the period, underscoring the correspondence between nation, household, and property rights. In the age of colonization, the rights of settlement and perpetuation of economic interests flowed precisely from such strands of legitimation, especially as the right to colonial dominion was founded unfailingly on the notion of rightful property. Even a brief survey of the parliamentary debates surrounding the establishment of the rule of the East India Company as a chartered, mercantile corporation would demonstrate that these rights were secured as the *bona fide* property of a corporate body politic, through which all claims to settlement, territory, and revenue were justified.

Attacks against the Company's mercantilist monopoly were rebutted through the assertion that these rights had been rightfully purchased from the Crown and Parliament in return for a promise of an annual territorial revenue for England of close to seven million pounds sterling, command over an army of sixty thousand men, and the disposal of the lives and fortunes of thirty million subjects.[32]

It was this contractual foundation of overseas possession that underwrote the continuity between the company Raj and the British nation, consonant with values shared by a burgeoning landed gentry: ownership, inheritance, and succession. In the latter half of the eighteenth century, particularly in the wake of the French Revolution, many, even in the colonies, felt threats to this order. Burke, in his *Reflections on the Revolution in France* (1790), written as a warning to the Whiggish aristocracy to shun the ranks of English radicals, phrased these concerns in no uncertain manner:

> The power of perpetuating our property in our families is one of the most valuable and interesting circumstances belonging to it, and that which tends the most to the perpetuation of society itself. It makes our weakness subservient to our virtue; it grafts benevolence even upon avarice. The possessors of family wealth, and of the distinction which attends the hereditary possession . . . are the natural securities for this transmission. . . .[33]

This particular rendition of the Lockean theorem of a commonwealth, the live "bond of wealth and law" among the natural subjects of the state, significantly informed the idea of overseas dominion.

Given the fiscal and military exigencies in the era of imperial and national rivalry with other European powers, notably France, there was a profound need to rearticulate the basis of dominion. The image of a monopolistic, acquisitive, profit-generating corporation would not have guaranteed legal sovereignty to the administrators of the Company. The inheritance of the early colonial empire in India was thus founded on the idea, forcefully put forward by Thomas Pownall in his pamphlet the *The Right, Interest, and Duty of the State as Concerned in the Affairs of the East Indies,* that the East India Company was indeed the true landlord of the dominions of the state.[34] The idea of delegated rule, trusteeship on behalf of the Crown, and the very responsibility of colonial rule were emphasized precisely at the time when the Company was being arraigned in Parliament and in public for corruption, misgovernment, and malpractice and made to answer for the great Bengal famine of 1771 that had led to the starvation and death of millions. This was a common basis for the conservative sentiment, notably expressed by Burke, beseeching the Company to fulfill its solemn covenant towards the inhabitants of India.

The quest for territorial revenue in eastern India, as the history of Bengal should remind us, led to a profound revolution in landed society, known to historians of the Company as the Permanent Settlement, a series of revenue experiments aimed at the standardization of land tenure and expected to change the face of the agrarian countryside of eastern India. Ushered in during the period of Lord Cornwallis as governor-general, this was an effort to improve the collection of land revenue by creating a society of landed estates in the Bengal countryside. Historians have seen this decision, which included an appeal to physiocracy, as instrumental in severing the feudal ties of Indian society in order to inculcate a new sense of enterprise in landed property. Ranajit Guha points out that the advocates of this momentous land settlement in eastern India shared a common regard for the sanctity of private property.[35] Philip Francis, for instance, one of the main architects of this policy, referred to the Company's territory in Bengal as an "estate" to be tended to like any other back home in England.

Since Englishmen were not allowed as individuals to settle in British India, the landed wealth of the Company was to be entrusted to a newly created class of improving landlords recruited from among the natives. They were to be the harbingers of Whig patrimony on the shores of Bengal. Behind this administrative and fiscal apparatus for the improvement of Indian society, E. P. Thompson suggests, lurked contemporary Whiggish notions of oligarchy. Even contemporary critics of the project failed to caution against the attempt to transplant the agrarian bourgeoisie of England on to Indian soil. Landed estates were indeed the only and true foundations of dominion, which, as Thompson put it, "gave security to exclusive rights in property, and property was the proper station not only for planting turnips but also for planting political interest."[36] The vision of improving estates was not just a matter of class prejudice of the rural gentry refashioned by mercantilists in India who were enchanted with the stability of measured, delimited, and cultivated land as the stronghold of property—it refracted on a much wider basis the idioms of colonial expansion.

The vision of estates in the English countryside replanted in colonial India is crucial to an understanding that accompanied it, namely, that the Indian subjects of the East India Company were bereft of the two fundamental qualities that rendered Englishmen free: liberty and property. The notion of the unfreedom of colonial subjects in India was profound among British administrators of India, if not always explicit in the early ethnography of Indian society. Alexander Dalrymple, however, hydrographer to the Admiralty and the Company, argued in a remarkable passage on the Company's role in India that the natives were not capable of enjoying the freedom reserved for their colonial conquerors. I have discussed this passage at greater length in the first chapter of this book. Dalrymple further contended that since Indians did not make their own laws and also lacked a true corpus of ancient jurisprudence, they were not free agents and thus had no say in their own governance. The very fact that they had acquiesced to British rule was testimony to the fact that the Indians simply did not possess that *"force and elevation of mind"* which has been so distinguishable in the British char-

acter."[37] To the extent that Indians had been conquered, they were tanta-
mount to slaves in principle, though not in practice.

These references to Indians as subservient were not accidental. Questions
of freedom, liberty, and servitude were crucial in this period, when the tide of
debate over chattel slavery was rising. The West Indian islands had been fully
annexed by this period, and the slave trade was at its height. The poignant
issues of slavery and abolition provide a moral direction in the conception of
benevolent despotism in India, which was seen as more realistic than liberal
and equitable rule. Opposing and complementary views of despotism and
slavery played an important role in the ethnography of Indian society in this
period, especially as the East India Company grappled with the prevalent
forms of bondage and servitude continued within the ranks of elite Indian
households. As Indrani Chatterjee has pointed out in a recent study, various
form of servitude in India remained invisible or unheeded, as they did not sat-
isfy the criterion of the plantation model in the eyes of the colonial reform-
ers.[38] Much of the discourse on subject formation discussed here tended to
disregard the internal differentiation of Indian society in favor of broad gen-
eralizations about governance and subservience.

DESPOTISMS ABJECT AND EXCESSIVE

Colonial narratives of despotism in India reveal a troubled affiliation between
the dominant authors of empire and their subordinate subjects. The assertion of a free, benevolent, improving, paternalist, consciously authoritative
agency on the part of the British in India fabricated, in a curious inversion of
the idea of dominion, a diabolical image of Indian despotism. It was represented most conspicuously in India in the figure of the Moor, the old invader
who had been forcibly removed from his seat not just because he happened to
lose in decisive battles but also because he had forfeited his right rule through
degenerate actions. And beneath the Moor in the natural-historical ladder of
existence there was the Gentoo, or Hindu, consigned to timeless and irredeemable slavery in his own nation and abode. I argued earlier (Chapter 2)
that the two-nation theory of India had been already advanced in the imperial historiography of India. Such histories, ironically, precipitated timeless and
iconic representations that animated ethnological discourse of Indian difference. The very archetypes, I shall argue below, can be read as perversions of
racial anxiety that found new articulations in the Indian context.

Gilles Deleuze and Felix Guattari, in their highly stylized renditions of
the imperial, despotic state, help us detect two vital conceptual moves: first,
the deterritorialization of authority exceeding the boundaries of traditional
political communities, and second, the reconstitution of a direct and overarching filial relationship with its constituents, sites, and subjects.[39] Invoking
this argument for colonial India, *mutatis mutandis,* one may suggest that in
claiming to alter Indian society in a radical fashion or, at the very least, replace
the preceding regime of the Mughals, the new state was in a position to absorb

and supersede all former alliances, engrossing to itself the entire economy of affiliation. In other words, the colonial power stood to usurp the social and sexual foundations of paternalist authority that had sustained the ruler-subject relationship in pervious polities.

This particular theme of domination is most characteristic of oriental-ism, beginning with the colonial administrative ethnography of primitive overlords and village republics, and can be traced all the way to the grand Marxian construct of the Asiatic mode of production, positing the ultimate fetishistic character of power. Such projections of domination, needless to say, were hardly fulfilled in the context of imperial formations in early colonial India. What interests us here, nonetheless, is the overt repression of intimacy established through the figure of the despot and the slave. Here lies an important source of the fear of miscegenation and also, perhaps, the fear and erotic rush of nativism: enticements of a transculturation that would find its way into literary imagination. The story of the lotus-eaters in Greek mythology shares something here with the infamous English nabob engulfed by India. In this fear there was not much that was new, as we shall describe at much greater length in the next chapter, for in the case of both Ireland and North America in the seventeenth century, familiarity with what were considered to be inferior ways of life had presented the repeated danger of Englishmen turning "degenerate" or savage.[40]

Much has been written about the body of knowledge produced by ori-entalist perceptions of Indian society but not about the immediacy of this revulsion and attraction to despotism. Almost all early accounts of life in India under the aegis of the East India Company indicate the carnal threat posed in the enticement of adventure, wealth, and opulence. A pamphlet arguing against the vile monopoly of the Company admonished the abundance of wealth in the East thus:

> this expence, this luxury and profusion of all those connected with the present East India monopoly, is rather of natural consequence of their situation, than of any evil or criminal intentions. Any body of men, especially in the present state of society, will, it is to be feared, ever prefer their own individual good, to the general advantage. But when men are tempted to the acquisition of immense private wealth, by means and opportunities which are even hurtful to the interests of their country, can it be expected that they will have so much patriotism or self-denial, as to resist the tempta-tion? . . . Can we wonder, then, at the anxiety of those who possess an exclusive trade to India, by which they acquire immense individual wealth, are at the same time enabled to live in all the profusion and luxury of princes. . . ? Luxury not only molli-fies, but depresses and debases the mind, and renders those who are immersed in it, incapable of any elevated sentiment, of any useful, active, or patriotic exertion.[41]

Much of this danger was posed by the Indian climate itself, promoting licen-tiousness and indolence, which supposedly robbed mankind of true freedom.

Read in another way, the influence of the peculiarly depraved and ostentatious life in India was feared as being capable of generating profligacy beyond the normative, domestic economy, a condition that threatened the assurance of a higher Anglo-British identity.

A regulated household was considered to be as important as an ordered political economy for the temperance of elemental passions. As early as 1775 we find Francis Fowke writing to his nephew stationed in Benares (north India) about his sister, who was on her way to join him in India, hoping that she might be lucky enough to find a husband and that she would conduct herself with propriety there, eschewing unnecessary "pomp and splendour."[42] John Walsh would write to his niece with the advice that in matrimony the best feminine qualities were those of frugality, providence, and "modest and plain manners."[43] At the same time, young men in the colonial cities of India, were often hard-pressed to find women who were "noble," "well-bred," and possessing "high honors."[44] These letters of the Fowke family between England and India make it clear that frugality and moderation were values very much encouraged for young people leaving Britain for India in search of a career.[45] But this was not always possible for men stationed far away from women of their own kind. By the end of the eighteenth century, with the decline of spectacular fortunes among Company servants, a number of Englishwomen seeking matrimony in India found themselves also unable to find suitable matches.[46]

The author of the *Sketches of India* published in 1816 claimed that the Indian environment and Indian women made it difficult for Europeans to maintain the characteristic moral restraints that upheld the sanctity of marriage and family back home. The climate made one prone to excessive sexual intercourse, while the guiles of native women ensnared the lonely and unsuspecting new arrival from England quickly and often.[47] A desirable marriage was difficult in India for the lack of a substantial number of British or European women, which inevitably led to liaisons with concubines, after the native fashion. The company of Indians, who were endowed with prodigious sexual appetites on account of the climate and "passionately devoted to a luxurious and idle life," thus encouraged irreparable moral decay among the newly arrived Britons.[48] In her advice to young Englishwomen traveling to India in the early nineteenth century, Emma Roberts was anxious to advocate the virtues of domestic economy and dispel a widespread belief that ladies led an "indolent life" in India, surrounded by "crowds of servants" or even slaves "entertained to do their bidding."[49] Although it was quite possible for European women to avoid all domestic drudgery and the cares of housekeeping, Roberts advised "active and industrious habits, and an acquaintance with useful things."[50]

Despotism on the whole, while posing a threat to the moral fiber of the British in India and their national character, also cast the previous rulers, the Mughals (Moors) in appropriately unfavorable light. The same author of the

Sketches expressed his horror at the state of the Mughal Empire in the early nineteenth century thus:

> The secret memoirs of the court of Delhi would unfold scenes of depravity unequaled perhaps at Rome, in the worst days of her worst emperors. Now one, who has not visited this fallen and vicious capital of the East, can possibly conceive of the ardour with which every species of profligacy is encouraged; nor the many shapes it Proteus-like assumes, to accommodate itself to the various wishes and tempers of individuals.[51]

Even during their days of grandeur, the Mughals seemed to have not been particularly clement or enlightened. The Reverend William Tennant, a chaplain in the military, during his tour of the Hindu holy city of Benares on the riven Ganges in 1797, in looking at ruins of temples concluded that Muslim aggression in India was far more awful and destructive than the invasion of the Goths and Vandals who overthrew the Roman Empire and extinguished the science and arts of Europe. While these were gradually reestablished in Europe, India had never recovered. They remained in the "same gloom of ignorance as in the turbulent periods of Mahomedan conquests."[52] For Tennant, as for many of his contemporaries, the advance of "the Mahomedan race" in India was a calamitous watershed succeeded by the "most ferocious bigotry and rapine."[53] Under such protracted tyranny carried out over centuries, the native Hindus had been reduced to what Tennant described as "domestic slavery," by which he meant the prevalent institution of bondage in the household and in society at large.

Repression had further stymied the evolution of enlightened institutions among the Hindus, whose predilection to hierarchy and servitude was legion and whose ancient laws afforded little or no regard to the natural rights of man, perpetuating "a system of slavery more complex than any yet recorded in history."[54] Under the yoke of Moorish tyranny, Dalrymple wrote, farmers and collectors of taxes had stripped the tiller of the soil of his natural rights, reducing him to bare subsistence.[55] Advancing the natural-rights doctrine to inquire into the original state of the inhabitants of India and the consequence of tyrannical authority on the part of the Moorish conqueror, he stated:

> The occupiers of land among the Hindus were originally fixed in the possession of them, on principles of equity; they might have enjoyed affluence and amassed wealth, but the simplicity of the earlier ages did not lay sufficient restraints upon the hand of power to secure them from future oppression. The Moors have left the occupier no more of his original right than the name.[56]

The despot amassed all the usufruct of nature; hence no form of property was safe in his hands. Writing in defense of the reform of landed wealth in India during the era of the Permanent Settlement, Thomas Law asserted that the edicts of the Mughals were nothing but capricious and tyrannical, produced only through the violation of natural rights.[57] Despotism, to be sure, was not endemic just to India. Forms of servitude in India, for observers like Tennant, were reminiscent of slavery under the Romans and fealty of the early medieval times in Europe, and it is possible to suggest that the trope of despotism in the accounts of many British observers in India was in part a complex historical repudiation of their own versions of the European past. In India it had also assumed the form of a master-slave narrative.[58] Indigenous regimes, it was proclaimed, had never enjoyed a rightful basis for dominion. At the same time, many assumed that the ingrained obligations of servitude among Indians left little room for progress. Tennant reasoned that although the abolition of slavery was indeed a noble object—and "tenderness to slaves as well as to every creature dependent on our care . . . one of the precepts which dignifies our benevolent religion"—there was not an urgent need to save the Hindus of India. Rather, it was important to recognize the "reciprocal duties between master and servant" laid down in their scriptures, and the fact that freedom and liberty were empty words as far as they were concerned.[59]

The idea that despotism in India was a result of Muslim tyranny and Hindu slavery deeply influenced the fundamental racial configuration of Indian society. Explanations of despotism appear contradictory when studied closely; some aspects were attributed to climate, some to manners and customs, and some to history. Alexander Dow tried to get around this problem in his *History* in an ingenious fashion:

> The seeds of despotism, which the nature of the climate and fertility of the soil had sown in India, were, as has been observed, reared to perfect growth by the Mahommedan faith. When a people have been long subjected to arbitrary power, their return to liberty is arduous, and almost impossible. Slavery, by the strength of custom, is blended with human nature; and that undefined something, called public virtue, exists no more. . . . The simplicity of despotism recommends it to an indolent and ignorant race of men.[60]

There had never been any "national or political freedom" in India, reflected Tennant, for "pure despotism, under the veil of theocracy, has ever been the only government in Hindostan."[61] This, then, was an innate form of subjection, where punishment and persecution were tolerated with silence, and idolatry of the ruler was equal to his oppression.

The British in India became convinced that despotism was founded on the principles of fear and indolence, and it came to be commonly believed that an authoritarian government would best serve the natives of India. A paternalist state seemed to be the remedy for despotic excesses. There had been arguments for a more forceful body politic in England; they were reinforced in the context of colonial India. John Bennet put forth the value of a regulative state:

> There never was, nor will be, any such thing as living without Government in the world: and Government implies superiority and subordination . . . it is the duty of the chief ruler, or Governors of every State, to regulate the different orders and degrees of its peo-

s every member of the Body Politick be happy and useful in his respective sta-
\ a perfect harmony and concert kept up and preserved throughout the whole.[62]

..onial body politic provided an even more compelling case, one
..iere the subject population was already divided along historic and religious
lines. This would set the context in which the notorious biracial theory of
Indian history, discussed previously, found wide acceptance. The concept of
race here, as I argue in the next chapter, has to be qualified as being a product of contemporary and generalized notions of the effect of climate on natural development and a discourse that privileged diversity and difference of
nations within the Chain of Being without positing overt or essential biological determinates. By the second half of the eighteenth century, the ideas
of racial superiority and inferiority had been established in scholarly circles.[63]
This learning itself was continually being questioned as the new frontiers of
empire began to acquire an unprecedented number and variety of subjects
and Britain emerged as the repository for these new gains in knowledge.
Hence it was possible for Lord Kames to contemplate the human species
from his native Edinburgh and add to the theories of Comte de Buffon with
ethnological comparisons between the origins of Negroes, Hindus, and
Europeans. The expansion of empire, however, called for a much more contingent sociology of knowledge.

GENTOOS AND MOORS

William Watts, a participant in the Battle of Plassey and senior member of
the Calcutta Council, in an otherwise innocuous text provides an archetyp-
ical account of the racial divisions of the East Indies:

> The two great nations, inhabiting this part of the Indies, differ widely from each other in
> their complexions, languages, manners, disposition, and religion. The Moguls who are
> commonly called Moors or Moormen, are a robust, stately, and, in respect to the origi-
> nal natives, a fair people . . . they are naturally vain, affect shew and pomp in everything,
> are much addicted to luxury, fierce, oppressive, and, for the most part, very
> rapacious. . . . The Gentoows [sic], or native Indians, are of a swarthy aspect . . . less war-
> like, but more active and industrious than the Moors . . . a mild, subtle, frugal race of
> men, exceedingly superstitious, submissive in appearance, but naturally jealous, suspi-
> cious, and perfidious; which is principally owing to that abject slavery they are kept in by
> the Moors.[64]

The Moor was thus unruly and disruptive, while the Gentoo was the natural
slave: a submissive and ideal domestic subject with whom a direct political
relationship could be forged under colonialism. Moors were seen as outsiders
to Indian history and society, as belonging to a different racial configuration,
in Dow's terms, the product of a "a continued influx of strangers from the
Northern Asia."[65] Dow saw the Islamic faith itself as "peculiarly calculated for
despotism," a religion that "enslaved the mind as well as the body."[66] Such

devotion endowed men with unlimited power over the family, wives and con-cubines, and children who were brought up to view the father as the "absolute dispenser of life and death." Islam thus "habituated mankind to slavery."[67]

The manner of the Hindus, on the other hand, had resigned them to a despotic state of government. "Tranquility is the chief object" of the Hindus, wrote Dow, their "happiness consists in a mere absence of misery."[68] The warm climate of India and the fertility of the soil made their subsistence easy, and over centuries they were even able to accumulate a degree of wealth: "notwithstanding their abstinence and indolence, they were in some degree industrious . . . their own arts, and the natural productions of their country, rendered them opulent."[69] Because of the accumulation of wealth, however, this "peaceable and harmless race of men" became the "objects of depredation to the fierce nations of Northern Asia."[70]

The Mughals were the last of such intruders who destroyed all possibil-ities of settled authority, regular collections of revenue, and rendered the Indian polity bereft of all equity and reason. Disinvesting the Indian politi-cal landscape of the Moorish regime would thus free the reproductive capac-ity of Indian society for the sustenance of the British Empire. Robert Orme, the officially appointed company historian, emphasized the reproductive plenitude of Indian society, relating it to the effects of climate. Due to the extreme mildness of climate, sustenance was easily afforded; "productions peculiar to the soil of India" wrote Orme, "exceedingly contribute to the ease of various labours."[71] The fertility of women in India, according to Orme was extreme, and the propensity of men to propagate their species was equal to it. Gentoos may thus take as many wives as they want, and this plurality in sexual union does not produce the effect of enervating the reproductive spirit and decreasing the number of inhabitants over time, as noticed in the more severe climates of Europe.

Robert Orme's account of the government and people of India, a truly remarkable tract which is part of his *Historical Fragments,* can be studied as one of the earliest ethnographic accounts of India where the natural history of the Indians is directly implicated with the project of imperial dominion. Parts of it were composed soon after his arrival in India, at a time in which British ter-ritorial possessions were just beginning to take shape; it betrays a wishful tax-onomy of the inhabitants of India in their natural environment, reduced at times to caricature as future subjects. Orme's Anglocentric prose unravels the sexual economy implicit in the British-Indian imperial imagination.

Orme was perhaps the first to locate in the figure of the submissive Hindu the weakest section of the domestic hierarchy, signified by both the inferiority of the slave and the passivity of women. The body of the Gentoo was weak, his livelihood easy. As Orme observed, "people born under a sun too sultry to admit the exercise and fatigues necessary to form a robust nation" were natu-rally weak in their constitution. In Book Five of the *Fragments,* in the section entitled "Effeminacy of the Inhabitants of Indostan," Orme mustered his observations to reach a resounding conclusion, where he proposed at least two registers of effeminacy. The first was the physical appearance and strength of Indians. Hair color, shape of the lips, shape of the eyes and eyelid, and nostrils were compared with the features exhibited by the "Coffrees" of Africa, the nations of Malay, the people of Tartary, the Spaniards, and the Portuguese, and in distinction from these, the inhabitants of northern Europe. The physical attributes of Indians for Orme were a direct function of the climate, a point on which he seemed to take Montesquieu, Ferguson, and Millar at face value. Orme emphasized in particular the severity of the monsoons, which affected the "texture of the human frame." Thus races residing in the northern and western extremes of the subcontinent were comparable in stature, muscularity, and robustness to Europeans, while the mingling of monsoon and extreme heat in the great plains and river valleys throughout the rest of India produced "a race of men, whose make, physiognomy, and muscular strength, convey ideas of an effeminacy which surprises when pursued through such numbers of the species, and when compared to the form of the European who is making the observation."[72]

Thomas Colebrooke (1795), a more careful observer of domestic life in India, had a more measured approach to the question of climate affecting the racial features of Indians, but it was based on similar principles of distinction:

> Picturesque beauties, unknown to level countries, are not more remarkable in the elevated tracts than the characteristic features of a race of people distinct from the inhabitants of the plain. Beyond Bengal the inhabitants of the northern mountains betray by their countenance a Tartar origin: descending to more fertile regions in the plains which skirt the hills, they people the northern boundary of Bengal. On the eastern hills of Bengal, and in the adjacent plains, the peculiar features of the inhabitants declare with equal certainty a distinct origin. . . . In the mixed population, of the middle provinces, the observer readily distinguishes the Hindu from the Mahommedan.[73]

Mountstuart Elphinstone, scholar-administrator and governor of Bombay, would explain in his *History of India* the variations of manliness, character, and appearance within the subcontinent as combined effects of the "peculiarities of place and climate, and perhaps, varieties of race."[74] Elphinstone's account, composed after he returned to England from service, demonstrates the resilience of eighteenth-century sexual and racial classification. The great defects of Hindu character, he reasoned, arose from moral causes, but also from physical constitution, soil, and climate. Heat need not necessarily enervate the mind and the body, but in India it was accompanied by a fertile soil requiring little labor for cultivation, making it possible for a relatively lesser effort to "support an almost indefinite increase of inhabitants."[75] Despite a degree of variation in the state of "listless inactivity," the Marathas of the west were hardy and laborious in comparison with the Bengalis of the east, who "are more effeminate than any other people of India." The "love of repose" was a "characteristic of the whole people"; their indolence matched their timidity, from which all their vices were derived.[76] On the overall character of the Hindus of India, Elphinstone concluded:

> Their great defect is a want of manliness. Their slavish constitution, their blind super-
> stition, their extravagant mythology, the subtleties and verbal distinctions of their phi-
> losophy, the languid softness of their poetry, their effeminate manners, their love of
> artifice and delay, their submissive temper, their dread of change, the delight they take
> in puerile fables, and their neglect of national history, are so many proofs of the absence
> of the more robust qualities of disposition and intellect throughout the mass of the
> nation.[77]

Such observations reflect an aversion to proximity and also an implicit anxiety that unnecessary concourse with Indians would result in the loss of manliness among Englishmen, which, for a commercial and trading nation, as Lord Kames had warned a century before, was a distinct threat to its political ambition.[78] The sexual connotations of these arguments are not too far to see; yet the filial relationship consummated between the colonizer and the colonized is ambiguous, suggesting the possibility of incestuous desire lodged within paternalist instincts of domination. However problematic and elusive the historical record of the psychology of this relationship might be, these narratives in themselves help us tie together the overarching desires of colonial occupation.

Images such as these played a signal role in shaping the attitude of the British towards Indians and or Hindus as permissive, tolerant, and unfortunate victims of oriental despotism. Here is an example from the average prose of a less-known commentator, deliberating on the "avarice of successive Mahommedan plunderers" and how it was perpetuated by the Hindu frame of mind, immured in timeless institutions and hierarchies such as caste:

> In short, whatever, could warmly interest the feelings and strongly agitate the pas-
> sions of men; whatever inflames hope or excites terror; all the engines of a most
> despotic superstition and of a most refined policy were felt at work for the purposes
> of chaining down, to the prescribed duties of his cast, the mind of the bigoted Hin-
> doo; to enforce undeviating obedience to the law, and secure inviolable respect for
> the magistrate. Hence his unaltered, his unalterable, attachment to the national code
> and the precepts of the Brahmin creed. As it has been in India from the beginning, so
> will it continue to the end of time and the dissolution of nature: for the daring culprit
> who tramples on either, heaven has no forgiveness, and the earth no place of shelter
> or repose.[79]

Even observers on the ground such as Tennant were wont to see Hindus as a people whose manners and customs, arts, modes of living, and dress had undergone very little change in two thousand years. They seemed to appear to the English exactly as they had appeared to the Greek historian Arrian.[80] Splitting Indian society and history into two distinct races, however controvertible such a simple thesis might have seemed to latter-day colonial ethnologists, nonetheless helped the British to secure themselves as outsiders, and not unwanted invaders, in India. In the Victorian era, the British would further divide various parts of the Indian population into martial and nonmartial races and incorporate such classification into the composition of the army.

An initial dichotomy of the subject population, marked by the opposing attributes of domestic and unruly, settled and nomadic, effeminate and martial, can be seen in other parts of the colonial world as well. A very similar set of descriptions, for example, emerged in Southern Africa in the late eighteenth and early nineteenth centuries, of the "Hottentots" and "Kaffirs." Both groups had been considered as general divisions of the Negro race by early observers such as John Livingstone and Keith Johnston.[81] These classifications were based rather superficially on missionary accounts of native African religion and language, "Kaffir" being adopted from the Arabic "infidel," and "Hottentot" from the Dutch for a barbarian "who stutters and stammers" (a reference to palatal clicks in the Khoisan languages).[82] On the Anglo-Dutch frontier of the Cape, Africans closest to the European settlements would be regarded as the servile and amenable "Fingoes" as opposed to the wild and rapacious "Kaffirs." This frontier typology of the unruly Kaffir on the one hand, and the Hottentot and Fingo on the other, was further reinforced during the outbreak of the Kaffir Wars of the 1840s between the colonists and the tribes of the interior.[83]

The racial markings of progress should not, however, be viewed simply as products of the high meridian of empire and the introduction of Afro-Asiatic types into its colonial margins. There were examples much closer at hand in Ireland and Scotland. Thomas Pennant, naturalist, indefatigable traveler, and arguably one of the foremost amateur ethnographers of Scotland and Wales, following in the footsteps of Defoe, Martin, Johnson, and Boswell, would express a very similar sentiment about the Highlanders. Pennant's descriptions of 1769 seem *prima facie* carried over from notions prevalent centuries before, for instance, in the chronicles of John of Foroun, that the inhabitants of the coastal lowlands were a people "domesticated and cultured," while those in the Highlands and the islands were "wild and untamed."[84] In the eighteenth century such praise or taint acquired a very different flavor, enjoined by new ideas of gentrification and measures of political and economic progress.

THE INDUSTRIOUS SUBJECT

Most European observers in India during the formative period of British rule were directly or indirectly concerned with the domestic economy of government, particularly as they viewed the production of wealth as tied to manners, morals, arts, and manufactures. Orme's account of the effeminacy of Indians was to large extent derived from his attempt to describe the manufacturers and artisans of eastern India, who seemed to be languid and desultory yet succeeded in turning out great quantities of extraordinary textiles, one of the very reasons that had attracted the East India Company to this part of India in the first place. This particular skill, Orme explained disingenuously, was a result of their general lack of strength and robustness. Given their effeminate disposition, the most popular source of livelihood among a large section of the rural population of India was the manufacture of cloth. Men in India excelled at spinning and weaving, tasks that, in Europe, were best done by women. Indian weavers were deprived of the tools and machine skills available in England or other parts of Europe, and they did not work in manufactories, yet the clothes they turned out were of exceptional quality. The manufactured products of Bengal fetched ten times the price of European products in the world market. Orme accounted for such remarkable skills by the fact that the Indians in the form of their laboring bodies possessed qualities unique to women and children:

> As much as an Indian is born deficient in mechanical strength, so much is his whole frame endowed with an exceeding degree of sensibility and pliantness. The hand of an Indian cook-wench shall be more delicate than that of a European beauty. The skin and features of a porter shall be softer than those of a professed *petit maitre*.[85]

This was, of course, particularly true of the women who helped in the making of silk garments, as they drew the raw silk from the pod of the worm into various different degrees of fine threads, a process accomplished only through the "exquisiteness" of their feeling and the touch of their fingers, which was far more subtle than the "rigid clumsy fingers of an European."[86]

A capable if unyielding government under the Mughals, as William Tennant admitted in his discussion of the reign of Emperor Akbar, had indeed encouraged native industriousness. A new "moral discipline" that had been established, although it was not compatible with the personal or civil liberties of the people, nonetheless, had led to "virtuous habits":

> Under the protection which it afforded to the people; and from the security of property which it effected, the industry of the Hindoos was stimulated to some degree of activity; and agriculture, manufactures, and internal commerce arose to a degree of prosperity equal, perhaps, to what they enjoyed under the ancient princes of their own race.[87]

Habituated to submissive toil, the peasants bore the relatively mild and equitable state taxes during this period with "great ease and cheerfulness."[88] Tennant argued, however, that the Mughals were nowhere near as efficient as the British in the execution of warfare and in the protection of the peace and property of their subjects, and that it was indeed unfortunate that the British inherited a country where even these institutions had declined. British rule in India, established "on the scattered fragments of society, and the mere wreck of empire," could not promise a strong encouragement to industry and manufacture overnight.[89]

Tennant and Henry Thomas Colebrooke, commenting on the general state of husbandry in India, rued the fact that despite the blessings of a fertile soil, mild climate, availability of a variety of grains, and abundance of agricultural labor, the husbandry of India under the British remained in a state of backwardness. In his *Remarks on the Present State of the Husbandry and Commerce of Bengal* (1795) Colebrooke, Sanskrit scholar and a firsthand observer of rural India, remarking on the natural diversity of the country, compared the "neat habitations" of the peasants in hilly regions to the "wretched huts upon the plain," asking why it was that "the richest productions and most thriving manufactories, contribute to the general comfort of the people at large, while the wealth earned by industry is diverted into other hands than those of the industrious."[90] The reasons for this, according to Colebrooke, were the precarious legality of tenures, overcrowded villages, want of proper public roads, and, above all, "want of enclosures," or secure property in land.[91] Indian cultivators did not understand a calculated succession of crops designed to reduce drain on the nutrients of the soil; the Bengal farmer had never contemplated planned cropping beyond a single year.[92] Colebrooke's verdict was gloomy:

> An ignorant husbandry, which exhausts the land, neglecting the obvious means of maintaining its fertility, and of reaping immediate profit from the operations which might restore it; rude implements, inadequate to the purpose for which they are formed, and requiring much superfluous labor; this again ill divided, and of consequence employed disadvantageously; call for amendment.[93]

Read otherwise, the Indians were indeed capable of being restored to a much more efficient and vigorous state of industry. Colebrooke believed that the land under tillage could be vastly expanded in India, supporting not only agriculture but "more numerous and extensive manufactures, than now employ the labour of our Asiatic subjects."[94] But there was little outlet for expanded produce and "no inducement for greater industry"; markets were inadequate and exertions went unrewarded.[95] Colebrooke pinned the situation, characteristically, on the habits of humble subsistence ingrained in the character of the rural inhabitants:

> The necessaries of life are cheap, the mode of living simple; and though the price of labour be low, a subsistence may be earned without the uninterrupted application of industry. Often idle, the peasant and manufacturer may nevertheless subsist. A few individuals might indeed acquire wealth by diligent application; but the nation at large, doomed to poverty by commercial limitations, can apply no more labour than the demand of the market is permitted to encourage.[96]

Tennant's suggestions were quite similar. He pointed out that such long neglect was the result of the lack of spirit among the producers. Crops such as tobacco, sugar, indigo, cotton, mulberry, and poppy, which had great commercial use, were seldom considered as alternatives to staples.[97] What crippled enterprise in Hindustan was the lack of capital and the division of labor resulting from it; peasants were responsible for every aspect of the productive process, from the planting of the seed to the transportation of the produce to the local market.[98]

The same primitive attitude and lack of innovative spirit seemed to be true of the manufacturers and artisans. Colebrooke marveled at the "simple tools" employed by the Indians, coarse and inadequate, so much so that it was surprising that they would even attempt their use.[99] And it was only "the long continuance of feeble efforts" that in the end enabled them to accomplish their task. Their routine success was vexing: "we cannot cease to wonder at the simplicity of this process, contrasting it to the mechanism employed in Europe."[100] Also curious was the ability to switch from one art or occupation to another, which was "not so much a proof of ingenuity and ready conception, as the effect of slow and patient imitation" characteristic of a society where versatile habits had to be acquired to compensate for imperfect division of labor and the "want of capital."[101] Manufacturers and artists worked entirely on their own account; they made their own tools and took their wares to market by themselves. The fluidity of occupations and the lack of clearly demarcated professional skills between craftsmen and peasants, farmers and weavers, according to Colebrooke, led to improvident use of time and idleness. What was required was a genuinely capitalist spirit:

> If Bengal had a capital in the hand of enterprising proprietors who employed it in husbandry, manufactures, and internal commerce, these arts would be improved; and, with greater and better productions from the same labor, the situation of the labourers would be less precarious, and more affluent: although the greatest part of the profit might vest with the owners of the capital.[102]

The deficiency of capital, then, was the "bar to all improvement" in Bengal, and this could be remedied only by the encouragement of "rational enterprise."[103] Tennant detected the same indolence and "want of industry" in India that prevailed among Roman Catholic countries of Europe, except that the Hindus were much more of a "listless and unambitious race."[104] The most obvious flaw in the Hindu character was of course caste, a "powerful obstacle to social and political improvements." Caste robbed a man of "the possession to which nature or inclination may have bent his talents" and also "every motive of honest ambition to excel in that sphere where his birth has fixed him."[105] Emulating the better orders of society in Europe had been the "grand spring" of both industry and improvement, and wherever such emulation was not thwarted, it modeled and arranged "the whole structure of society." In observing India, Tennant came to the conclusion that in the whole of Asia the "conditions of individuals remained unalterable, so does the state of society." Tennant was echoing Robertson a few years earlier, suggesting that the British would see in India exactly what the Greeks had found. Nothing, in effect, had changed over the centuries: "The simple dress of the Hindoo, his rude hut, and his feeble instruments of agriculture, are the same at present as they were two thousand years ago; and if the same causes continue to operate, they must remain for many ages without amendment, and without change."[106]

Tennant prophesied that just as Britain had proved immeasurably advanced in the arts of warfare over the Indians, especially the Hindus, so they would in the realm of cotton manufacture. In a few years it was probable that all the manufactured produce of India would "bear hardly any proportion to that of Great Britain, and that too in the very article of which the Hindoos have had the exclusive possession for so many ages, and that in the same fabric which they were deemed the only people of sufficient ingenuity to execute."[107]

LABORING BODIES

Ideas of domesticity and work permeated much of the discourse on the progress of subjects under a paternalist empire. These observations have a long provenance, as I have indicated before, some of which can be readily found in the descriptions of the Scots and the Irish. A reading of such prejudice in the context of British India forewarns that it was often the English themselves who foisted their own versions of class, status, and hierarchy on societies based on very different principles.

In North America during the seventeenth century, the Indians were often classed into two groups: those of the "better sort," and those who were most common. These divisions reflected English society of the day, increasingly being cleft into the gentry and the rest, with the lower orders regarded as a vast service class.[108] In this familiar mirror, the American Indians emerged as the possible subjects of exploitation, which in itself was in part an inspiration for the burgeoning ethnographic interest in the life, manners, customs, morals, religion, and implements of Indians. Even the positive accounts of observers such as William Wood and Thomas Morton were full of expectation that Indians should for the sake of their advancement be incorporated into the new settler society.[109] Karen Kupperman has shown how the English in many respects were dependent on the very domestic economy of the American Indians for survival, and many thought of them not as irredeemable savages but merely low-born natives whose improvidence and laziness, stealing, vengefulness, cowardice, and sexual promiscuity would one day be assuaged.[110] These English settler accounts converge on what Kupperman has described as the "tractable Indian who would willingly jettison his own culture and religion in order to accept what the English saw as their own superior religion and culture."[111]

A century later, such questions of amenability of the Scots and the Irish emerged in Britain itself. Samuel Johnson, on his tour of the Scottish Highlands soon after its subjugation at Culloden, was reportedly moved to compose an ode in Latin containing a prompt sketch of the people:[112]

Pervagor gentes, hominum ferorum
Vita ubi nullo decorata cultu
Squallet informis, tugurique fumis. . . .

Through nations wild, a hardy race,
Where life no cultivated grace,
No elegance can know;
But shrinks abashed from human eyes,
And in the smoky hovel lies. . . .[113]

Thomas Pennant's sketches of the Highland people, written during his tour of Scotland a couple of decades after Johnson, convey some of these very same images but reflect the kind of concern the Puritans had about the natives of the east coast of North America. In his account of Inverness, Pennant describes the Highlanders as "indolent to a high degree" but also generous, capable of hospitality, forbearing, and surprisingly free of national bigotry.[114] In some parts of the country, he remarked, they were indeed dispersing, breaking away from their clans and chiefs, "finding that their good conduct afford them better protection . . . than any their chieftain can afford."[115] Chiefs, too, were discovering the "benefits of industry," dismissing retainers, and able to mend their oppressive and tyrannical ways. Pennant's remarks often pause on the dire poverty rather than the legendary ferocity of the Highlanders. In Aberdeen he encounters unusual squalor:

> The houses of the common people in these parts are shocking to humanity, formed of loose stones, and covered with clods, which they call devish, or with heath, broom, or branches of fir: they look, at a distance, like so many black molehills. The inhabitants live very poorly, on oatmeal, barley-cakes, and potatoes; they drink whiskey, sweetened with honey. The men are thin, but strong; idle and lazy . . . are content with hard fare, and will not exert themselves farther than to get what they deem necessaries. The women are more industrious, spin their own husbands' clothes, and get money by knitting stockings, the great trade of the country.[116]

Again, the emphasis is on the lethargy of the poor, their acceptance of their lot in life, and suggestions for change. Even though the writer of these lines is a naturalist—Pennant was a well-known zoologist—the domestic economy of the natives receives a great deal of attention.

John Carr, touring the south and southwest parts of Ireland during the beginning of the eighteenth century, had a similar opinion about the nature and causes of poverty, related to the national character, an "unenvied independence in her wants and inconveniences."[117] Rent that one could secure with "common good husbandry and prudence" and provide for the tenant and family in England did not offer much comfort here in Ireland.[118] The farmer was half-naked and his wife and family in rags. Carr's account is exceedingly dismal:

Without being slaves in fact their condition is little better than vassalage in its most oppressive form. . . . Depressed to an equality with the beast of the field, he shares his sorry meal with his cow, his dog, and his pig, who frequently feed with him, as his equal associates, out of the same bowl. . . . This sense of degradation, and conviction that his wretchedness has scarcely any thing below it in the scale of human penury, frequently led the unhappy peasant to mingle in those unfortunate tumulus which have so long, and so fatally, retarded the improvement of his country; and when he beheld how hopeless were the exertions of rebellion, to rush forward in the scene of slaughter, uncover his head, and bow it to the bullets of his enemy.[119]

Yet, working with few materials, the peasantry of Ireland was successful on account of their ingenuity and with proper returns could be induced to work hard. Many were endowed with vigorous frames and were keen, even though deprived of "all avenues of useful knowledge." Carr also found them trustworthy, innocent, modest in their sexual appetite: characters that a conscientious government could perhaps reform "to the great purpose of augmenting the prosperity of the country, and the happiness of society."[120] Such accounts of the Scots and the Irish accentuated the Anglocentricity of British identity; in India the distinction between English and Briton was less important.

The simplicity and primitive toil of the populace, especially Hindus, still evoked a comparable response. There was some measure of enthusiasm about the prospect of improvement in India, to be brought about by the institution of property and security in land under a beneficent and impartial government. At the same time, although it was widely acknowledged that they were capable of reform and improvement, of aspiring to the benefits of freedom and property, the introduction of certain aspects of high civilization that the English possessed had to be restricted and calibrated. Dalrymple took the most direct position on this, and exhorted: "we cannot permit the Indians to enjoy the whole of our freedom."[121] The establishment of freehold tenure in the land revenue settlements of India was not desirable, as the Indians would then be able to claim a legal status that would weaken the very colonial authority that had proven to be beneficial to them; and further, freehold tenures would not impart "real freedom" but rather aggravate their licentiousness and indolence. Dalrymple argued, in effect, that, given the debilitating consequences of a warm climate, labor would not sustain production beyond subsistence unless compelled by an external authority, in this case the firm and guiding hand of British rule.[122]

Artists who visited India in this period—William Hodges, Ozias Humphry, Thomas and William Daniell, James Forbes, Sir Charles D'Oyly, Balthazar Solvyns, and Arthur Devis—also made attempts to depict the lives, manners, and customs of Indians faithfully as objects of curiosity that might soon be lost to the world. Solvyns described his lengthy series of sketches of Indian life as an attempt to record things of "beauty and novelty" in Hindustan that might invoke the curiosity of Europeans and pique their interest in the "habits, manners and features of the various tribes."[123] In the introduction to *A Picturesque Voyage to India* (1810), Thomas Daniell enjoined artists to advance the "liberal spirit of curiosity."[124] The Daniells landed in Calcutta in 1786 and proceeded to tour India extensively in the next few years. By their return to London in 1794, they had been to Srinagar (Kashmir), Garhwal, Lucknow, Jaunpur, Benares, Bihar, Madras, and Bombay. These journeys inspired the much-viewed colored engravings known as *Oriental Scenery,* which appeared in two parts in 1795 and 1798.[125] Many of these plates presented native Indians as insignificant figures dwarfed by an imposing landscape, following the injunctions of the picturesque in composition. An example of this would be the typical watercolors of George Chinnery or the quick wash-and-pen pieces of William Hodges, where figures in the foreground were there not as subjects but to augment the landscape.[126] It became widely popular, especially for amateur and ambitious young artists, to follow the Reverend Gilpin, who had laid down the definitive rules of proportion, distance, and foreground.[127]

One of the guiding principles of such composition, explained by Warren Hastings himself, the governor-general of India, was that things which were "beautiful in themselves always leave something of their effect in representation," for human imitation must "fall short of Nature."[128] The picturesque quality of objects was based on the reverse principle: real substance "naturally disgusts by its deformity" but is nevertheless rendered beautiful through artistic composition. Indians, even when they were not mere accents to the landscape, were subjects visually transformed through inflections of the roving, picturesque eye. This reduction seems to have reinforced them in their traditional roles as docile bodies of labor, timeless and impervious to progress. Of all the artists who portrayed the domestic life of Indians, Arthur William Devis stands out perhaps as the most prolific, and his sketches and paintings of peasants and artisans, rich in detail, bear out aspects of the British view of their Indian subjects unlike any other.[129]

On route to India, his ship, the East India Company's messenger ship the *Antelope,* survived an attack from native islanders off the north coast of New Guinea (in which Devis was injured and disfigured) and was subsequently wrecked in Palau (Pelew).[130] Devis made a few sketches during his exile in the island, which were used afterwards to illustrate an official narrative of the disaster, George Keate's *An Account of the Pelew Islands.*[131] Keate writes that the shipwrecked crew of the *Antelope,* who despaired of being "cut off for ever from the society of the rest of the world," were much surprised to find among the natives of the island a "human race of men."[132] What most caught the eye of the captain, Henry Wilson, and also Devis, was the domestic life and economy of the islanders, which, according to art historian Mildred Archer, left a deep impression on Devis's mind and led to his sympathetic portrayal of Indian village life.[133] Keate's account of the natives and their nakedness, unadorned lifestyle, and simplicity was perceptive:

> In a country where no aid could be obtained from the assistance of iron tools, and where every thing which was convenient and useful could only be produced by much time, labor, and patience, and at last fashioned by such poor means as necessity, stimulating invention, by slow degrees brought about, it will not be expected that their domestic implements would be numerous.[134]

Keate proceeded to judge the disposition and character of the natives from their "uniformly courteous and attentive" behavior towards the English. Their mutual intercourse was civil, women were treated well, and all were engaged in peaceful pursuits of fishing and agriculture; their daily sustenance required that none were indolent or idle. And yet, concluding his observations on the general character of these people, Keate noted: "however untutored, however uninformed, their manners present an interesting picture to mankind. . . . We see a despotic government without one shade of tyranny, and power only exercised for general happiness, the subjects looking up with filial reverence to their King."[135] Arthur Devis would express a similar sentiment when he came to paint the Indians.

Devis spent his early years in India traveling widely in Madras, Bengal, and Bihar.[135] William Jones, whose portrait he painted in 1793, patronized him for a while; he also made drawings for the Dent landowning family. Devis wanted to publish by subscription a series of prints, at least twenty-six of them, "illustrative of the arts, manufactures, and agriculture of Bengal" from his work, a project in which John Biddulph, an affluent patron, supported him.[136] Among Biddulph's papers has been found *A Descriptive Catalogue of a few Asiatic Subjects, Illustrative of the Agriculture, Arts and Manufactures of Hindoostan,* published later, which provides some illuminating details behind Devis's evocative scenes of Bengal village life.[137] These constitute an extensive array of subjects, including, agriculture, ironwork, carpet weaving, sugar milling, corn husking, brazier's work, spinning of cloth and corn grinding by women, work at the mint and at the essayer's, and the manufacture of paper, saltpeter, muslin, and salt.[138] What distinguishes Devis's approach from Solvyns and his better-known series of 250 ethnographic etchings is that they are in-depth, rather than quick studies, and seek to capture the essence of these newly found exotic subjects, a peculiarly *human* picturesque. Notes in the catalogue elucidate Devis's approach. The ploughshare, "faithfully represented" in the "Hindoo Ryot, or the Indian Labourer," takes on a different light:

> Those who have visited the East can testify, with what truth the cattle, the plough, and the Hindu laborer, are represented . . . the simplicity of this first and most necessary instrument of husbandry must surprise Europeans: it is formed entirely of wood, and put together with some degree of ingenuity; but as it was found to answer the purposes of the first agriculturists who settled in India, so it has continued to descend without improvement to their posterity.[139]

Devis was clearly captivated by the assumed antiquity of these practices. The introduction to *Treading Out the Corn,* where an Indian laborer drives four oxen to tread corn (wheat) spread on the threshing floor, mentions that such floors are frequently mentioned in Homer, the Bible, and the Mosaic laws. Similarly women in the act of grinding the corn are described as using stone mills "of a very ancient date," possibly the same alluded to in Xenophon's *Cyropaedia* and also the same method that might have been used in ancient Judea. The sugar mill seems to have been unchanged for two millennia.

One might well conclude that these studies contribute to a rich ethnography of work in India, and that the artist has tried to be as accurate as possible. Thus the catalogue elaborates that *Spinning* in the exhibit is supposed to represent "domestic employment of the women in the middle rank of life in India."[140] *Weaving Muslin* is described as "an exact representation of a whole family so employed: painted on the spot in Santipore,"[141] while at the same time fine Indian linen is seen as an ancient tradition that can be traced to biblical references and to ancient Egypt as a conduit for the trade in cloth between the Levant and the East. *A Loom,* very similar in composition to the above and part of the same series devoted to the study textile manufacture, is also an exercise in detailed observation (Figure 4, Devis, *A Loom with the Process of Winding the Thread*). Various members of the same family, grandfather and grandsons, are shown at work, naked to the waist, using both hands and feet with great dexterity to work reels, threads, shuttles, spindles, and earthenware. The room is dark except for the light that comes through a door

Figure 4 Arthur Devis, *A Loom with the Process of Winding the Thread.* Courtesy of the Harris Museum and Art Gallery.

just opened. It is as if the artist had just walked in on this intimate and age-less scene. It is possible to imagine that the manufacture of cloth once again constitutes the trope of absolute difference between Britain and India along the lines of manliness and progress, very much reminiscent of Robert Orme's comments discussed earlier in this chapter:

> The beautiful muslin, which the ingenuity of our countrymen, with the most expen-sive and complex machinery, cannot surpass that fabricated in the rude manner here depicted; the delicate touch, and fine finger of the effeminate Hindoo, gives a degree of softness and flexibility to the thread, which no machine the art of man has yet formed, can at all equal.[142]

ETHNOGRAPHY AND THE ALLEGORY OF CONQUEST

The scientific description of British India that began in earnest in the early years of the nineteenth century could not easily set aside the deprecatory and condescending views of Indians as unlikely imperial subjects. It has been the argument of this chapter that the first impressions of the origins, organization, institutions, behavior, and progress of Indian society were inflected with the inconsistent presumptions and deep-seated unease of conquest. The assurance of a lasting *pax Britannica* led to the emergence of new, objective forms of knowledge; but these forms were still susceptible to the subterranean allegories of the struggle for dominance. Systematic ethnography, a tool of what Bernard Cohn has termed the "investigative modalities"[143] of colonial social science, emerged in India from the tangle of travel, reportage, sketch, observation, and survey. Rather than sanction-ing general views of Indians, these later official descriptions, subsumed under statistical accounts and surveys, focused more comfortably on the task of routine administration.

There are common threads between these later surveys and the early leisurely observations that we have discussed before, but in many important ways the expansion of empirical knowledge about British Indian topography, produce, customs, industry, and history was coextensive with a new phase of expansion of the colonial state. Roots of this can be found in Britain itself, in Pennant's tours of Scotland and Wales, Samuel Johnson's *Journey to the Western Islands of Scotland in 1773*, Fraser's *Essay on the Origins and Antiq-uity of the Scots and Irish Nations* (1800), and Carr's *Stranger in Ireland* (1806). More specific attention to political economic prospects may be found in David Loch's *Essay on the Trade, Commerce and Manufactures of Scotland* (1775), Col. William Fullarton's *General View of the Agriculture of the County of Ayr* (1793), and Heron's *Observations Made in a Journey Through the Western Counties of Scotland* (1792), a mode which was much more methodically pursued in John Sinclair's *Statistical Account of Scotland* (1791–1797), containing extensive information drawn from parishes and small localities with the direct view towards the improvement of commerce.[144] Francis Buchanan Hamilton's tours and journals of travel in the eastern parts of British India undertaken in the early years of the nineteenth century fall within this slightly later genre and speak to the new confidence of East India Company's territorial possessions and a great and renewed interest in the economic potential of these once-prosperous parts.

It was Governor-General Wellesley, after the British conquest of Mysore, who noticed Hamilton (born and educated in Scotland), a surgeon in the medical service and an avid natural historian, geologist, and botanist, and selected him to carry out an investigation into the state of agriculture, arts, commerce, civil history, natural history, and the antiquities of the ceded and allied countries in southern India.[145] In 1807 the Court of Directors decided to proceed with a statistical survey of the Bengal Presidency with Buchanan as the officer in charge. The directions that were issued from the governor-general provide a glimpse into what may be termed both an improving and extractive official vision of the Indian heartland. Buchanan was prohibited from traveling beyond the Company's territories, but he was allowed to consult natives of adjacent countries for further information.[146]

He was entrusted with a formidable task of inquiry that, given the resources at his disposal, seems surprisingly ambitious. He was to furnish a topographical account of each district, including its area, soil, geography, weather, history, and antiquity. He was also asked to provide an account of the "condition of the inhabitants; their number, the state of their food, clothing, and habitations; the peculiar diseases to which they are liable together with the means that have been taken or may be proposed to remove them; the education of youth; and the provision or resources for the indigent."[147] He was to inquire into the religious practices of the inhabitants of these parts, their number, their progress, the "most remarkable customs" of the tribes, the resources commanded by priests and chiefs, and the conditions that might "attach them to Government, or render them disaffected."[148]

On the subject of natural productions of the country, Buchanan was directed to note fisheries, forests, mines, and quarries; in agriculture he was to find out the different kinds of vegetables cultivated for food, forage, medicine, and intoxication, and their impact on land under the plough. He was to compare the implements of husbandry, manure, water control, breeds of cattle and other domestic animals, fences, farms, labor employed in farms, and most important, the state of landed property and tenures. He was also supposed to examine the progress in fine and common arts and the state of manufactures in each district. The court was interested in a detailed account of the variety of goods manufactured and in ascertaining "the ability of the country to produce the raw materials used in them."[149] The situation of artists and manufacturers, rates of their labor, their economic position relative to cultivators of land, their consumption and sales, and the potential for new manufacture to be introduced in these districts were all to be recorded in detail. He was also to find out about the state of commerce by traveling to fairs and markets and to witness how money, weights, and measures were regulated, how goods traveled on land and by water, and whether the internal transportation could be improved.

Francis Buchanan indeed proved to be an indefatigable traveler and procurer of information. During his tour of the Shahabad district, traveling from Patna to the fort of Chunar, he reputedly traveled some 820 miles, seven per day on average, moving his camp about 57 times in the process.[150] He did not have good internal maps: charts from earlier surveys of Bengal were unreliable, and there were no plans to consult for Bihar save those in the second edition of Rennell's *Bengal Atlas* (1781).[151] He had, therefore, also to act as surveyor and drew a large number of charts himself, often improving considerably upon James Rennell.

The seemingly exhaustive statistical compendia of Buchanan indicate the remarkably large empirical appetite of the East India Company's state. We can approach his work as a combination of ethnography and political economy, where the intrinsic and essential features of Indian subjects have been replaced by the value placed on their location, labor, products, and environment. If Robert Orme's observations are manifestly prejudicial, Buchanan's are remarkably factual on the surface. Indeed, as a later commentator, Charles Oldham, points out, he seldom expresses his views but resorts to statements made by his informants, scrupulously noting down the "traditions of the illiterate country folk and of the so-called aboriginal races, who . . . often preserve genuine tradition more undefiled and reliable than the literate population of the towns and persons versed in the Brahmanical texts."[152] Whether such a claim is fully merited or not—and although it seems likely that Buchanan's informers were village and tribal heads who were summoned and discharged rather peremptorily, given the length of the task at hand—Buchanan's questions seem to have been at least directed at the common people of India, the primary recipients of the East India Company's patrimony. These accounts anticipate a degree of maturity on the part of the colonial state and its will to muster the particulars of its expanding domains.

During the period of this evolving British view of India and Indians, the domains of the economy and the body politic, as Mary Poovey has suggested, had not quite been disaggregated back in Britain.[153] The abstraction and incorporation of Indians into a singular social body to be classified, enumerated, and measured suggests an early development in the exercise of autonomous knowledge in the institutions, practices, and discourses of the colonial state. Francis Buchanan's repertoire thus brings us to a provisional resolution of these questions, because it departs from the earlier, more anxious accounts of Indians as subjects of Britain reduced to overbearing despots or effeminate slaves. With such assurance towards the empirical permanency of India, the pitfalls and uncertainties of the traveling gaze, including what

Chloe Chard has adroitly described as its intimate and feminizing effects, were laid to rest in the official discourse.[154]

Questions of the domestic economy of empire in India, one might assume, still continued to wreak disorder from within. How such problems persisted outside the penumbra of the state and governance is beyond the breadth of this study. Needs of the colonial state in the long run transformed the nature of the engagement between Britons and Indians. Thus even the most meticulous and seemingly intimate details of Indians and Indian society could be digested as official knowledge of the state, adding another dimension to the distance from the life-world of the governed. Later in the century, the agents of this transformation tend to disappear from the historical record reinforcing the anonymous power of the colonial state.

The exploitative logic of the colonial political economy, however, could not have functioned without reference to overt, masculine modes of authority learned through the social and familial context of the English household, where assertive identities were nurtured in the nexus of dominant and subordinate relationships. In the light of new studies emerging on the relationship between masculinity, family, household, and the state, it may be inferred that reconfigurations of patriarchal authority within the colonial world could not have taken place without these various intimations of gender inequality back home. Anthony Fletcher's long-term study of domestic values and masculine conduct in England helps us underscore how social divisions were mapped onto the categories of gender, creating future, predetermined roles, reinforced in a flurry of literature on the conduct and comportment of women and also of men.[155] It would be a stretch simply to pin the attitudes and conduct of men who came to rule India solely on expectations that society imposed on them during their early lives in England, but allegories of domesticity in the classification of Indians during the early years of British expansion point to the articulation of new authoritative personas forged both at home and abroad. Injunctions laid out in texts circulating throughout the eighteenth century indicate a long term provenance of formations that must have been tested in India, including the *Art of Governing a Wife* (1747), *An Enquiry into the Duties of Men in the Higher Ranks and Middle Classes of Society in Great Britain* (1794) and *Enquiring into the Duties of the Female Sex* (1797) by Thomas Gisborne, and William Fleetwood's *Relative Duties of Parents and Children, Husbands and Wives* (1794).[156]

So far the debate over domestic ideology and the early Victorian household has not been seen in the context of colonial domesticity in India.[157] It seems appropriate, however, that historians of the British in India heed John Tosh's recent contention that historic shifts in the domestic order taking place between the late eighteenth and the early nineteenth centuries redefined both the character and affective life of men as well as the rites of passage from boyhood to young adulthood.[158] Relationships that were articulated and reenacted during early moments of the colonial encounter exhibit some of these familiar passages of identity, and even hypostatize them, in the context of political authority changing hands in India and shifts in the modes of subjection that placed a handful of young Britons in charge of a vast and complex order. How far they became accustomed to this new order and how successfully they con-figured their masculine and racial identities in Indian exile, are subjects for the chapter to follow.

5

The Decline of Intimacy

The effeminacy of subject races articulated by Robert Orme persisted as subtext in much of the nineteenth century colonial accounts of Indians, alongside biological race, social Darwinism, and even early eugenics, as cumulative and residual mythologies of origin under colonial rule. Emasculated and enslaved subjects of the British Empire, as I have argued, were not simply products of explicit racism or mere props for the dramatic maleness of Englishmen in the tropics. In the period of heightened imperial expansion, caricatures of new subject populations inevitably attended the "naturalization" of colonial subjects. It took a long time for the Company to determine the proper place of Indians in the great map of empire. Even in 1836, a select committee appointed by the House of Commons to consider what measures ought to be adopted for native inhabitants of countries of British settlement explained its task thus:

> The situation of Great Britain brings her beyond any other power into communication with the uncivilized nations of the earth. We are in contact with them in so many parts of the globe, that it has become of deep importance to ascertain the results of our relations with them, and to fix the rules of our conduct towards them. We are apt to class them under the sweeping term of savages, and perhaps, in doing so, to consider ourselves exempted from the obligations due to them as our fellow men.[1]

Obligations of imperial rule thus encouraged systematic and scientific examination of non-European races. During the very beginning of the East India Company's venture in India, Sir James Mackintosh had professed a comparably apposite view of history as a vast museum of mankind where all specimens of human nature could be studied.[2]

Such knowledge was the province not merely of naturalists, but law-givers, statesmen, moralists, and political philosophers as well. Laws of nature regulated the actions of humans, and the scientific understanding of the duties of mankind could derive only from the accumulated knowledge of human nature, and not from theology or metaphysics. Here the repatriation of Aristotle's ideas of *genus* and *species* and attempts to understand the natural order in systematic fashion in the writing of Descartes, Hobbes, and Locke played a very significant part.[3] The Scottish enlightenment, as we have seen earlier, had put forward a four-stage theory of the progress of mankind. This mode of thinking implied human improvement along a linear pattern, with history itself dictating how and when rude nations would graduate into polished ones. At the same time, along with what Lovejoy calls the "temporalization" of the Great Chain of Being, the distinction and linking of species would come to dominate the field of biological inquiry.[4] The impact of naturalists such as John Ray, Montesquieu, and Comte de Buffon led to a sea change in thinking about race and racial difference as external qualities. As the horizon of European observers expanded, urged on by imperial expansion, new empirical findings and their interpretation created conflicting accounts of racial difference.

In the eighteenth century there would emerge two competing explanations of racial diversity. Both, as Richard Popkin points out in an influential essay, were posited by scholars who grappled with biblical accounts of human origins. One strand of reasoning derived from the pre-Adamite theory of Isaac la Peyrère (1596–1676), which essentially stated that a vast majority of the people in the world were outside the purview of the Bible and the history of the Jewish people, and thus had origins independent of the descendants of Adam.[5] This would lead directly to polygenetic accounts of race. The other was the contention that all humans had a common ancestry. Buffon (1749), in his *Histoire Naturelle,* had argued that mankind is not composed of species essentially distinct from each other and that it was originally one that had spread throughout the habitable world, undergoing changes on account of climate, diet, mode of living, diseases, and admixture of blood. This argument was carried further by Blumenbach (1776), who posited that there were indeed five principle varieties of mankind—Caucasian, Mongolian, Ethiopian, American, and Malay—but only one species. In addition, the debate about continuity versus the gradation of different varieties of human beings had not by any means been resolved during the period under consideration. Climatic explanations once championed by Montesquieu still enjoyed currency and, in the light of significant incidence of early mortality in the colonial tropics, they lingered in discussions of disease, degeneration, and racial character through the nineteenth century.

Monogenetic explanations of racial diversity, while accounting for a common provenance of humankind, nevertheless accentuated the hierarchy of races, placing Caucasians—a term adopted by Buffon—at the summit of human achievement in terms of beauty, intelligence, and civilization. They also led to degeneracy theories of the nineteenth century, developed by Lord Kames, Oliver Goldsmith, and Blumenbach, which presented Europeans as models of human perfection and every other race as subject to deterioration from that ideal form. The detection of degenerate features in various human types had become a part of the naturalist debate. Lord Kames, for instance, attempted to improve on Buffon's idea of the unity of the human species, arguing that distinctive physical features and characteristics of different races had persisted across the world largely irrespective of the variations in climate, food, and geography.[6] Kames could thus compare the character of the African "Negroes" to the Indian "Hindows," arguing that the former were inferior, habituated to the primary fruits of nature, and thus liable to be enslaved, while the latter were more industrious only by degrees in a less severe tropical climate.[7] There were certain ways of life that simply corrupted and blighted the progress of natural man. Humanitarian and antislavery crusaders also supported the notion of degeneracy in order to explain why certain people were stuck in the lower stages of history and why darker races as a rule were inferior to whites. Just as Buffon had believed that the effects of degeneracy could be in theory reversed over a few generations if the afflicted could be rehabilitated in Europe, his successors would come to the conclusion that Europeans, too, placed in unsavory habitats, would loose their physical and mental vigor.

Contrary to what Popkin calls the "liberal racism"[8] of the humanitarians conceding a common ancestry to all humans and the potential for improvement, other theorists of natural classification posited an immutable hierarchy of races. Polygenetic explanations of race not only persisted but gained strength, especially in North America, through the mid-nineteenth century.[9] Even more important for our purpose, less scholarly and more popular versions of human difference, inhering in skin color, geographical distance, technological backwardness, and the very fact that much of the inhabited earth had been subject to European mastery, reinforced the appeal of race as a prime criterion of human worth.

In the case of British India discussed below, the ideas of separation and segregation were indeed buttressed as Anglo-Britons became familiar with the territorial possession and governance of India. While there was on the one hand a degree of official empathy with Indians, especially Hindus who had supposedly been delivered from the tyranny of the Islamic rulers, there was also common aversion. Indian climate and Indian ways of life were seen as inherently weakening of the human frame. Racial ideas in this context were, of course, contingent on the political and cultural specificities of the interchange between rulers and the ruled. Just as colonial occupation would further the racial divide, race itself played an important role in sorting out the physical and emotional proximity of Britons and Indians. Just as skin color and appearance marked the visible segregation of the rulers and the ruled, people who straddled the divide—brokers, servants, native wives and concubines—continued to threaten the sanctity of the colonial-racial hierarchy.

This chapter explores these founding versions of racial imagination and difference, especially as they intersected with other barriers that kept colonial societies such as British India in place: blood and sex. In tracking such dissemination of racial ideology, especially toward the end of the eighteenth century, one needs to step away from some common associations that are Victorian in terms of history, Darwinian in terms of bio-ideology, and politically contemporaneous with the high meridian of empire. This is thus an examination of the racial divide in India during a formative period of British rule, when the distinctions between nation, race, and subject had not yet hardened into civilizational and biological certitudes. Forms of inequality within the state and society in England had always shaped ideas of colonial rule as much as the encounter with people newly incorporated into the empire. In the figurative denial of civilization, sovereignty, property, and liberty to the mass of inhabitants within the newly expanded reaches of empire in the later eighteenth century, various inferior subjects and the many criteria of their lowliness were authored: timid and rebellious savages, noble and ignoble barbarians, sturdy and effete workers, indentured bodies and slaving bodies, docile and treacherous subjects, Indians and Irishmen, the Negro, the Kaffir and the Fingoe, the Moor and the Gentoo. These were hardly objective conclusions, but the gendered and sexually laden aspects of such nomenclature are clues to the conflicted racial self-image of conquering and civilizing Britons.

Recent work on the relationship between the sites of bourgeois sexuality in Europe and ideas of race has emphasized the many-stranded legacy of colonialism. Some historians have offered a straightforward explanation of the formation of male identity, as in the case of young men in search of sexual exploits in the colonies;[10] others have suggested an underlying sublimation of sexual danger and the threat of racial difference within the walls of the European domestic scene.[11] Thus, according to Robert Young, perceptions of race were tied to the hidden articulations of sexual desire.[12] There seems to be a degree of truth in all of the above formulations. I suggest in this chapter, however, that neither the conduct and needs of men nor the threat to domesticity defined within the precincts of the colonial bungalow address the complex ramifications of race in British India as an ideological and substantive category of experience.

In a general sense, it might well be argued, as John Tosh and Michael Roper have, that prevalent idioms of English and British masculinity were maintained in the age of high imperialism through the assertions of difference and superiority vis-à-vis other races.[13] There were many during this period who considered English manhood as an exemplary civilizing ideal, a repository of noble qualities such as courage, independence, and veracity, attributes Macaulay found so lacking among Bengalis. Along with these overt projections of masculinity, British racial identity in India was also implicated in normative ideas of family and the domestic order away from their home country. Arguments to this end follow from the last chapter, where I have indicated how ideas of the household became pivotal to the discussion of the state and the body politic in colonial India. The misadventure of the English household in early British India and a sense of indefinite siege on the part of the English as dominant representatives of empire framed the discourse on race and also contributed to the sanguinary lines intended to keep different subject groups in place.

Historians of India and the British Empire have long regarded the last decade of the eighteenth century as a significant divide. This was a time when the Company government began to discourage in earnest liaisons and marriages between Englishmen and Indian women, to remove the sons of "mixed blood" from service in the civil and military departments, and to encourage the presence of Anglo-British white women.[14] The significance of this dispossession is crucial to the history of the colonial divide in India, which requires a careful sifting of Anglo-Indian social formations and attention to particular histories of the relationship between blood, inheritance, race, and sexuality. The reason India never became a major settler colony, or indeed produce a significant population of mixed Indo-Anglican descent within a more widespread mestizo society can be traced back to the eroticization and racialization of cultural difference.

ANARCHY, DEGENERATION, AND THE COLONIAL PROJECT

In the first decades of the rule of the East India Company, however, the government in India was considered to be in great disarray. The English had inherited a despoiled, tyrannical, and fragmented government of Moorish conquerors. As Warren Hastings pleaded during his trial, the political confusion in India could be redeemed only if all of the British acquisitions could be brought together under a "uniform compact body by one grand and systematic arrangement," an arrangement that would "do away with all the mischiefs, doubts and inconveniences, both to the governors and the governed."[15] Only with the full assumption of power could such an unsettled state of society be brought to order and rescued from the "unavoidable anarchy and confusion of different laws, religions, and prejudices, moral, civil, and political, all jumbled together in one unnatural and discordant mass." In fact, the distinction between state and civil society as in England simply did not obtain in India. As Burke saw it, the English nation in India was no more than a "seminary for the succession of officers" and a republic without a people.[16] The inevitable consequence of this situation was that the power of office was arbitrary in India, and the ruling class of Englishmen was held together by an *esprit de corps* that was neither entirely of England nor indigenous to British India. It was this very ruling "caste" that became progressively aloof in India, a cohort steadfastly carrying on with the idea that devolution of power was quite unnecessary, even meaningless to a degree, as the very foundations of the new state could not be controlled or opposed by a people who understood neither their language nor their laws. The late eighteenth and early nineteenth century was a period in which the British formally acknowledged their territorial acquisition in India, and public trials of illustrious company servants such as Warren Hastings brought home to the British public the romance, exoticism, and strangeness of Indians. There were vigorous debates in Parliament over the future of British rule in India and the limits of the East India Company's sovereignty, the question of European settlement and plantations in India, and the juridical and administrative segregation of Indians and Britons. Such questions shaped British-Indian society at large.

What is quite remarkable in this accusation of imperial profligacy is an unprecedented public condemnation of British moral conduct in India, after the fact of military conquest (1757–64) and the establishment of a revenue-extracting state (1765), led by the likes of Edmund Burke. The inquisition into the affairs of the East India Company, followed by a series of parliamentary acts, has been characterized by Francis Hutchins as the rise of a "just idea of rule."[17] This new moral accountability of government in this era also subtended a new configuration of the possibilities of colonial society and the self-awareness of the English presence in India, which relates as much to the anxiety of race as to the predicament of cultural assimilation. This is nowhere as clearly depicted as in the satirical descriptions of newly enriched Anglo-Indian nabobs, emblematic of the emerging deep-seated misapprehension of colonial societal order, which, unlike that in the New World, could not be established *ex nihilo*. The pilloried nabob, akin to the sugar baron from the West Indies, was the subject not just of jealousy and contempt but also of misdirected moral outrage. Clive, who epitomized for the enemies of the Company at home the reprobate life of English adventurers in India, himself reviled Anglo-Indian Calcutta as "one of the most wicked places in the universe" where "corruption, licentiousness and a want of principle seem to have possessed the minds of all the civil servants" who had become "callous, rapacious and luxurious beyond conception. . . ."[18] Wealth was corrupting anywhere, but wealth in India led to moral degeneration.

The arrival of the nabobs in England and their attempts to purchase titles and respectability with their new found wealth were derided mercilessly by sections of the public and the press in London. They were satirized in the Haymarket production of *The Nabob, or Asiatic Plunderer* in 1772 and, according to a line engraving from 1797, given the epithet of "Count Roupee."[19] In a later era, Macaulay condemned Gen. Richard Smith of the eighteenth-century Calcutta circle who had already been lampooned in Forbes's play *The Nabob* as "an Anglo-Indian chief, dissolute, ungenerous, and tyrannical . . . hating the aristocracy yet childishly eager to be numbered among them, squandering his wealth on pandars [*sic*] and flatterers. . . ."[20] There was quite a demand for caricatures in England; booksellers such as

William Holland in London specialized in sketches of traders and members of the *nouveau riche,* and also of nabobs as social misfits.[21] Young Englishmen in India were commonly expected to be nonchalant, conceited, spoiled by servants, and easy victims of moneylenders and middlemen. James Moffat's *Scene in the Writers' Building, Calcutta* (1811) is a well-known example, where just such a youngster sits with his legs on the table smoking a native hookah, while servants ply him with luxuries and outstanding bills.[22]

During the impeachment of Hastings, Burke had strenuously disputed the common assumptions of what he termed as "geographical morality," which amounted to the principle that the private and public duties of men were governed by the degrees of latitude and longitude. Geography and climate rivaled divine providence and the laws of human society, and it was supposed that after Englishmen had crossed the line of the equinox, their virtues simply expired.[23] James R. Martin, surgeon and medical topographer, considered the issue of disease and sickness relative to the causes and consequences of moral character, especially in the colonial tropics. "The soil and inhabitants . . . always react with each other," wrote Martin:

A sober, industrious race of inhabitants, for example, will have a greater desire to improve their country than men of a contrary character, and will also possess greater physical power to carry their desire into execution. Place such a body of men in a district over-run with noxious weeds and timber, and fast degenerating into a morass; and can there exist any rational doubt that they will clear it sooner, and longer preserve it in that improved state, than men of a different disposition? Place in a similar situation, or even in the district thus improved, a body of men who are idle and intemperate, and the immediate result will be, that the soil will deteriorate for want of proper care, the weeds will re-appear, the drains will become obstructed. . . .[24]

The poisoned weeds and congested drains here, of course, are thinly veiled allusions to the miasmal environment of eastern India, especially Bengal. Left to itself, such an environment would not be able to sustain the proper sources of nutrition, leading to unhealthy inhabitants with diminished physical powers disabled progressively from being able to remedy the causes of their own evil. Martin believed that without proper precaution, such effects would surely tell on the newly arrived English in India.

These were standard ideas of contemporary medical topography. Martin was explicitly drawing on the work of Dr. John Hennen the elder, who had written extensively on military surgery and also on medical topography. Hennen had postulated that a slothful and squalid population was the invariable characteristic of an unhealthy country.[25] Thus for Martin, the morally degenerate character of the Bengali—his timidity, insensibility, cruelty, habits of falsehood and perjury, "physical uncleanliness," obscene worship—was a peculiar affliction of the climate and environs of Bengal, and was not quite as pronounced among other Hindus from further north and west. It was expected, then, that colonization and the presence of Europeans would, through the example of their vigorous action, education, and moral character, usher in a change in the basic behavior among the people.

The nineteenth century would become known, as Nancy Stepan has put it recently, as the "tropical century."[26] Imperial powers of Europe had penetrated the coastlines of all major continents, leading to an unprecedented exploration of geography, flora, and fauna. What had once been the province of the amateur scholar-adventurer became the province of naturalists, many of whom were commissioned to set up botanical gardens, experiment with rare plants, and expand the pharmacopoeia of Europe.[27] Interest in natural history grew in Britain from natural theology and the idealization of nature in an overwhelmingly industrial society. It drew the attention of a leisured middle class that sought exotic specimens for their gardens. Much of this precipitated the idea of a prototypical "tropical nature" identified by humidity, heat, plenitude, and excess, traits supposedly intensified in the Torrid Zone.[28] Many of its connotations were negative, most visibly in regard to the African tropics, where death and disease were proving to be rampant during expeditions to the West African coast. The contrast between the civilized, temperate world and the wild tropics would become ingrained, as Stepan shows, in scientific and naturalist discourse by the middle of the nineteenth century, producing racialized and sexualized stereotypes of the degenerate tropical body.[29] Many of these conclusions, however, had been anticipated in British India a few decades earlier.

Here too, the human body became an anxious litmus test for the colonial venture. As I discussed in the preceding chapter, Indian bodies had been depicted as feminine and docile, in contrast to those of Britons. Physical features were thus quickly translated into racial characteristics and considered as direct results of climate and pathology. European bodies, on the other hand, were seen as peculiarly vulnerable in the Indian tropics. Tennant came to the conclusion while in Calcutta (1796) that the climate of all tropical regions, and especially that of India, was "unfavorable to European constitutions."[30] The combination of heat and moisture proved equally fatal in Calcutta or Batavia, corroding European restraint and probity, leading eventually to enervation. In India the debate over the tropics was initiated by the military medical establishment, and their views were somewhat different from the naturalists of a later era. Contemporary medical opinion stated that the heat of the climate accelerated the circulation of bile, producing fever, dysentery, nervous and paralytic disorders, and a general malaise that universally produced a "sallow and livid complexion" among Britons in this part of India.[31]

These ideas of climatic effect were more than supported by the fear of premature mortality. On this score the record of fatalities among new arrivals in India, especially in Bengal, the primary seat of British rule, was abysmal. Martin's account of numbers of European troops who lost their lives from "endemic causes" in the army cantonments of Fort William, Dum Dum, Berhampore, and Dinapore between 1828 and 1834 shows that 1,386 soldiers either died or were rendered invalid.[32] Such a grave loss, according to Martin, could have been ameliorated by the judicious stationing of the troops with the view to preservation of their health in the tropics. The most authoritative voice on this subject at the time was Dr. Robert Jackson, whose suggestions on military logistics and service in the West Indian colonies had become the standard reference by the time of Martin's survey. Jackson had attempted to demonstrate that it was not fatigue from labor under the tropical sun but indeed the state of lodgments and habits of soldiers that affected their chances of survival.[33] Martin agreed readily with Jackson that the happiness, health, and morale of the troops depended on how effectively they were acclimatized to their foreign post and where they were placed.

Chances of survival depended, military authorities Sir John Moore and Jackson proposed, on neatness and cleanliness, regularity of diet, frequent baths, moderate consumption of alcohol, constant exercise, discipline, parades, and inspections. It was not advisable to lounge in barracks, where the air was of a poor quality and exposed the human frame to indolence and enervation. Labor and discipline were the proven safeguards against idleness and temptation. Intoxication from alcohol, Martin noted from contemporary reports, was the bane of the European soldier in India, extremely difficult to redress despite the rules of confinement, court-martial, and frequent, severe, physical castigation.[34] Addiction to spirits in an exhausting climate was potentially fatal, often leading to death by *delirium tremens* ("horrors"), endemic fever, organic lesions, or dysentery.[35]

In the tropical colonies, where external causes for disease were rampant, internal vigilance was of the essence. It was thus advisable not to neglect proper nutrition, including animal food, and not to succumb to native habits such as the smoking of the hookah, which was reputed to affect the digestion, nerves, and heart. Caveats such as these became equally applicable to the civilian population of the British-Indian presidencies, who, in the light of equally severe death tolls, began to support similar moderation and discipline as in the garrisons. In his account of the East Indies, Alexander Hamilton, says that he observed 460 burials in the space of five months.[36] The average annual mortality rate in Calcutta in the twenty years between the years 1759 and 1779 was 212.4, and between 1786 and 1800, a space of fourteen years, 164.21, during a period in which the European population in the whole of Bengal amounted to around five thousand.[37] Sailors made up a substantial portion of these numbers—they were allegedly victims of their own "irregularities and intemperance" rather than the climate itself—followed by children, especially the "very delicate progeny" of unions between Europeans and Asiatics.[38] These numbers speak for themselves in regard to the apprehension with which many Britons must have considered a career in the coastal strongholds of the British Empire such as Calcutta. In order to counter the degenerative effects of unsanitary places and noxious vapors, Europeans had to conduct their lives with regularity and with due temperance:

The malignant climate of India, and the uncertainty of life in a region where it is so frequently cut off by disease, has produced among some individuals, the spirit of extravagance, which in Batavia the same cause has created among the parsimonious Dutch. This spirit, however, is more than counterbalanced by the habit of saving, monthly, a small portion of their allowances, to enable them to revisit their native country, and there to support their advanced life and declining years. . . .[39]

Moral defects in the colonial context thus acquired a directly physical dimension. The very same causes over the centuries that had allegedly produced despotism and slavery in the East threatened also to consume the founders of British rule in India. In fact, during the public trials of company servants, as we have noted before, Clive and Hastings had been accused of despotism supposedly endemic to the Orient, which in itself provided a justification for their excessive behavior.

DOMESTIC DISLOCATIONS

The fear of degeneration was tied from the very beginning of British concourse with India to the lifestyle of company factors, servants, and soldiers who had been absorbing facets of indigenous culture over a period of more than a hundred years in the cities and ports of the country. What was most visibly at stake was the state of their domestic affairs, their extravagance, ostentation, and their sexual relationships with native women. What little work has been done on the subject, notably the studies of Pervical Spear and Kenneth Ballhatchet, indicates a relatively uncharted history of English settlements in India, a period during which both marital and extramarital relationships between European men and local women were tolerated and even encouraged.[40] Modes of dress, cuisine, smoking of the hookah, modes of entertainment all suggest that British subjects could, given time, be assimilated into Indian society and culture. Even in the later eighteenth century, company servants lived with their "unofficial" Indian wives and mistresses (*bibis*). Writing in the early years of the nineteenth century, Capt. Thomas Williamson defended such behavior from the charges of libidinousness and licentiousness by asserting that they were simply the product of the "disparity in numbers between British men and British women in India."[41] He opposed the idea of shipping out English and Scottish women to be married to company men in India, arguing that it was indeed cheaper to engage a harem of Indian mistresses. Williamson even provided details for his readers on how to finance the upkeep of a Hindustani woman and also how an Englishman should conduct himself as her lover and companion. Numbers available are irregular, especially for the eighteenth century, but it appears that in the 1750s the ratio of European women to men in Bengal, including Britons, was roughly one to eight.[42] Williamson himself estimated that there were 250 European women in Bengal and about 4,000 men, a proportion of about one to sixteen.[43]

Even in the early nineteenth century, when European women began to arrive in somewhat greater numbers, British society in India tended to be overwhelmingly male and evidently bachelor in character. John Blackiston, who served in the East India Company's army between 1812 and 1814, described the first ball after a fleet arrived from Europe as an opportunity for the display of newly arrived young maidens who set their sights on prospective partners stationed in India.[44] The rank and property of the suitors— from a member of council or general to an ensign or assistant surgeon—were minutely graded. This assessment of matrimonial prospects, according to Blackiston, was akin to the auction of "king's stores in a dockyard"; the fairest lot were quickly reserved for civilians of high office or highly ranked officers of the staff and others weighed their chances with prospects down the rank. Prospects of matrimony for any European woman was very high: "Should she possess any pretensions to beauty, she is soon snapped up; for the scarcity of the article prevents people from being very fastidious in their tastes. If of the true European white, she is almost sure to go off tolerably well. . . ."[45]

In the seventeenth century it was not uncommon for factors to induce soldiers to marry native women because it was too expensive for the Company "to import women for their white subjects."[46] An order from the Court of Directors of in 1688 plainly suggested to the factors to "induce by all means you can invent our soldiers to marry with the Native women, because it will be impossible to get ordinary young women as we before directed to pay their own passages. . . ."[47] Percival Spear notes in passing the temporary marital unions between soldiers and Christian or Eurasian women, whose children lived with their "pariah or prostitute mothers" and after reaching their adolescence "disappeared into the interior" or "drifted into the bazaars."[48] In contrast to this were the unions of wealthy Anglo-Indian officers, whose Indian wives were permanent members of the household and presided over an extended *zenana* (literally, female quarters).[49] The offspring of such families, curiously referred to as "natural children," were given an opportunity of education and, if their skin color permitted, attempted to blend in with the greater society of metropolitan London.

Such practice had become widespread in the eighteenth century. Lt. Col. Skinner, Major Hyder Hearsay, and James Forbes were well known for their marriages into Indian aristocratic families. Others, like William Hickey of Calcutta, were noted for their attachment to native mistresses. Hickey writes fondly in his memoirs about his "cheerful and sweet-tempered Jemdanee," whom he lost in childbirth, a "gentle and affectionately attached . . . girl" with a "strong natural understanding, with more acuteness and wit than is usually found among the native women of Hindostan."[50] She left him with "a fine, strong, healthy-looking male child" who was then entrusted to the care of Mrs. Turner, the wife of Hickey's business partner, who adopted him into her large family and procured a nurse for his care. Many older men with civilian appointments in India who had already been married declined to bring their wives or children with them, instead taking up instead Indian companions. Philip Francis, John Shore, Robert Grant, and James Rennell all lived with Indian women, and many like Rennell had "natural" children by them alongside their legitimate children from previous or subsequent European or British wives.[51]

Such women, often marginal and of questionable value to the respectable Anglo-Indian household, have remained outside the pale of received histories, especially as records of their marriages and baptisms remain ambiguous and scattered.[52] Some of them tended to be of Portuguese or Luso-Indian extraction, but most were Muslim women of purportedly aristocratic background, owing to the fact that it was more likely for members of the Muslim service elite to mingle with Europeans, rather than Hindus, whose caste and communitarian codes prevented physical contact. Most of these women were not baptized and retained their former lifestyle of the *zenana.* In his study of the Anglo-Indian community in eighteenth-century Bengal, S. C. Ghosh concludes that Christian marriages between Britons and Indian women consecrated by baptism were rare and that most often Britons resided with Indian women out of wedlock.[53] Wills and testaments from this period providing for survivors who were Indian women describe them as mothers of the children of the deceased, as housekeepers, and simply as Hindustani women, but almost never as wives. Irregular unions with Indian women led to many such undocumented, unofficial households that would continue during subsequent years of the much more rigid separation between Indians and Britons as a suggestion of what colonial society in India might have been like without strictures on interracial association.

During the period of ascendancy of company rule, particularly toward the end of the eighteenth century, such mixed Anglo-Indian households were beginning to be looked upon with disdain. Soon after the British victories in India, administrators in the newly established presidencies, while admitting irregular unions of Englishmen and natives, began to impose restrictions on marriages. By the first decades of the nineteenth century, the company of native women, especially of entertainers and prostitutes, was seen by observers from England to have the most baneful effect on the English character. In the early nineteenth century, as witnessed by Captain Williamson, native female companions of company servants were excluded from all official and public gatherings. Their presence was clearly seen as detrimental to the image and comportment of the colonial Anglo-Indian society.[54] In her travels Mary Sherwood commented on the association of young Englishmen in India with the infamous "nautch-girls" and lamented on how these "once blooming boys, who were . . . slowly sacrificing themselves to drinking, smoking, want of rest, and the witcheries of the unhappy daughters of heathens and infidels."[55]

Syed Hassan Shah's Persian "novel," *Nashtar (The Surgeon's Knife)*, written in 1790 and translated into Urdu by Sajjad Hussain Kasmandavi, is written from the perspective of an officer of the East India Company who falls in love with a dancing girl by the name of Khanum Jan, who is employed for the entertainment of officers.[56] Hasan Shah, who worked as a clerk for a nephew of Sir Eyre Coote and was stationed at Kanpur during the Rohilla Wars, had seen the life of a cantonment firsthand. The story provides a glimpse of the kind of intimacy that was once possible between young Englishmen and professional Indian women, especially through social gatherings under the auspices of music, dance, and entertainment.[57] The history of such sociability is all but missing in the English accounts and records, and it remains to be fully understood to what extent and in what numbers Britons assimilated to the courtly cultures of northern India during the twilight era of the later Mughals. Williamson's account seems to indicate that Englishmen and their *zenanas* were not looked upon with any particular disrespect by Indians. Women who lived with company officials and their kin often did not distinguish between marriage and cohabitation.[58]

In one respect at least, the new rulers had adopted the lifestyle of the Indian elite. Over the course of the eighteenth century, the Anglo-Indian household had been stretched; in some cases it was further extended to incorporate an Indian-style retinue. Even without direct Indian kinship, a large establishment was seen by some as necessary and by others as a pernicious aspect of the Indian influence. Young Britons were often surrounded by an immoderate number of servants, bearers, middlemen, and sycophants. These were the unavoidable additions to households that grew around successful company officials. John Blackiston gives a graphic account of the scene that accosted the new arrivals from England in Madras:

> The swarm of natives who assail you on landing, with testimonials of character, as fair as had once been the paper on which they were written, each endeavouring to fix himself upon you as your dubash or factotum, and actually quarrelling like vultures for their prey, would give him who judges by the surface of things but an unfavourable opinion of the people among whom it is his lot to be thrown.[59]

Burke spoke at length on the figure of the go-between, the "black banya" as a testament to the moral anarchy of the European household in India:

> He is a domestic servant. He is generally chosen out of that class of natives who, by being habituated to misery and subjection can submit to any orders, and are fit for any of the basest services. Having been themselves subject to oppression, they are fitted perfectly—for that is the true education—to oppress others. They serve an apprenticeship of servitude to qualify them for the trade of tyranny. They are persons without whom a European can do nothing.[60]

Most natives who attended Englishmen were considered to exercise an undue influence over their households. Thomas Motte, a confidant of Clive, wrote in 1766 that bearers from Orissa who flocked to Calcutta formed a formidable "commonwealth" and had "made themselves masters of the conquerors of Hindustan."[61] They were known to be outrageous thieves and yet refused to have their living quarters examined by Englishmen, which they maintained would instantly defile their caste status. They had taken full advantage, thought Motte, of the "heat of the climate and the indolence of the English"; they could as easily refuse to carry their master's palanquin and let him walk "till he dies of a fever."[62] An orderly middle-class household was the site of respectability, happiness, and discipline, but despotic customs of the Orient in India thwarted this possibility. In his oriental memoirs James Forbes observed:

> This system of oppression, so completely pervades all classes of society under every form of oriental government, that it is almost impossible, out of the British dominions, to find an Asiatic of any caste or tribe, who, like the English *country gentleman,* in the middle walk of life, enjoys his patrimonial inheritance, surrounded by domestic happiness and rural pleasures.[63]

Most contemporary observers remarked on the immoderate number of servants that surrounded the Englishman in India. House rent and servant's wages constituted the most significant charge of housekeeping in Calcutta. Tennant remarks that soon after his arrival in India he lived with an Anglo-Indian family where he counted the number of servants to be a hundred and five, each and every one considered indispensable.[64] Extravagance was the norm even in relatively sober families. Added items of luxury in a warm climate, according to Tennant, multiplied the most laborious pursuits, where the labor of extra hands became quickly indispensable.[65] The hierarchy of servants tended to replicate the local order of caste and community, especially as far as Hindu employees were concerned, tending to a strict distribution of higher and menial tasks.[66] Toward the end of the century in particular, company officials seemed to maintain as a rule more hands than they could possibly require. William Hickey in 1783 had sixty-three, eight carrying sticks and a team of twenty to transport their employer in a palanquin; Thomas Twining in 1792 had forty-four men for travel alone.[67] There were women too, from domestic slaves to *ayahs* and wet-nurses. Emma Roberts warned prospective English sojourners in India about the ineptitude of the *"ayahs,"* or ladies' maids, and female servants in general recruited from the ranks of "idle and dissipated native women" who chose to enter European establishments.[68] It was feared that in such extended Anglo-Indian households, where personal valets and menservant (bearers) had unlimited access to the bedrooms of their masters and mistresses, the close proximity of natives would lessen the respectability of English women.[69]

It has been argued that the possibility of the development of a mixed society of Anglo-Indians and Eurasians located in the kin networks and households of India was checked by the introduction of increasing numbers of English and European women in the settlements. After the era of political reform introduced by Lord Cornwallis, the newly established Board of Control mandated that Europeans should not be allowed to settle freely in company territories, as the presence of a large body especially of the middle and lower classes would be detrimental to the respect and reverence paid by the natives towards the British as figures of authority.[70] Spear has suggested that this was the crucial turning point, during which there was a "widening racial gulf" that separated Englishmen from Indians. This seems at first glance to be the case, but a simple equation between the fear of the *déeraciné* and the restoration of conjugal relationships between white men and women in India needs further revision. Marriage with natives might have led to a degree of empathy towards the subject population but it would have hardly led to a new context for equality. Marriage itself was a patently hierarchical institution in both Indian and British society, and the history of Creole societies suggests that over time the mixture of blood and the variegation of skin color reinforced and even proliferated social rank and station. The incrustation of race in the pre-Victorian era, as Catherine Hall suggests, entailed unstable associations between notions of national exclusiveness and sexual identity whose historical and specific outlines still have to be mapped out beyond the usual analytics of ethnicity, gender, and class.[71]

One notable aspect of this process was surely the beginnings of a sense of a besieged domestic frontier within the walls of the Anglo-Indian household, the paternalist implications of which spread through the extended colonial-political economy. At some indeterminate point in early Victorian India, the vignette of the orderly colonial household would be rendered secure and even inviolable, with servants and maids as the safest native companions English men and women could have. Thus later in the century Colesworthy Grant could put together letters to his mother in the form of *An Anglo-Indian Domestic Sketch* (1849), in which various servants of the house were featured: the Khidmutgar, the Bawurchee, the Mushalchee, the House Bearer, the Durwan, the Mehtur, the Ayah, the Dhobee, the Durzee, the Hookka Burdar, and so on.[72] He noted that a "great gulf . . . exists between Europeans and their dependents" and that Anglo-Indian children "seldom see anything in the manners of their parents towards the servants to impress their minds with any strong feelings of respect for them. . . ."[73] The natives were, after all, "with very rare exceptions, the *only servants* whom they see in the country. . . ."[74] In later Victorian times the relatively peaceable domestic frontier of British-India would begin to stand in dire contrast, especially after the Mutiny, to the general mistrust that continued to grow between the colonial ruling class and the natives. Treatises such as Flora Annie Steel's *Complete Housekeeper and Cook* that enjoyed much popularity in colonial household in late nineteenth century India have to be seen in such a historical context.

COLONIAL SOCIETY AND THE SANGUINARY DIVIDE

Regulation of the territorial possessions of the company-state was to a degree in complicity with the ordering of race, sex, marriage, and reproduction in

the last two decades of the eighteenth century. In order to explore this growing distance between the British and the natives in India, I turn to Winthrop
Jordan's signal analysis of the development of racial consciousness in early
North American colonial society. English settler society in this context dif-
ferentiated by statute the offspring of unions between whites and Native
Americans, and whites and Africans.[75] Interracial union was seen not only as
contrary to the laws of nature but also as the introduction of inferior blood
into the body politic in various proportions. In the absence of the genetic
theory of human reproduction, Jordan inferred, blood was indeed seen as the
virile essence that passed on the essential attributes of a society and race. In context of slavery, of course, the admixture of African blood was seen as instantly
contaminating, and thus for social and economic purposes the mulatto was
considered a Negro.[76] In the case of Native Americans, as Kathleen Brown
points out in a recent essay reconsidering Jordan's conclusions, the possibility
of assimilation through sexual union was seen as much stronger than in that of
Africans.[77] As she shows elsewhere, while sexual relations with Indian women
could be seen as an extension of commerce and exchange, and thus compatible with the rise of English dominance in northern America, those between
Englishmen and Negroes threatened the stable distinctions between slave and
free, especially as far as the law was concerned.[78] In the seventeenth century, a
white woman attempting to marry a Negro, Indian, or mulatto was handed
out exemplary punishment. The newly emerging legal definitions of race were
thus tied to the details of everyday practice in which the sexuality of women,
especially white women, was regulated.[79]

Since India was never considered a colony of settlement, the presence of
people of mixed origin did not directly threaten the rights of white British-born
subjects in India, as they did in the British West Indies or the Cape.[80] This
situation began to change in the era of the expansion of the East India
Company's territorial ambitions. It is possible that in the wake of the rebellions in the creolized Spanish Americas, the growing number of mixed-
blooded subject were seen to be particularly menacing. Scholars of Anglo-Indian
background in the modern era, such as H. A. Stark, have emphasized this
threat voiced in contemporary newspapers and travel accounts, such as that
of Viscount Valencia, who was in India between 1802 and 1806 and whose
Voyages and Travels reported on the state of the East India Company's eastern
possessions. Valencia saw a grave danger in the rising numbers of "half-
caste" children, the "most rapidly increasing evil of Bengal," who, by creating a "link of union" between the English and the natives, were eroding
the exclusive position of the rulers.[81]

Other more recent histories point out that the root of discrimination
against the East Indians, or Eurasians, as they were called at the time, lay
in the security concerns of the company-state, which was keen to hold on
to its territorial acquisitions in India in the face of European rivals.[82] It has
also been suggested that the rapidly rising career prospects in the govern-

ment of India alerted the Court of Directors and shareholders of the Company to the valuable source of patronage being usurped by Indian-born "sons of the Company" begotten through legitimate or illegitimate union with native women.[83] Traditionally a degree of support had always been extended to some of these "natural" children. Up until the 1780s it was customary among those who could afford it to send their Indian children for an education in England so that they might stand a good chance afterwards of being inducted into the covenanted and commissioned services.[84] Many servants of the Company expressed fatherly concern about the future of their natural children and made provisions to send them to boarding schools in England and afterwards secure for them an Indian career. Francis Fowke, for example, like many of his contemporaries, remembered in his will his Indian mistress and his natural children.[85] The Court of Directors was clearly concerned that young men of mixed Anglo-Indian descent would eventually dominate posts in the civil, military, and marine services at the expense of its own candidates from the home country. It thus acted to prevent children of Britons born of Indian mothers being sent to England for education.

These were surely legitimate concerns, especially the ones regarding the power of patronage reserved by the Court of Directors, but they still do not fully explain why between 1786, which marks the arrival of Cornwallis as governor-general of India, and 1791 there was a series of measures passed that would banish the sons of mixed blood as significant members of the East India Company's civil and military establishments. In the year 1783 a plan, endorsed by most officers and laid before the governor-general, for the support and education of orphans of army officers had been approved. This led to an expansion of the Bengal Military Orphan Society and its schools. In March 1786, however, the Court of Directors suddenly refused to entertain the society's proposal (1784) that the wards of the Upper Orphanage School of Calcutta, both British- and British-Indian born, be sent to Britain for further education. An order had been issued that only legitimate children born to European parents on both sides would be allowed to return to Britain. An even more rigid gesture followed in 1791, when John Turing, whose father was the commissioner of the Coromandel (Resident at Ganjam, Orissa) and mother was a southern Indian woman, was barred from joining the Company's army as a commissioned officer.[86] In April that year, the Court of Directors passed a resolution that no person of Indo-British or Eurasian extraction—"son of a Native Indian"— could be appointed in the civil, military, or marine services of the Company.[87]

In 1794, Governor-General Cornwallis drafted a plan for the amalgamation of the king's troops and the Company's army in India in which he laid down a fundamental principle that "the European and Native branches of the service . . . should be entirely separated"[88] and that no persons "who are not descended on both sides from European parents, can be admitted into the European branch of the service, except as drummers, fifers, or other musicians: nor can such persons be hereafter admitted on the establishment of European officers in Native troops."[89] Not only did this resolution bar the entry of East Indians into the Company army, it also led to the dismissal of members who had already distinguished themselves in the armed services.[90] These measures, to be sure, were not simply the result of capricious color prejudice or an unprecedented surge of racial ill-feeling. What seems to be most apparent is that the question of patronage was being revisited according to the emerging social divisions of British India, where a new and distinctive racial hierarchy was taking shape. Blood and patronage became directly related in the discriminatory practices of the Company; without doubt the basic tendency of this colonial policy was the differentiation rather than further aggregation of imperial subjects.

A similar prejudice along the lines of race surfaced in regard to the claims of widows and children of civil and military servants on the long-established charitable funds. Whereas in the 1780s and even during the Rohilla Campaigns, orphaned children born to European soldiers of native women were allowed primary education and monthly stipends, in 1797 it became exceedingly difficult to provide for the native offspring of even high-ranking officers.[91] Some were quick to send their sons to the Dutch Indies, particularly Bencoolen, for service.[92] The Bengal Civil Fund was all of a sudden closed to Indian women and their Eurasian children in 1804; similar measures followed in the military. In 1805 a major controversy emerged in the management of the Military Fund (or Lord Clive's Fund), a charitable institution founded by Robert Clive, whose financial support had once been extended to the native wives of European officers "in common with persons of European descent."[93] However, despite petitions to the Board disputing claims denied to widows "born in India," a widow seeking charity now had to make an affidavit that she was not of native blood, and her certificate of birth attested by a surgeon was crucial part of the application.[94] First in Madras and subsequently in Bombay, funds were disbursed only to children of unmixed European blood.[95] Article 14 of the proposed legislation for the Bombay Military Fund in 1810 guaranteed full benefits to wives and legitimate children of all officers in service at that time, but categorically stated that for all marriages contracted thereafter, it would be: "an indispensable qualification that both the parents of any and every claimant shall have been European, or of unmixed European blood, though born in other quarters of the world, four removes from an Asiatic or African being considered as European blood."[96]

It is clear that a routinization of colonial rule demanded the legal sanction for the separation of blood, although the incidence of sexual contact between Britons and Indian women continued through the early nineteenth century, especially in the army. The purity of blood, actualized through law, stood as a measure of racial autonomy that safeguarded the idea of an undiluted British community in India. Yet even a brief look at the history of the sexual conduct of the army, especially during long campaigns away from their bases, shows the continuing practice of British and European officers and cadets entering into liaisons with local native women, often resulting in offspring out of wedlock who were thereafter left behind in India with their mothers. By 1825 some of these women actually succeeded in petitioning the state for support for their children, appealing to the sense of justice and clemency of the Company.[97]

Thus in 1820 the commanding officer of the Sixty-Sixth Regiment, Royal Horse, was apprised by the government of Bengal of its "highly reprehensible behavior" in permitting fifty-five unmarried women and fifty-one children to accompany the corps leaving Ceylon for Bengal, as they could not be transported any further to St. Helena or Europe.[98] The Bengal government complained that they had to make arrangements for these women to return to their relations in Ceylon, rather than leave them to "starve or obtain a livelihood by vice in Bengal."[99] Responding to the charges that the local authorities had to encounter a degree of embarrassment in procuring provision and maintenance for these women and their orphaned children, the CO seemed to ascribe this conduct on the part of his men to have grown out of "the *local habits* incidental to the country." Twenty-seven of these children, who were proven to have Europeans as their mothers, were sent to the Military Asylum in Chelsea; the rest remained in India.[100] Similar situations were reported with His Majesty's Sixty-Sixth and Seventy-Eighth regiments, and the Twenty-Fourth and Fifty-Ninth regiments of Light Dragoons.[101] In 1812 the governor of Mauritius had already expressed his concern over the "deserted families" of the king's officers, asking the Crown to defray the expenses of their upkeep. In certain instances it was difficult to take the children away to their designated orphanages in Calcutta and Madras, or in some cases to England, as their mothers were unwilling to let them go.[102]

Orphans would remain a visible reminder of the limits of communal proximity between the British and the Indians, presenting a lingering social problem for the British government in major Indian cities.[103] Despite all efforts to the contrary, the community of Eurasians continued to grow in India, especially in Bengal. In 1822 it is estimated that in Calcutta there were 2,254 Europeans and 10,884 Eurasian men, women, children.[104] Ricketts put the number of people of mixed origins for the whole of Bengal in 1830 at 20,000.[105] J. R. Martin noted in 1837 that there were still more Eurasians than Englishmen within the actual precincts of the city of Calcutta.[106]

CONFLICTED HIERARCHIES: BLOOD, RACE, GENDER

In the light of what has been said above, it may be argued that while the colonial state tried to enforce the separation of blood with mixed success, administrative rhetoric simply acknowledged the divide as absolute. Colonial and colonized subjects could in this way be naturalized in official terminology through the category of race as a primordial, unchangeable entity, much like the essence of a nation or civilization. Contemporary terms[107] such as "legitimate," "illegitimate," "European," "Eurasian," "native," and "half-caste" to describe the status of children in India thus all denoted a degree of divergence from a pristine natural state.

There was a great deal of disagreement about the consequences of the running of English into native blood. It is clear that British attitudes toward such admixture varied predominantly according to the gender of the offspring. Eurasian women appealed to Englishmen in India; they were even considered eminently nubile. Many Indo-British and half-caste women were raised by the orphanages of Madras and Calcutta so that they would be able to "earn a respectable livelihood" and even provided with a modest dowry if they could marry their way out.[108] Eurasian families of Madras even in the 1830s tried their utmost to socialize with young English gentlemen and offer their daughters in marriage. Such liaisons were common, according Albert Hervey, an ensign in Madras from 1833 to 1843:

> officers belonging to regiments stationed in Madras are frequently thrown amongst these dark-eyed bewitching syrens, and are very liable to become smitten with their charms. I must say the young women are very pretty, notwithstanding their color. The consequences of associating with them are almost inevitable. Young, unthinking ensigns and lieutenants easily fall into the trap set for them. . . .[109]

The presence of native blood in these "pretty, handsome young women, full of Oriental ardour"[110] was seen as a mark of explicit sexuality. In a quatrain dedicated to a "beautiful East Indian" in the *Asiatic Journal* of 1816, Thomas Moore exhorted:

> Oh for a sun-beam rich and warm
> From thy own Ganges' fervid haunts
> To light thee up, thou lovely form
> All my soul adores and wants![111]

This tribute was consonant with the natural sexual attractiveness of Indian women for contemporary Englishmen. "Nature seems to have showered beauty on the fairer sex throughout Indostan" wrote Orme in his *Fragments,* "with a more lavish hand than in most other countries."[112] The author of *Sketches of India* offered that the "Hindoostanee women . . . are in general exquisitely formed, after the truest models of symmetry and beauty" and that it was no surprise that otherwise prudent Englishmen fell victim to their charms.[113] Marriages took place between well-positioned Englishmen and Eurasian women even through the 1820s. The *Bengal Hurkaru* of March 1825 reported that many "elegant and accomplished half-Indian girls" had been respectably married, "whose blood may soon mingle with that of the proud nobility of England; and *en passant,* will not degrade it either."[114] At the more profane end of the scale, contemporaries reported the widespread practice by Europeans of keeping concubines in India, tacitly sanctioned by British-Indian society. The author of the *Sketches* calculated that at least one third of unmarried Englishmen in India kept native women as sexual companions and among them about half had fathered children through such illegal liaisons.[115] It was partly due to the climate of India, which resulted in a "great propensity to sexual intercourse" and a certain "fever of the blood" hitherto unknown to these "frigid sons of Europe."[116] The young servants of the Company were thus quickly infatuated and wont to form easy attachments with native women, leading to children, debt, and ruin.

And yet the possibility of a widespread colonization of India through a dispersion of European blood would not be admitted by contemporaries. Implicit in this denial was the conviction that men of mixed blood remained in the last instance unfit for official patronage, gentlemanly office, and rank because of their racial provenance, and also the deep-seated assumption that Europeans and Indians were furthest apart in racial terms. Sir Robert Grant, son of the philanthropist, abolitionist, and statesman, Charles Grant, who had spent the first eleven years of his life in Bengal (and later became governor of Bombay), wrote during the period of the passage of the Regulating Act in 1813 that Europeans should be: "for a very long course of time . . . divided by the strongest marks of distinction from the original inhabitants."[117] He assumed that an unbridgeable difference "arising from diversity of colour, genius, manners, opinions, and institutions" existed between the two communities, which was further confirmed by the "essential incompatibility between political authority and political subjection" as well as "hereditary feelings and recollections" that could neither be renounced nor reconciled.[118] For centuries then, the "purely Indian" and the "purely European population" would continue. And even if there were to be a large number of people of "mixed order" with various gradations of "race and privilege," as in the Americas, they would clearly identify with the European lineage.[119]

This order would prevail, according to Grant, not so much because people would prefer to claim a "nobler descent" but because the mixing of blood could only happen where the father was European and the mother Indian, and it was "consonant with both nature and with experience" that the character of the offspring will be dictated by the father's blood. Grant had difficulty imagining that white women would ever marry Indian men. European women in India were relatively scarce, and the prospects of an "Oriental haram" added to the "obvious degradation" resulting from such a union could inspire in them nothing but horror and disgust. The colony, he concluded, must not, then, descend by degrees into the native population, but laid out as a society of "distinct and separate" entities. Although Grant did not mention the British Caribbean, his prospects for the colonization and settlement of India were pointedly contrary to the experience in the West Indies. Here the mixed-blood population had been further reclassified. The progeny of white fathers and black mothers became known as mulattos, those of whites and mulattos as mestizos, and the offspring of whites and mestizos as castizos.[120] The entanglements of race and economic servitude in the plantations had created a society of color gradations quite unlike that of India, which continued to be governed along much more closely supervised principles of segregation, at least on paper.[121]

Restrictions on European migration into India and the ownership of landed property had been justified on the ground that such an influx would further deprive the natives of their place in the economy. It was also argued that a precipitous rise in the number of whites would tend to degrade the character and exclusivity of the British inhabitants in the eyes of the natives.[122] By the turn of the eighteenth century, a genuine debate about the possibility of opening up India to colonial settlement was already taking shape, which would gather further impetus with the end of the Company's exclusive monopoly on East Indian trade in 1813 and the rise of the policy of free trade. With the end of the Anglo-French rivalry and peace in Europe, it was also becoming more difficult to justify the sequestration and close supervision of Europeans in the major Indian cities.[123] In the 1830s there were many in England who demanded that India be opened up to a new flow of British subjects. Thus a reviewer of Peter Auber's *Rise and Progress of British Power in India* (1837) wrote with a degree of aggravation with respect to Pitt's India Bill that "the colonization of India was rigidly prohibited, lest an infusion of British blood and British spirit might render the country impatient of the necessary yoke of a committee of merchants."[124] Despite a few voices in support of opening up the country to the general subjects of Great Britain, India of the company Raj remained largely impervious to civilian settlement.

Racial worries continued to permeate the question of European and British subjects and their status in India. While maintaining that a clear separation of Indians and Britons was inevitable, Grant commented at length on the acclimatization of more than thirty thousand British subjects residing in India from their early youth, some from their very childhood. They gradually become habituated and even attached to the "climate, manners, and the mode of living, which belong to the country" he wrote, observing in passing that some "enter into less reputable connections with the native races."[125] This contradiction between the inescapable fact of miscegenation and the assertion that a full-blooded ruling race would continue untainted in India set the context for a lengthy uncertainty about the hierarchy of various subject races in the Indian context. Along with the eventual denial of intimacy between Englishmen and Indians, one can detect the beginnings of a particular aversion towards people of mixed blood, anticipating aspects of the latter-day eugenic doctrines, that helps to explain the peculiar severity with which the Eurasians of colonial India were marginalized.

THE "INTERMEDIATE TRIBE"

The very presence of a body of subjects of mixed blood entailed a potential threat to the legitimacy and exclusiveness of the ruling community. On the point of law, the Supreme Court in Calcutta held that the legitimate off-spring of a British-born subject and a native Indian woman was a British subject, while illegitimate children of such parents were Indians.[126] Thus an English officer of the East India Company who consorted with native women could father both Indian and British subjects, and the widow of an English officer returning to England with her children had to leave behind in India a child of her husband from a previous marriage to a native woman.[127]

The *Asiatic Journal* of 1825, addressing the legal disabilities under which the Eurasians of India suffered, declared that the "whole fabric" of Britain's "Eastern Rule" was anomalous and unprecedented. Not only were the Eurasians denied posts in military and civil society, but also the "very circumstances" of their birth made them "outcastes in the eyes of their superstitious fellow nations".[128] This was not only prejudicial but also "cruel and unjust."[129] These were also the grounds on which the East Indians of Bombay petitioned the Court of Directors of the East India Company opposing the resolution passed by directors of the Bombay Military Fund in 1833 that that widows of "mixed-extraction" and children of mixed blood may not be allowed to partake of the benefits of the fund.[130] The East Indian community of Bombay thought that such a resolution "cast a stigma not only on those who suffer in their immediate persons . . . but also on every individual of the class which by implication it proscribes as a *degraded* body."[131] Since many East Indians had held commissions and had risen to the highest ranks in the army, it was often the case that their own sisters had married brother officers of European descent. The new regulation in such cases worked "to the prejudice of the weaker sex, so characteristically barbarous" that it appeared "singularly out of place" in an institution the patrons and members of which belonged to a "highly civilized nation."[132]

What the East Indians found particularly onerous was the charge against widows of mixed origin, "calculated to discourage illicit and immoral connections." The rule, they argued, was aimed not so much at the "moral nature" of such sexual relations, permitted or illicit, nor even to protect the conventional degree of rank bestowed on the respectability of a woman's mother's family. It was based rather on an "animal standard" which implied that without a certain proportion of European along with Asiatic and African blood flowing in their veins, these women were physically degraded.

Eurasians in India thus labored under the accusation that there must be some "inherent defect of body or mind" in the offspring of mixed descent. An order passed as early as 1786 that proscribed the wards of the Upper Military Orphanage in Calcutta from being educated in and settling in England, explained that it was "a political inconvenience because the imperfections of the children, whether bodily or mental, would in process of time be communicated by intermarriage to the generality of the people in Great Britain, and by this means debase the succeeding generations of Englishmen."[133] Five years later a crucial proviso in the regulations adopted by the Court of Directors on November 9, 1791, barred their participation in the higher and covenanted offices in the civil and military services: persons receiving any such appointment could not be "the son of a native Indian."[134] In 1830, the Christian residents of Calcutta, born of European fathers and native mothers, petitioned Parliament complaining of the disqualifications to which they had been subjected ever since the first settlement of the East India Company.[135] They had been summarily excluded from privileges that both the natives and the Europeans enjoyed: they could not serve in the civil, military, or marine departments, nor could they hold the king's commission in India. They were not even allowed to hold any office of trust or emolument.

When this petition asking for rights of Eurasians in India came up before the House of Lords in 1830, Lord Ellenborough did not think that it was a favorable time to discuss the issue, but said that he felt, as all must, "for the unfortunate situation of the class to which the petitioners belonged."[136] Although it was desirable that their conditions be improved as much as possible, the "principles essential to the maintenance of British Government in India," however, could not be violated. In response to a question from the Earl of Carlisle, who asked if there was any difference between the children of half-castes and the half-castes themselves, Ellenborough confirmed that the children of mixed parents were indeed natives, and in that capacity eligible to all the offices in the service to which all Indians were eligible. It was clearly the sense of the House that, as illegitimate offspring of European fathers and native mothers, the Eurasians could never amount to much and should not be given privileges beyond nominal civil rights.

The same petition on the floor of the House of Commons elicited a certain degree of sympathy for the plight of the East Indian community in India. Sir James Mackintosh warned against the consequences of debarring good, faithful Christians from holding respectable administrative offices. Branded as an inferior class, the East Indians would be "visited by evils of a deeper dye."[137] C. Pote, a member of the East Indians' Petition Committee, which met in the Town Hall of Calcutta (1831) to receive John Ricketts, their agent to the British Parliament, admonished that legislation disqualifying Indo-Britons from service would "degrade that class below what the vilest barbarism and ignorance could effect . . . degrade them below their self-esteem . . . left for the support even of the rudest savages."[138] John Ricketts himself voiced at these meetings the fear that "political degradation" inevitably implied a "moral degradation."[139] Judging by the high standard of living enjoyed by Englishmen in India at the time, the abject financial plight of many of these East Indians made them particularly vulnerable to these charges.[140]

Quite apart from the curious history of the dispossession and plight of what was to become the future 'Anglo-Indian' community in India, I find such discussions richly illuminating in that they reveal contemporary attitudes toward racial degradation and degeneration beyond the accepted doctrines of natural history. It is clear that victims of sanguinary and racial discrimination often had to submit to such standards, especially as the question of extraction further implicated status, rank, and class in colonial society. A contemporary observer remarked that "the British blood and the native blood in their veins are alike hateful" to Eurasians.[141] Pote, who so vociferously defended the innocence of his fellow East Indians in the Town Hall of Calcutta, based his genuine outrage on the fact that his people were being denied the true birthright of British subjects and were subjected to "contumely and scorn" even though they "stood in many ways in the relation of consanguinity to Britons" and therefore were in effect under the protection of the "noblest, freest and the most enlightened government of the modern and ancient world."[142] Again, blood and civilization were being seen as much the same thing.

Thus both official policy and unofficial attitude stood in the way of Eurasians being accepted within the ranks of colonial society. While British observers in India deprecated the fallacies and injustices of the indigenous caste system, the rules of patronage and racial purity had precipitated a new caste hierarchy among Anglo-Indians. The calibration of blood became of vital significance for the colonial order in India. For Eurasians, blood became an insurmountable barrier.

ATTRIBUTES OF SUBJECT RACES

The very premise that native Indian blood was defiling and spoiled the rights and liberties of trueborn British subjects elucidates the early racial configuration of colonial India. I have already noted how the question of degeneracy was entangled with questions of reproduction and gender. The taint of native blood devolved around the racial character of native women themselves. The author of the *Sketches* (1816) feared the "vast and increasing number of *demi-bengalees*" in Calcutta, who were "characterized by all the vice and gross prejudices of the natives, but devoid of their pusillanimity."[143] They inherited all the "faults and failings of the European character, without its candour, sincerity or probity."[144]

While the ascriptions of blood and character conferred on English the genuine attributes of an advanced civilization, they also produced the negative racial profiling of native subjects. In the remaining section of this chapter I shall explore the way in which the colonial discourse on race derived and also diverged from the prevalent natural history of the races of mankind. Given the limits of conjugal English domesticity in colonial India and also the fear of wanton dissipation of blood, both manliness and racial exclusivity were jealously defended. It is hardly surprising in this context that the dependent Indian subjects would appear childlike or effeminate in the eyes of imperial rulers.

As we have already seen, the assertion of a free, benevolent, paternalist, authoritarian colonizing agency produced a split image of the generic Indian subject: the slavish Gentoo (Hindu) and the despotic Moor (Muslim). Many British observers believed that the Muslims of India had degenerated to a point where they were incapable of maintaining legitimate rule in India, while the Hindus had been reduced for centuries to the status of dependent subjects. Despite the respect given by orientalist scholars for their sacred texts, the bodies, habits, and characters of living Hindus were looked upon with a mixture of odium and curiosity. William Carey, a Scottish missionary known for his benevolence and friendship with the natives of Bengal, could still remark that the Hindus lacked the "ferocity of American Indians" but were "abundantly supplied with a dreadful stock of low cunning and deceit."[145]

Along with the categorical repression of sexual and social intimacy between the rulers and the ruled, the need for authoritarian treatment of Indians became further entrenched. Indian despotism was beginning to be considered as of natural, even biological origin. The litany of despotism and slavery in British descriptions of India can also be seen as an exercise far in excess of its administrative, discriminatory convenience. Rather, these were signs of the enormity of the colonial responsibility thrust on a handful of mostly young Britons in India, especially the fear of native insubordination at home and in the barracks. Tennant noted the difference between Hindus and Muslims in both domestic service and the Company's regiments. The Moors were "proud, dissolute, and vindictive," untrustworthy, and much less "manageable" servants compared to the Hindus.[146] Deep-seated inequalities between kings and their subjects, it was believed, had characterized the Indian polity centuries prior to the arrival of the British; they were the consequence of climate and character. The fear was that Indian nature might never be amenable to British governance and that in ruling India, the true character of the English, or indeed that of Britain, right eventually be lost.

Debauchery threatened the moral fiber of the British and their national character, to the extent that it was a result of endemic despotism. The British presence in India was supposed to break the spell of oriental tyranny, and yet the very discourse of despotism kept alive a generic master-slave narrative that legitimated rightful conquest. The division of subject races in India could, then, naturally be regarded as the extension of its inherently flawed polity.

Colonial ideas of race derived in part from the writing of natural historians that predated biological determinism. By the second half of the eighteenth century, ideas of natal distinction had gained ground across Europe, especially in relation to Africa and Africans.[150] Kant had divided mankind into four races: White, Negro, Hunnic, and Hindu, each delineating particular physical and moral character.[151] Linnaeus, more directly attuned to stereotypes flowing from imperial expansion had classified men as Wild, American, European, Asiatic, and African.[152] Europeans were fair, sanguine, and brawny, their manner gentle, acute, and inventive, governed by laws. Asiatics were sooty, melancholy, and rigid, severe, haughty, and covetous in manners, and governed by opinions.[153] Georges Cuvier (1817) regarded race as the "hereditary peculiarities" of the fixed varieties of the human species, divided roughly by skin color: Caucasian or white, Mongolian or yellow, and Ethiopian or black. Caucasians were the progenitors of high civilization, Mongolians were civilized but stationary, and Negros were in a state of "utter barbarism."[154] Chevalier de Lamarck divided man into six groups, adding Hyperboreans and Malayans to Cuvier's list, and speculated upon the possible mastery of one race over the others, just like man against other animals including the higher apes.[155]

Such taxonomies were carried back and forth between European scholars and amateur scholar-administrators in India. It came to be commonly assumed in India that, as already discussed, the natives were indeed two distinct racial groups, one autochthonous and the other a later arrival. The original "Moors" of India were considered a race apart, despotic, capricious and warlike, while the Hindus were seen as generally meek, submissive, servile, and accepting of their subjugated status. The previous chapter has shown how Orme emphasized the production and reproduction of the Hindus, relating their character and conduct to the effects of climate. Indolence was peculiar to the soil of the country, as was fecundity and fertility.[156] Curiously, excessive sexual union did not deplete their reproductive spirit or decrease their numbers, as was noticed in the more severe climates of Europe. Orme's climatic explanations, following Buffon's theory of the degenerative effects of nontemperate latitudes, also seem to parallel Lord Kames and Oliver Goldsmith. In the figure of the Hindu the weakness of the race was most clearly manifest, signified both by the inferiority of the slave and the passivity of women; as Orme observed, "people born under a sun too sultry to admit the exercise and fatigues necessary to form a robust nation" were naturally deficient in their constitution. Orme compared the hair color, shape of the lips, shape of the eyes and eyelid, and nostrils of the Hindus to features of the Kaffirs of Africa, Malayans, Tartars, Spaniards and the Portuguese, who in turn were compared to inhabitants of northern Europe.

These descriptions of physical attributes comes close to a theory of racial degradation, especially the assertion that the severity of the monsoons affected the "texture of the human frame" permanently. Thus races residing in the northern and western extremities of the subcontinent were comparable in stature, muscularity, and robustness to Europeans, while the mingling of monsoon and extreme heat in the great plains and river valleys was productive of races whose physiognomy and muscular strength made them more like women.[157] By the beginning of the nineteenth century, such curiosities about Indians had become foregone conclusions. Thus Martin, the medical topographer, could heartily concur with James Mill that the "languid and slothful habits of the Hindoo" were a product of both climate and the wretchedness of government.[158] There was little to be done about such things: "When we reflect on the habits and customs of the natives, their long misgovernment, their religion and morals, their diet, clothing, and above all, their *climate,* we can be at no loss to perceive *why* they should be what they are."[159]

FURTHERING THE RACIAL DIVIDE

The idea that a majority of Indians were inherently unfree created a lasting impression. Robert Grant wrote in 1816 that the Hindus could not be "like the negroes, personally slaves," and that a distinction ought to be made between "personal and political servitude."[160] At the same time; "the feebleness and timidity of the Hindoo confer on the Englishman a moral superiority, which does not differ in kind, though it greatly differs in degree, from the dominion of a personal master, and which, unless subjected to powerful restraints, is not perhaps less susceptible of abuse."[161]

John Crawfurd, onetime British Resident at the court of Java, wrote in his *Free Trade Pamphlet:* "The Indians know not what freedom is; they are for the most part a timid, often an effeminate, and as a nation a feeble race of semi-barbarians."[162] A report on the East India Company's charter published in 1832 declared: "The Hindoos, it is true, have not had iron fetters, on their wrists and ankles like the slaves of the West-Indies, but they have for centuries fetters of the mind, far more efficacious for the debasement of the immortal spirit of man . . . it must be a matter of astonishment that they possess so many amiable qualities in spite of the mental and bodily slavery to which for ages they have been subjected."[163]

Colonial India was thus seen as a deeply fissured civil society. According to Robert Grant, the "associated community of British and natives" presented one of the "most curious and interesting spectacles ever witnessed."[164] Here were "two races of men" distinct in origin, language, complexion, dress, manners, customs, and religion, and completely "disproportionate in energy both of body and mind." On the one side there was "extreme feebleness of frame joined with extreme effeminacy, dependence and timidity of spirit," while on the other there was "vigour, hardiness, courage, enterprise and ambition." Now only was such inequality natural, argued Grant, but both groups were aware of the fact that the "feeble race is politically subject to the stronger." Hindus had become in common usage the archetypal subject race.

Colonial perceptions of race, of course, did not always dovetail with laws of natural history that would place subjects in the appropriate hierarchy of creation, but borrowed freely from various ideas of climate, degeneracy, blood, and civilization, factors that both complemented and contradicted one another. The racial divide in India continued to encourage polygenetic accounts of difference among subjects of empire even while theories of the common origin of mankind began to dominate the scientific community in Europe. Climatic ideas of race that were in circulation in the 1830s continued well into the latter half of the nineteenth century. One in particular was the medical contention that "unmixed European stock" could not survive more than two generations in the Indian plains and deltas, which was why surgeons advised that children should be sent back to England after the age of five or six.[165] Heat and dust in the plains and the noxious vapors of the coastal cities would become climatic stereotypes, at the base of which lay the fear of atrophy of culture and emasculation far away from home soil.

During the period under consideration, however, the commonplace view was that all Indians were inferior in various degrees to Europeans, and Britons in particular. As Emma Roberts observed in her advice to outbound cadets, European residents in India not only "despised native opinions" but also treated natives with "rude indifference" and arrogance. Contempt often led to outright hatred:

> . . . a considerable portion of Anglo-Indians entertain the strongest aversion to the people whom they have alienated by their haughty and imperious manners. A black fellow, the invidious epithet with which they designate every native, however high in the scale of intellectuality, is, according to their opinion, scarcely superior to the brute creation. . . .[166]

She suggested that new arrivals try to "think well of the natives," acquaint themselves with the local language as much as possible so that they avoid their commands being misunderstood or disobeyed, and refrain from outbursts of rage and indiscriminate beating of domestic servants.[167]

Similar incidents of racial antipathy occurred in the army, especially after 1797 with the rigid separation of the native and European officers of the infantry enforced by Cornwallis.[168] John Briggs in his popular letters of advice written to a young person starting out in India, warned against the indiscriminate abuse of "natives as a whole race" designated by the "absurd appellation of black fellows."[169] Briggs attempted to expose the fallacy that a darker skin, the effect of tropical climate, was in itself a sign of inferiority, but he was aware that such was the prevalent view of most Europeans traveling to the East. Similar descriptions can be found of Indians who were transported to England as servants in the eighteenth century, especially in notices for the sale or apprehension of those who had fled: "black Indian boy," "black servant boy," "East India black," "East India tawney black," and "runaway Bengal boy" were phrases that appeared in papers such as *The Tatler,* the *London Gazette,* and the *Morning Chronicle,* alongside "Coffree boys" from Africa.[170] It can be argued that familiarity with Indians back home in England as domestics, servants, *ayahs,* and *lascars* (seamen), people whom Rozina Visram terms the "chattels of empire" indeed sharpened the popular ideas of color and race as exterior signs of inferiority.[171]

East Indians or Eurasians were also liable to be branded with the mark of a corrupted race, depicted as proud, lazy, indolent, extravagant, ignorant, and miserable. Bishop Heber had described the financial burdens of supporting a large number of "European poor and half-castes" in Calcutta who led a life of considerable distress.[172] Agents of charitable societies only furthered the circulation of such epithets. A sympathetic reader wrote to the editor of the government *Gazette* in 1830, contending that their indolence was a "moral result from their physical condition."[173] Blackiston recorded the fact that people of rank would seldom deign to marry a woman who had a "mixture" of Asiatic blood.[174] Captain Hervey observed that the European community in Calcutta distinguished themselves from Eurasians by calling them by the Hindustani epithet of "Chee-Chee" (shameful) while refering to themselves as "Koi-Hai" (notable), and declared that the man who married a half-caste was "a fool to be pitied" and that he "would rather marry an Ourang-outang."[175]

In the course of the nineteenth century the experience of empire mediated the turn away from these shifting categories of racial distinction, borne out of natural history and common watchwords of administration, toward race as an unbridgeable biological divide. The Industrial Revolution further strengthened the image of a conquering, civilizing, technologically advanced nation rather than one conquering race among many—Briton rather than Anglo-Saxon, Celtic, or Teutonic.[176] Racial distinction and hierarchy had been systematized and reinforced through the scientific study of race, especially craniology and craniometry. The empirical findings of racial science in Great Britain, as much as slavery and the colonization of the nonwhite world, contributed to deep-seated and abiding moral, intellectual, and physical values that Britons readily attributed to the different branches of humankind.[177] The work of natural historians, anatomists, and physical anthropologists that had become popular over the years, especially in other countries of western Europe, also contributed to new formulations of the relationship between state, society, and the individual. Science had legitimated race as a formative force that moved in human society through processes of degeneration and regeneration, and as a fundamental factor that separated humans from the rest of the animal kingdom and people of Caucasian blood from Asians and Africans.[178] The biological distinction of higher and lower races would become intimately tied to notions of exclusive national character and would have a significant impact on racial identities *within* European societies.[179] In the case of Britain, the Indian empire provided an immense context for a rehearsal of domestic national identities.

How the historical progress of nationhood became analogous to the progressive natural development of man in the later Victorian era is a question beyond the historical period under review here. The development of nation *as* race was articulated, perhaps not altogether accidentally, during the greatest extent of Britain's Asiatic empire by anthropologists such as Kelburne King in tracts such as *An Inquiry into the Causes that Have Led to the Rise and Fall of Nations* (1876), where he dismissed geography, climate, forms of government, and religion as factors that brought about the predominance of nations, and argued in favor of the merging of superior races to produce a dominant stock. The discovery of common protohistorical Aryan ancestry complicated the picture, but the fallen state of the Hindu civilization could be explained by the fact that centuries of Moorish tyranny had corrupted the character of these Aryans, producing parasitic and unmartial rajas. India was thus caught not in a barbaric but a savage state, or as Sir Henry Maine had it, in a state of arrested development.

The relative wildness or timidity of subject peoples was therefore a reflection of the ambiguity of the colonial ideology of race as blood and the unstable association of national, imperial, and racial identities. I have tried to suggest in this chapter that an important way in which racial differences were being articulated in the late eighteenth and early nineteenth centuries was through new definitions of the colonial domestic order. The regulation of both casual sex and marital union between Indians and Britons was a response to the uncertainties of a creole or mestizo society on the American or West Indian model that could not be tolerated in a colonial dependency of great national-imperial and strategic importance. In such a situation, the figure of the Indo-Briton could stand only as a dispossessed and marginal figure. In this, the history of colonial India can be placed alongside the history of colonial North America in a previous century, where, despite the long existence of a "sexual frontier"[180] between colonists and Native Americans, the idea of racial segregation emerged triumphant despite all the evidence pointing to persistent if furtive crossings of racial boundaries. In order to locate this conceptual and physical divide, we need more attentive studies of the early years of colonial encounter in India when crucial links were established between the search for paternalist authority, domestic order, sexual moderation, and national exclusivity, anticipating stable and enduring templates of colonial and imperial belonging.

Afterword

T he union of England and India, John Seely told Cambridge under-
graduates during his lectures of 1881 and 1882, was the "strangest,
most curious, and perhaps most instructive chapter of English history."[1] This
was an empire, similar to that of Rome, where the English were not only the
rulers but also an "educating and civilizing race." Yet the conquest of India
and the subjugation of two hundred million by an English trading company
was "strange and anomalous."[2] "Our acquisition of India was done blindly,"
thought Seely; nothing of such significance ever done by Englishmen "was
done so unintentionally, so accidentally, as the conquest of India."[3] Seely's
observations recapitulate an age-old paradox, one that still haunts the historical memory of Britain's Indian adventure: India, the most important
acquisition of the British Empire, did not in fact belong to it.

This anomaly bears directly on the question of Britain's identity during
the period of imperial expansion discussed here, a question that was not settled
even during Victorian times. Thus Seely and his contemporaries referred to the
empire as a "Greater Britain" whose constituency could be subject to debate.
New revisions in the history of collective, national reckoning seem to suggest
that we have indeed neglected many conflicted aspects in the development
of the empire-nation that date back to the century of the Seven Years War,
the War of American Independence, Anglo-French rivalry, and Britain's
Indian conquest. Linda Colley has noted the complexities of national sentiment and its curious relationship to other modes of political and social
accountability during these decades of military crisis.[4] Expressions of righteous patriotism were common enough on occasion, especially when the
enemy was France or Jacobinism. The American revolutionary war, which did

witness an outburst of national feeling and animated English wrath against treasonous, colonial Americans, however, led to other, more disputed and complex questions of who could be an Englishman in the colonies and who could not.[5]

Much closer to home, the question of Ireland and Scotland and the intimate histories of the loss and reconfiguration of nationality within the substantive core of the First Empire before the loss of Britain's American possessions still needs further elaboration. Some of this difficulty follows, as David Armitage has rightly identified, from the myopic, insular, and largely Anglocentric historiographical legacy of the British Empire.[6] Accession of the Highlands, along with the acculturation of the Scottish Lowlands, and the incorporation and disenfranchisement of Ireland are episodes of the imperial history that are only now being considered as integral to the larger Atlantic empire.

It is clear that selective historical narratives of these constituent parts have been crucial to the relationship between England and Great Britain. For Seely's generation, one was the natural extension of the other: imperial expansion as a sign of the organic maturity of the English nation-state. Nevertheless, the essential character of the British Empire at its greatest extent was English. Seely regarded the historical passage from England to a "Greater Britain" as that of a boy attaining manhood but fundamentally the same entity: "For the original England remains distinctly visible at the heart of Greater Britain, she still forms a distinct organism complete in herself, and she has not even formed the habit of thinking of her colonies and her Indian Empire along with herself."[7]

A reconsideration of Anglo-Scottish, Anglo-Irish, and even Anglo-American history seems to be vital to the excavation of the intricate striations that intersperse English and British ideational formations in the age of empire.[8] And yet the Anglo-Indian extension of the very same process, however marginal or abortive it may appear at first sight, has remained largely outside the purview of these considerations. The divisions of historiography, curiously enough, have remained in some respects close to the racial divides of the empire itself. At the end of the day native blood could not be admitted into British ranks in Hindustan, whereas even in the Scottish Highlands, English blood was seen as capable of converting the wild to civilized ways. During his tour of Scotland, undertaken not long after the suppression of the rebellions, Samuel Johnson, found the erasure of difference part of a natural historical process:

> Such are the effects of habitation among mountains, and such were the qualities of the
> Highlanders, while their rocks secluded them from the rest of mankind, and kept
> them an unaltered and discriminated race. They are now losing their distinctiveness,
> and hastening to mingle with the general community.[9]

This clearly was not possible in India.

It has indeed been suggested by some, as I discuss in Chapter 1, that the farthest reaches of the history of the empire-nation may be found in settlements tied to England through the kinship of language, blood, and culture. It is this very distinction, which is based on the idea that only a certain kind of colony inherited the critical and intimate aspects of the mother country, that has perpetuated the impression that the case of British India is an exception. Why this has been the case is best understood, as I have argued throughout, in the inherent limitations in the formation of singular identities: race, empire, and nation.

It is important for the imperial and even post-imperial historiography to maintain that India left little or no impression on Britain. The danger that Pitt had presented before Parliament in 1782—that corruption in the ranks in India was beginning to poison British politics and British senators were "no longer the representatives of British virtue but of the vices and pollutions of the East"—still lingers in the historical memory of empire.[10] Seely was confident that England had indeed been able to break the spell of India and had "stoutly refused to be influenced by her."[11] Much the same sentiment has recently been expressed in Lawrence James's popular history of the British Empire, where, once again, the pernicious influence of India on the British character during the early years of the Company is revisited. In the days of the East Indian fortune hunt, writes James: "it appeared that those responsible for India underwent a moral transformation, abandoning British habits of mind and codes of public behavior and embracing those of the subcontinent."[12] Such degradation was of course strenuously reversed in the subsequent decade.

It has not been the purpose of this book to argue that India did after all transform Britain's national character or moral fiber or to suggest that Indian history should somehow be repatriated to the larger history of the British Empire. It is rather to reflect on how the question of national identity, often treated as a discrete and unchanging substance, has led to some crucial blind spots in British-Indian historiography. Britishness, if there was ever such a thing, we cannot presume to have been simply a primordial inheritance but a conscious creation, based on difference, whose criteria must have shifted throughout history and which was shaped in the period under review according to popular reckoning of patriotism and empire. We have to investigate much more carefully, therefore, the murky terrain between domestic ideas of the imperial nation and expatriate formations of national-imperial exclusivity. In this the Indian archive remains of great value. The historical contemporaneity of Britain's Indian exploits with the aftermath of Culloden and the suppression of the clans in the Scottish Highland, as well as the United Irish Rebellion of 1798 and the 1802 Union with Britain, suggests at the very least that the Indian experience belongs to the same field of inquiry. Identities generated in the struggle over the Gaelic Pale thus should be peculiarly instructive to historians of India.[13] The unread correspondence between colonial metropolitan experiences of Dublin, Edinburgh, Calcutta, and Madras could well be the task of future histories.

Confronted with the responsibility of ruling India, the British began to regroup into tightly knit expatriate communities. This had been to a certain extent the effect of narrow patronage that the directors of the Company had tacitly encouraged over the years. After the era of reform under Cornwallis and especially during Wellesley's time, when the British-Indian army had fully secured the territory of the East India Company, Britons began to settle down. With the regular education and training of civil servants at Haileybury, and also with a larger number of men from public life resorting to India, a close tie began to develop between service families.[14] This was in effect comparable to that in the military, where service and life at the cantonment, as new research suggests, created a garrison state to an extent set apart from the rest of British India, especially subsequent to 1857.[15] As Britons closed their ranks to native society, an expatriate, inward society of a new, middling sort would emerge in India whose allegiance and association to England were often tenuous and whose relationship to India was rigidly encoded.

High rates of mortality, injury, and disability in the army, and also the incidence of mental illness, point toward a community in semipermanent exile. The strains of India might have disrupted the emotional stability of some unfortunate Britons. It is of course difficult to judge whether such cases were more frequent than in other colonies. But records of the Beardsmore facility in Calcutta and the Madras Hospital, along with those of Pembroke House in Hackney, Warburton's White House in Bethnal Green, and the Holly House in Hayton, show that among the institutionalized were soldiers, gunners, army captains, private soldiers, storekeepers, and civil servants.[16] Until the year 1819, insane patients had been detained in Indian hospitals, but with a rise in numbers of the mentally unstable, the Court of Directors arranged to have Dr. Rees of Pembroke House, Hackney, place a majority of them in his asylum. The insane, it was directed, should not be kept in India any longer than was "absolutely necessary" and should be "sent home at once."[17]

It is in this context of a seemingly transient yet carefully regulated society, wary of its appearance to the people over which it ruled, that a distinct sense of Indian Britishness might have surfaced. Scattered literature at first glance suggests an elegiac tone in such articulation, conveying simply a sense of longing rather than vaunted assertions of race and civilization. This is perhaps best expressed in run-of-the-mill poetry such as *Lines Written in a British Burial Ground in India,* published in *Blackwood's Magazine* in 1821:

> No father here, beside the ancient church,
> May shew his sons their honour'd grandsire's tomb,
> Or point the spot where near that sacred dust
> Would he recline, his worldly labours done. . . .
> Behind yon shrubs, in corner verdant spread,
> Lies a crowd of nameless graves: the soldier there,
> Whose vigour pined before the Indian sun,
> Now uncomplaining sleeps. . . .[18]

War and death were perhaps the most common experiences that urged a sense of belonging. Thus also R. Farmer's *The Soldier: An Historical Poem,* lamenting the loss of Indian and English blood in war, expressed the ardor of empire:

> Nor these scenes alone must publish
> Britain's civilized rage;
> Tibet's mountains will proclaim it
> To the world's remotest age. . . .[19]

Sentiments of the imperial nation are indeed clues to the more enigmatic aspects of seemingly common identities. In this book, however, the emphasis has been overwhelmingly on the political nature of the national character, which simply cannot be understood without reference to the colonial state, its expression of sovereignty, and the forging of British India as a definitive geopolitical entity. The embodiment of difference according to the rules of gender, blood, and race, studied in some detail in these chapters, can thus be seen as also subject to forces within the same political field. How far a history of the Indian colonial experience contributes to a better understanding of Britain itself is a question that cannot be fully answered here; but a retrospect of its distant Indian empire implicates, if anything, the innermost episodes in the story of the island nation.

Notes

NOTES TO INTRODUCTION

1. Political letter, June 13, 1813, India Office Records (IOR) Home Miscellaneous (HM) 708, Part 1, pp. 132, 134.
2. Extract, political letter from Bengal, October 18, 1809, IOR, Board's Collections (BC), F/4/312, no. 7118.
3. Ibid.
4. Lord Lake to Wellesley, August 4, 1803, Kanpur, IOR, HM 485, p. 177.
5. Lord Lake to Wellesley (reply to secret official dispatch no. 4), August 8, 1803, Camp near Imlai, IOR, HM 485, pp. 191, 194.
6. Letter to His Majesty Shah Alam, October 8, 1803, IOR, HM 485, p. 398.
7. Ibid.
8. Extract, Bengal Public Consultations (BPC), October 10, 1809, IOR, BC, F/4/312, 7137.
9. Charges brought against Muhammad Bahadur Shah, ex-king of Delhi by Fred. J. Harriott, deputy judge-advocate general and government prosecutor, Delhi, January 27, 1858. See H. L. O. Garrett, ed., *The Trial of Muhammed Bahadur Shah,* Lahore: Punjab Government Records Office Publications, 1932, p. 2.
10. Translation of Sunnud (*sanad*) granted to Colonel Robert Clive, IOR, HM 191, p. 44.
11. Memorandum respecting the claims of the king of Delhi, IOR, HM 708 (Part 1), p. 53.
12. Ibid. p. 91.
13. See the account of presents sent by His Majesty Shah Alam to His Majesty King George by the hands of Lord Clive and delivered to Captain Swinton by Munir-ud-dowlah, IOR, HM 134, p. 123. Also, the letter of Emperor Shah Alam to Sir Elijah Impey, March 5, 1777, IOR, HM 134, pp. 127–132.
14. Extract, political letter, June 13, 1823, IOR, HM 708, pp. 139–140.
15. Ibid; extract, political letter of September 1, 1825.
16. Ibid; extract, political letter of July 3, 1828, p. 141.
17. Ibid., p. 142.
18. *Sketches of India,* pp. 103–104.
19. Ibid. p. 110.
20. J. Z. Holwell, *Interesting Historical Events Relative to the Province of Bengal and the Empire of Hindoostan,* 2nd ed., London: Becket and De Hondt, 1766, p. 181.
21. I have discussed some of these issues at much greater length in *Empire of Free Trade: The East India Company and the Making of the Colonial Marketplace,* Philadelphia, PA: University of Pennsylvania Press, 1998, pp. 80–81.
22. "Extracts concerning the constitution of the Empire of Indostan," extract of letter from Bengal December 29, 1759, IOR, HM 191, pp. 111–112.
23. Ibid. p. 113.

24. Speech, February 27, 1769. See Sir Henry Cavendish's *Debates of the House of Commons during the Thirteenth Parliament of Great Britain,* vol. 1, London: Longman, Orme, Brown, Green & Longmans, 1840–1843, p. 261.

25. Letter of Clive and the Select Committee to the Court of Directors, September 30, 1765, cited in Walter Kelly Firminger, ed., *The Fifth Report from the Select Committee of the House of Commons on the Affairs of the East India Company,* Calcutta: R. Cambray & Co., 1917, vol. 1, p. viii.

26. Speech on the opening the impeachment of Warren Hastings, February 15, 1788, *Writings and Speeches of Edmund Burke,* ed. by P. J. Marshall, Oxford: Clarendon Press, 1991, vol. 6, p. 281.

27. Ibid., pp. 281–282.

28. See Huw V. Bowen, "A Question of Sovereignty? The Bengal Land Revenue Issue, 1765–67," *Journal of Imperial and Commonwealth History,* 16, 1988, pp. 155–171.

29. Letter of February 23, 1829, IOR, HM 708, p. 145.

30. Letter to the Board of Control, October 11, 1831, Bedford Square, London, IOR, HM 708, p. 155.

31. Letter of R. M. Martin, March 3, 1834, Waterloo Place, London, IOR L/PJ/1 17, no. 3.

32. Roy to Charles Grant, President of the India Board, November 7, 1831, Bedford Square, London, IOR, HM 708, pp. 183–184.

33. Ibid., p. 190.

34. Ibid., p. 191.

35. Ibid., p. 195.

36. Ibid., p. 198.

37. Letter of the India Board (Board of Control), December 1, 1831, IOR, HM 708, p. 239.

38. William Cavell, Secretary, Political Department on Rammohan Roy's letter to Grant, November 15, 1831, IOR, HM 708, p. 224.

39. Ibid. pp. 226–227.

40. On the circumstances surrounding Rammohan Roy's death, see Upendra Nath Ball, *Rammohun Roy: A Study of His Life, Works and Thoughts,* Calcutta: U. Ray, 1933, pp. 319–322.

41. Roy to Charles Grant, IOR, HM 708, p. 197.

42. See Hallam's passages on the execution of Mary, Queen of Scotland. Henry Hallam, *The Constitutional History of England from the Accession of Henry II to the Death of George II,* 5th (London) ed., New York: Harper and Brothers, 1870, p. 99.

43. Ibid., p. 100.

44. See the Copy Book of Letters Issued to Governor General Warren Hastings by the Resident at the Durbar (court) at Murshidabad, Bengal in the intervening period of September 29, 1772–March 2, 1774, vol. 1, p. 134, West Bengal State Archives, Calcutta (WBSA).

45. Firminger, *The Fifth Report,* pp. xiv–xvi.

46. Letter of Thomas Kelsall to John Cartier, May 13, 1770, Dacca, in Copy Book of Letters of the Resident at the Durbar of Murshidabad, Bengal, December 27, 1769–October 1, 1770, WBSA, p. 64.

47. Extract, political letter from Bengal September 2, 1807, IOR, BC, 1810–1811, vol. 297, F/4/297, no. 6851.

48. John W. Kaye and G. B. Malleson, *Kaye's and Malleson's History of the Indian Mutiny,* 2nd edition, London: 1892, p. 4.

49. Walter Bagehot, *The English Constitution,* Oxford: Oxford University Press [1867], 2001, p. 7.

50. Ibid., pp. 9, 44.

51. See, for instance, George L. Mosse, *The Struggle for Sovereignty in England: From the Reign of Queen Elizabeth to the Petition of Right,* New York: Octagon Books, 1968, pp. 6–7.

52. See F. W. Maitland, *The Constitutional History of England: A Course of Lectures Delivered,* Cambridge: Cambridge University Press, 1920, pp. 298–300.

53. On the rise of neo-Whiggism, see John Kenyon, *The History Men: The Historical Profession in England since the Renaissance,* Pittsburgh, PA: University of Pittsburgh Press, 1984, pp. 40–41.

54. Kenyon, *History Men,* pp. 44–45.

55. Alexander Dow, "A Inquiry into the State of Bengal with a Plan for Restoring that Province to its Former Prosperity and Splendor," in *The History of Hindostan,* London: Vernor and Hood, Cuthell and Martin, J. Walker, Wynne and Scholey, John Debrett, Blacks and Parry, T. Kay, and J. Asperne, 1803, p. xcviii.

56. Attributed to Samuel Davis, district judge and agent to the governor-general in Benares in north India.

57. *Debates at the East India House, during the Negociation for a Renewal of the East India Company's Charter, Held at Various Courts of Proprietors of East-India Stock in the Year 1813,* London: Black, Parry and Company, 1813, vol. 1, pp. 26–27.

58. Firminger, *The Fifth Report,* p. viii.

59. Ibid., p. x.

60. "Lord Cornwallis Receiving the Sons of Tipoo Saib," in *A Descriptive Catalogue of a Few Asiatic Subjects, Illustrative of the Agriculture, Arts, and Manufactures of Hindoostan, Painted by A. W. Devis,* Westminster: G. Smeeton, 1821, pp. 1–2.
61. Ibid., pp. 3–4.
62. Ibid., p. 14.
63. Mark Wilks, *Historical Sketches of the South of India in an Attempt to Trace the History of Mysoor from the Origin of the Hindoo Government of that State to the Extinction of the Mohammedan Dynasty in 1799,* vol. 3, London: Longman, Hurst, Rees, Orme, and Brown, 1817, p. 449.
64. John Dryden, *Aureng-Zebe,* ed. by Frederick M. Link, Lincoln, NE: University of Nebraska Press, 1971, p. 52.
65. "Histoire de Nader Chah, Connu Sous le Nom de Thamass Kuli Khan, Empereur de Perse," in *The Works of William Jones,* vol. 11, Delhi: Agam Prakashan [1799], 1980, pp. v–vi.
66. John Malcolm, *Persia: A Poem,* 2nd ed., London: John Murray, 1814, pp. 6–7.
67. John Malcolm, *The History of Persia from the Most Early Period to the Present Time: Containing an Account of the Religion, Government, Usages, and Character of the Inhabitants of that Kingdom,* vol. 2, rev. ed., London: John Murray, 1829, p. 23.
68. On the popularization of George III and British nationalism see Linda Colley, "The Apotheosis of George III: Loyalty, Royalty and the British Nation 1760–1820," *Past and Present* 102, 1984, pp. 94–129; Colley, "Whose Nation? Class and National Consciousness in Britain, 1750–1830," *Past and Present* 113, 1986, pp. 97–117. See also Colley, *Britons: Forging the Nation 1707–1837,* New Haven, CT: Yale University Press, 1992, pp. 195–236; and James J. Sack, *From Jacobite to Conservative: Reaction and Orthodoxy in Britain, c. 1760–1832,* Cambridge, UK: Cambridge University Press, 1993.
69. See Ernest Kantorowicz, *The King's Two Bodies: A Study in Medieval Political Theology,* Princeton, NJ: Princeton University Press, 1957; also John Cannon, "The Survival of British Monarchy," Prothero Lecture, July 3, 1985, *Transactions of the Royal Historical Society* 36, 1986, pp. 143–164.
70. On the adaptability of royal institutions of the later eighteenth century, see Marilyn Morris, *The British Monarchy and the French Revolution,* New Haven, CT, and London: Yale University Press, 1998, pp. 187, 192–193 and *passim.* For a general overview of the literature on the salience of European monarchies, see Cynthia Herrup, "Beyond Personality and Pomp: Recent Works on Early Modern Monarchies," *Journal of British Studies* 28, 1989.
71. Bernard S. Cohn, "Representing Authority in Victorian India," in *An Anthropologist among the Historians and Other Essays,* Delhi: Oxford University Press, 1990, pp. 633–634.
72. Henry St. George Tucker, *Memorials of Indian Government,* ed. by John William Kaye, London: Richard Bentley, 1853, p. 484.
73. Ibid.
74. Sir John Malcom, quoted in the *Memoir of Captain Dalton, Defender of Trichinopoly, 1752–1753* by Charles Dalton, London: W. H. Allen, 1886, p. 44, emphasis added.
75. Michael Duffy, *The Englishman and the Foreigner,* Cambridge: Chadwyck-Healey, 1986, pp. 31–39.
76. Eric Stokes, *The English Utilitarians and India,* Oxford: Oxford University Press, 1959, pp. xi, xiii.
77. J. R. Seely, *The Expansion of England,* ed. John Gross, Chicago and London: University of Chicago Press, 1971, p. 196.
78. Ibid.
79. Cited in "Notice of the Life, Writings and Speeches of Sir James Mackintosh," in James Mackintosh, *History of the Revolution in England in 1688,* London: Longman, Rees, Orme et al., 1834, pp. lxiv–lxv. Italics mine.
80. Anthony Pagden, *Lords of All the World: Ideologies of Empire in Spain, Britain and France c. 1500–c. 1800,* New Haven, CT, and London: Yale University Press, 1995, pp. 6–9.
81. David Armitage, *The Ideological Origins of the British Empire,* Cambridge and New York: Cambridge University Press, 2000, pp. 11–12.
82. For some more recent examples of this approach, see Kathleen Wilson, *The Sense of the People: Politics, Culture and Imperialism in England, 1715–1785,* Cambridge, UK: Cambridge University Press, 1995; also, Madhavi Kale, *Fragments of Empire: Capital, Slavery, and Indian Indentured Labor Migration in the British Caribbean,* Philadelphia, PA: University of Pennsylvania Press, 1998.
83. See Homi K. Bhabha "Signs Taken for Wonders," in *Location of Culture,* London & New York: Routledge, 1994, p. 113.
84. Ibid.
85. Frantz Fanon, *Black Skin, White Masks,* New York: Grove and Weidenfeld, 1967. For an extension of the psychological dimensions of the binary, colonizer and colonized, in the context of colonial India see Ashish Nandy's provocative arguments in *The Intimate Enemy: Loss and Recovery of the Self under Colonialism,* Delhi: Oxford University Press, 1983.

86. See, for examples, Catherine Hall, "Histories, Empires, and the Post-Colonial Moment," in *The Post-Colonial Question: Common Skies, Divided Horizons,* ed. Ian Chambers and Lidia Curtis, New York: Routledge, 1996; Antoinette Burton, "Who Needs the Nation? Interrogating 'British' History," *Journal of Historical Sociology,* September 1997, vol. 10, no. 3, pp. 227–248; and also her *At the Heart of Empire: Indians and the Colonial Encounter in Late-Victorian Britain,* Berkeley, CA: University of California Press, 1998; Mrinalini Sinha, *Colonial Masculinity: The "Manly Englishman" and the "Effeminate Bengali" in the Late Nineteenth Century,* Manchester: Manchester University Press, 1995; Philippa Levine, "Re-reading the 1890s: Venereal Disease as 'Constitutional Crisis' in Britain and British India," *Journal of Asian Studies* 55, no. 3, 1996, pp. 585–612; Jenny Sharpe, *Allegories of Empire: The Figure of Woman in the Colonial Text,* Minneapolis, MN: University of Minnesota Press, 1993; and Ann Stoler, *Race and the Education of Desire,* Durham, NC: Duke University Press, 1995.

87. Philip Corrigan and Derek Sayer, *The Great Arch: English State Formation as Cultural Revolution,* London: Basil Blackwell, 1985.

88. Apart from Percival Spear's somewhat dated *The Nabobs: A Study of the Social Life of the English in Eighteenth Century India,* London: Curzon Press, 1963, and Kenneth Ballhatchet's *Race, Sex and Class under the Raj: Imperial Attitudes and Policies and Their Critics,* New York: St. Martin's Press, 1980, there have been surprisingly few comprehensive histories of the social relationship between Indians and the English in the period prior to the maturity of British rule. Francis Hutchin's *Illusion of Permanence: British Imperialism in India,* Princeton, NJ: Princeton University Press, 1967, is largely focused on the nineteenth-century transformation of British attitudes towards India, while Thomas Metcalf's more recent *Ideologies of the Raj,* Cambridge and New York: Cambridge University Press, 1995, is an useful overview of recent research that deals more substantially with the Raj in the nineteenth century.

89. Linda Colley, *Britons: Forging the Nation, 1707–1837,* New Haven, CT: Yale University Press, 1992. On the debate over the geographical insularity of British history, see J. G. A. Pocock, "The Limits and Divisions of British History: In Search of the Unknown Subject," *American Historical Review,* vol. 87, no. 2, 1982, pp. 311–336; and also Bernard Bailyn, "The Challenge of Modern Historiography," *American Historical Review,* vol. 87, no. 1, 1982, pp. 1–24. None of these consider India seriously as an apposite site for a history truly British in content. For a summary dismissal of a continuity between the domestic and imperial history of Britain, see John M. Mackenzie, *Orientalism: History, Theory and the Arts,* Manchester: Manchester University Press, 1995.

90. Colley, *Britons: Forging the Nation,* pp. 144–145.

91. See Cohn, "The British in Benares: A Nineteenth Century Colonial Society," in *An Anthropologist among the Historians,* p. 458.

92. On this question see Elie Kedourie, *Nationalism,* 4th expanded ed., Oxford: Blackwell, 1993; Ernest Gellner, *Nations and Nationalism,* Ithaca, NY: Cornell University Press, 1983; Benedict Anderson, *Imagined Communities,* London and New York: Verso, 1911, reprint 1992.; Partha Chatterjee, *The Nation and Its Fragments: Colonial and Postcolonial Histories,* Princeton, NJ: Princeton University Press, 1993.

NOTES TO CHAPTER 1

1. J. G. A. Pocock, "The Limits and Divisions of British History: In Search of the Unknown Subject," *American Historical Review,* vol. 87, no. 2, 1982, pp. 311–336. See also Bernard Bailyn, "The Challenge of Modern Historiography," *American Historical Review,* vol. 87, no. 1, 1982, pp. 1–24. More recently, similar charges against the insularity of the historiography of the British empire have been leveled by David Armitage, *Ideological Origins of the British Empire,* "Introduction."

2. It is important to emphasize that the historical *formalism* at work in the colonial conception of rule in India derives from a wider of field of dominating endeavors in which the Anglo-Saxon nation contributed as an ensemble of signs and practices, subordinating nations within the generic Great Britain—the Welsh, the Scots, and the Irish. See, for instance, John Gillingham, "The Beginning of English Imperialism," *Journal of Historical Sociology,* vol. 5, no. 4, 1992, pp. 392–409; G. E. Aylmer, "The Peculiarities of the English State," *Journal of Historical Sociology,* vol. 3, no. 2, 1990, pp. 91–108; Rees Davies, "The English State and 'Celtic' Peoples," *Journal of Historical Sociology,* vol. 6, no. 1, 1993, pp. 1–14.

3. C. A. Bayly, *Imperial Meridian: The British Empire and the World,* London and New York: Longman, 1989, pp. 249–250.

4. Philip Corrigan and Derek Sayer, *The Great Arch: English State Formation as Cultural Revolution,* Oxford: Basil Blackwell, 1985.

5. For comparative study, see D. K. Fieldhouse, *The Colonial Empires: A Comparative Survey from the Eighteenth Century,* New York: Delacorte Press, 1967. Chartered companies have had a long and multiplicit history, leading to plantations and colonies as much as to trade, and in the nineteenth century for the direct purpose of colonial administration, as in the case of the Imperial British East Africa Company. See also Percival Griffiths, *A License to Trade: The History of English Chartered Companies,* London and Tonbridge, UK: Ernest Benn, 1974.

6. See Holden Furber, *Henry Dundas, First Viscount Melville, 1742–1811: Political Manager of Scotland, Statesman, Administrator of British India,* London: Oxford University Press, 1931, pp. 29–31

7. Suresh Chandra Ghosh, *The Social Condition of the British Community in Bengal 1757–1800,* Leiden, Holland: E. J. Brill, 1970, pp. 50–51.

8. Furber, *Henry Dundas,* p. 62.

9. Michael Fry, *The Dundas Despotism,* Edinburgh: Edinburgh University Press, 1992, p. 119.

10. See Adam Anderson, *An Historical and Chronological Deduction of the Origin of Commerce, from the Earliest Accounts Containing an History of the Great Commercial Interests of the British Empire,* vol. 3, London: J. White and Company, 1801, p. 3.

11. Edmund Burke, cited in a contemporary pamphlet, *Chartered Rights,* London: A. McPherson, n.d., p. 7.

12. *The Speech of Mr. Hardinge as Counsel for the Directors of the East India Company,* London: J. Stockdale, 1784, p. 10.

13. Thomas Pownall, *The Right, Interest, and Duty of the State as Concerned in the Affairs of the East Indies,* London: S. Bladon, 1773, p. 14.

14. Ibid., p. 47.

15. For references, see Huw V. Bowen, *Revenue and Reform: The Indian Problem in British Politics, 1757–1773,* Cambridge, UK: Cambridge University Press, 1991, pp. 22–26.

16. William Cobbett, "To the Thinking People of England on the Affairs of the East India Company," published in the *Political Register,* January, 1813; see John M. Cobbett and James P. Cobbett, eds., *Selections from Cobbett's Political Works,* London: Anne Cobbett, 1835, vol. 4, pp. 170.

17. Ibid., pp. 170–171.

18. Ibid., p. 171.

19. Dame Lucy Sutherland, *East India Company in Eighteenth Century Politics,* Oxford: Oxford University Press, 1952, p. 78.

20. I refer particularly to Philip Lawson, *The East India Company: A History,* London & New York: Longman, 1993. Also, Bowen, *Revenue and Reform.*

21. Quoted in Bowen, *Revenue and Reform,* p. 28.

22. Ibid., p. 15.

23. T. H. Breen, "Ideology and Nationalism on the Eve of the American Revolution: Revisions *Once More* in Need of Revising," *Journal of American History,* no. 84, June 1997, p. 28. In addition, see Dror Wahrman, "The English Problem of Identity in the American Revolution," *American Historical Review,* vol. 106, no. 4, October 2001, pp.1236–1262; also Kathleen Wilson, *The Sense of the People,* and Linda Colley, *Britons.*

24. On this, see Derek Sayer, "A Notable Administration: English State Formation and the Rise of Capitalism," *American Journal of Sociology,* vol. 97, No. 5, March 1992, pp. 1382–1415.

25. See IOR, HM, vol. 94, p. 160, letter from George Pigot, Stringer Lawrence, Henry Powney, Robert Orme, William Perceval, John Smith, Charles Bourchier, to Admiral Charles Watson, Fort St. George, Madras, August 20, 1756.

26. IOR, HM, vol. 94, p. 160. Copy of letter from Clive, Fort St. George, October 11, 1756 to Secret Committee of the East India Company.

27. Richard, Marquess Wellesley in his dispatch to the Court of Directors of the East India Company, Fort William, Calcutta, July 9, 1800, cited in George Bennet, ed., *The Concept of Empire: Burke to Atlee,* London: Adam and Charles Black, 1953, p. 64.

28. Anon., *Thoughts on the Present East India Bill: Passed into a Law, August 1784,* London: John Stockdale, 1784, pp. 3–4.

29. Nathaniel Brassy Halhed, *Letters of Detector on the Reports of the Select Committee of the House of Commons, Appointed to Consider How the British Possessions in the East Indies May Be Held and Governed with the Greatest Security and Happiness of the Natives May Best Be Promoted.* London: s. n., 1782, pp. 1–3.

30. Ibid., p. 2.

31. William Cobbett, "To the Thinking People of England on the Affairs of the East India Company," published in the *Political Register,* January, 1813; see John M. Cobbett and James P. Cobbett, eds., *Selections from Cobbett's Political Works,* London: Anne Cobbett, 1835, vol. 4, pp. 169–170.

32. Adam Smith, quoted in Anon., *A Demonstration of the Necessity and Advantages of a Free Trade to the East Indies,* London: C. Chapple, 1807, pp. 134.

33. *A Demonstration of the Necessity and Advantages of a Free Trade,* pp. 131–132.

34. IOR, HM, vol. 92, p. 133. Extract of letter to the Select Committee, May 17, 1766.

35. Philip Corrigan and Derek Sayer, *The Great Arch,* pp. 105–106.

36. J. Steuart, *Inquiry into the Principles of Political Oeconomy,* Edinburgh: Oliver and Boyd [1767], 1966, p. 16.

37. John Bennet, *The National Merchant: or Discourses on Commerce and Colonies,* London: 1736, p. 6. This very insight is repeated in a popular school textbook authored by James Mill, Jeremy Bentham, Samuel Ricardo, and J. S. Mill, *Elements of Political Economy.* See Corrigan and Sayer, *The Great Arch,* p. 218, fn. 6.

38. Keith Tribe, "The 'Histories' of Economic Discourse," *Economy and Society,* vol. 6, 1977, p. 326. See also his *Genealogies of Capitalism,* London: Macmillan, 1981.

39. See Adam Smith, *Lectures on Justice, Police, Revenue, and Arms: Delivered in the University of Glasgow by Adam Smith, Reported by a Student in 1763,* ed. Edwin Cannan, Kelley, and Millman, 1956, esp. 'Editor's Introduction,' pp. xi–xxxiv.

40. *The Writings and Speeches of Edmund Burke, Volume Five, India: Madras and Bengal, 1774–1785,* ed. by P. J. Marshall, Oxford: Clarendon Press, 1981, pp. 306–307.

41. Uday Singh Mehta, *Liberalism and Empire: A Study in Nineteenth Century British Liberal Thought,* Chicago: University of Chicago Press, 1999, p. 159.

42. This has also been acknowledged by critics who tend otherwise to caution against attributing too much agency to the East India Company in the political transformation of India. For a stimulating discussion, see C. A. Bayly, "The British Military-Fiscal State and Indigenous Resistance: India 1750–1820," in C. A. Bayly, *Origins of Nationality in South Asia: Patriotism and Ethical Government in the Making of Modern India,* Delhi: Oxford University Press, 1998, pp. 241–243.

43. Ronald Meek, *Social Science and the Ignoble Savage,* Cambridge, UK: Cambridge University Press, 1976, pp. 1–4.

44. Ibid., pp. 104–105.

45. Anonymous, *The Art of Governing a Wife,* 1722, p. 11.

46. John Cartwright, *An Appeal on the Subject of the English Constitution,* Boston and London: C. Stainpank, J. Johnson, 1797, pp. 62, 69.

47. Leonore Davidoff and Catherine Hall, *Family Fortunes: Men and Women of the English Middle Class, 1780–1850,* Chicago: University of Chicago Press, 1991, pp. 229–230.

48. Lawrence Stone, *The Family, Sex and Marriage in England, 1500–1800,* New York: Harper & Row, 1979, p. 146.

49. Thomas Pownall, *The Right, Interest, and Duty, of the State as Concerned in the Affairs of the East Indies,* London: S. Bladon, 1773, p. 19.

50. Ibid., p. 25.

51. Ibid., pp. 38–39. The right to possess unclaimed territory as the prerogative of an elect nation had precedence in earlier English encounters with "Indians" in New England, where the settlers were able to draw upon previous sociologies of wild, pastoral, unpropertied people—the Irish near home. See James Muldoon, "The Indian as Irishman," *Essex Institute Historical Collections,* vol. 3, no. 4, October 1975, pp. 267–289.

52. Ibid., p. 40.

53. Stephen Greenblatt, *Marvelous Possessions: The Wonder of the New World,* Chicago: University of Chicago Press, 1991, pp. 58–60.

54. Abbe Raynal, *Philosophical and Political History of the Settlements and Trade of the Europeans in the East and West Indies,* trans. J. O. Justamond, vol. 1, 2nd ed., reprint, New York: Negro Universities Press, 1969, p. 215.

55. Alexander Dalrymple, *A General View of the East India Company,* London: s.n., 1772, pp. 19–21.

56. See James Walvin, *England, Slaves and Freedom, 1776–1838,* Jackson, MS, and London: University Press of Mississippi, 1986, pp. 22–23.

57. James Walvin, *Slaves and Slavery: The British Colonial Experience,* Manchester and New York: Manchester University Press, 1992, p. 39.

58. A. O. Lovejoy, *The Great Chain of Being,* New York and London: Harper & Row, 1960, pp. 183, 227.

59. Lovejoy, p. 234, Linnaeus himself wrote *The Cousins of Man,* published posthumously.

60. It shall suffice here to refer to Foucault, *The Order of Things: An Archaeology of the Human Sciences,* New York: Vintage, 1973, pp. 128–131.

61. Anthony Pagden, *The Fall of Natural Man,* Cambridge, UK: Cambridge University Press, 1986, pp. 32–33, 49.
62. Anthony J. Barker, *The African Link,* London: Frank Cass, 1978, pp. 59, 66.
63. Ibid., p. 53.
64. For a fuller discussion see Philip Curtin, *The Image of Africa: British Ideas and Action, 1780–1850,* Madison, WI: University of Wisconsin Press, 1964, esp. Chap. 2, "The Africans' 'Place in Nature,' " *passim,* and pp. 38–46.
65. Ibid., pp. 363–375.
66. See Rozina Visram, *Ayahs, Lascars and Princes: Indians in Britain 1700–1947,* London: Pluto Press, 1986, pp. 13–15.
67. Ibid.
68. John Beames, *Memoirs of a Bengal Civilian,* London: Chatto & Windus, 1961, reprint, Delhi: South Asia Books, 1984, p. 64.
69. Muldoon, "The Indian as Irishman," pp. 267–268.
70. Noel Ignatiev, *How the Irish Became White,* New York and London: Routledge, 1995, pp. 34–59.
71. Ranajit Guha, *A Rule of Property for Bengal: An Essay on the Idea of the Permanent Settlement,* Paris: Mouton, 1963, pp. 98–99, 125.
72. Luke Scrafton, *Reflections on the Government &c. of Indostan: With a Short Sketch of the History of Bengal from the Year 1739 to 1756; and an Account of English Affairs to 1758,* London: Richardson and Clark, 1763, p. 17.
73. Ibid.
74. Ibid., p. 30.
75. Minute of John Shore, dated June 18, 1789, respecting the Permanent Settlement of the lands in the Bengal Province, in Walter Kelly Firminger, ed., *The Fifth Report from the Select Committee of the House of Commons on the Affairs of the East India Company,* Calcutta: R. Cambray & Co., 1917, vol. 2, app. 1, p. 1.
76. Ibid.
77. "Murray papers on the revenues of Bengal," IOLR, HM, vol. 68, p. 707.
78. Speech on Bengal Judicature Bill, June 27, 1781, *The Writings and Speeches of Edmund Burke,* vol. 5, p. 141.
79. Burke, Speech on Bengal Judicature Bill.
80. Robert Orme, *Historical Fragments of the Mogul Empire,* 1782, reprint, New Delhi: Associated Publishing House, 1974, p. 275. It is important to point out the irony of such observations as varieties of 'unfree labor' persisted in England through the nineteenth century and beyond. Compare D. Simon, 'Master and Servant,' in J. Saville, ed., *Democracy and the Labour Movement,* London: Lawrence and Wishart, 1954; and P. R. D. Corrigan 'Feudal Relics or Capitalist Monuments?' in *Sociology,* 11, 1977, pp. 35–63.
81. William Watts, *Memoirs of the Revolution in Bengal,* reprint, Calcutta: K. P. Bagchi [1760], 1988, p. 3.
82. Leonard Krieger, *An Essay on the Theory of Enlightened Despotism,* Chicago and London: University of Chicago Press, 1975, p. 49.
83. Adam Smith, *Lectures on Justice, Police, Revenue, and Arms,* p. 105.
84. Ibid., pp. 107–108.
85. John Brewer, *Sinews of Power,* New York: Alfred A. Knopf, 1989, p. 199.
86. *A Demonstration of the Necessity and Advantages,* pp. 105–106.
87. On this point, see Huw V. Bowen, "A Question of Sovereignty? The Bengal Land Revenue Issue, 1765–67," *Journal of Imperial and Commonwealth History,* 16, 1988, pp. 155–176.
88. Anderson, Adam, *An Historical and Chronological Deduction of the Origin of Commerce,* vol. 3, p. 350.
89. E. P. Thompson, *Customs in Common,* New York: New Press, 1993, pp. 170–175.
90. Thomas Law, *Sketch of Some Late Arrangements and a View of the Rising Resources in Bengal,* London: John Stockdale, 1792, p. 127.
91. *Sovereignty of the Law: Selections from Blackstone's Commentaries on the Laws of England,* Gareth Jones, ed., Toronto: University of Toronto Press, 1973, p. 118. This, for Blackstone, was a form of patriarchal authority: that of a husband (a petty baron) over his wife.
92. Marketplace reform produced far reaching changes in the relationship between traditional political authority and redistribution of resources within Indian society. See Sudipta Sen, *Empire of Free Trade: The East India Company and the Making of the Colonial Marketplace,* Philadelphia, PA: University of Pennsylvania Press, 1998.
93. T. H. Colebrooke, *Remarks on the Present State of the Husbandry and Commerce of Bengal,* Calcutta: s.n., 1795, p. 48.

94. Derek Sayer, "A Notable Administration," p. 1409.
95. Thompson, *Customs in Common,* p. 175.
96. Abbe Raynal, *Philosophical and Political History of the Settlements,* p. 443.
97. Burke in the speech on the Secret Committee, April 30, 1781. See *The Writings and Speeches of Edmund Burke,* vol. 5, p. 137.
98. Cited by Thomas Law, *Sketch of Some Late Arrangements,* p. xiii.
99. Seid Gholam Hossein Khan, *The Seir Mutaqherin or Review of Modern Times,* 1789, reprint, Lahore: Oriental Publishers and Booksellers, 1975, pp. 162–164.
100. Thomas Pownall, *The Right, Interest, and Duty, of the State,* pp. 44–45.
101. William Cobbet in the *Political Register,* April 16, 1808, cited in George Bennet, *The Concept of Empire,* p. 64.
102. See the debate on the "State of Affairs in India" of April 5, 1805 in T. C. Hansard, ed., *The Parliamentary Debates, from the Year 1803 to the Present Time,* London: Longman, Hurst, Rees, Orme, Brown etc., 1805, vol. 4, p. 251.
103. John Brewer, *Sinews of Power,* pp. 91–92.
104. Michael J. Braddick, *The Nerves of State: Taxation and the Financing of the English State, 1558–1714,* Manchester and New York: Manchester University Press; New York: St. Martin's Press, 1996, pp. 91–103; see also Jonathan Scott, *England's Troubles: Seventeenth-Century English Political Instability in European Context,* Cambridge, UK, and New York: Cambridge University Press, 2000, pp. 399–400; c.f. Brewer, *Sinews of Power,* p. 38.

NOTES TO CHAPTER 2

1. Much of the details of James Mackintosh's life in India are based on *Memoirs of the Life of Sir James Mackintosh,* ed. Robert J. Mackintosh, vols. 1–2, 2nd ed., London: Edward Moxon, 1836.
2. Mackintosh, *Memoirs,* vol. 2, p. 146.
3. Ibid.
4. The *Dictionary of National Biography* [hereafter *DNB*], ed. Leslie Stephen and Sidney Lee, vol. 12, London: Oxford University Press, 1917–, p. 619.
5. See Patrick O'Leary, *Sir James Mackintosh: The Whig Cicero,* Aberdeen: University Press, 1989, p. 81.
6. *Memoirs,* p. 216.
7. O'Leary, *Sir James Mackintosh,* p. 96.
8. Ibid., p. 78.
9. Mackintosh, *Memoirs,* vol. 1, p. 242.
10. See "Notice of the Life, Writings and Speeches of Sir James Mackintosh" in James Mackintosh, *History of the Revolution in England in 1688,* London: Longman, Rees, Orme et al., 1834, p. lix.
11. Ibid.
12. Ibid., p. 226.
13. Ibid.
14. Mackintosh, *Memoirs,* vol. 2, p. 156.
15. Mackintosh, *History of the Revolution in England,* p. 1.
16. Mackintosh, "Notice of the Life, Writings and Speeches," p. xxxix.
17. See Robert Orme's letter to Richard Smith, February 1, 1766. India Office Records [hereafter IOR] Orme MSS, vol. 1, p. 121.
18. The classicist historiographical tradition in Britain during the eighteenth century has been studied comprehensively in Mark S. Phillips, *Society and Sentiment: Genres of Historical Writing in Britain, 1740–1820,* Princeton, NJ: Princeton University Press, 2000, pp. 21–25.
19. Sheridan, *A General Dictionary of the English Language,* 2nd ed., London: Charles Dilly, 1789.
20. Mackintosh, "Notice of the Life, Writings and Speeches", p. xxxix.
21. Preface to "An Introduction to the History of the Life of Nader Shah," in *The Works of William Jones,* Delhi: Agam Prakashan [1799], 1977, vol. 12, p. 323.
22. Edward Said, *Orientalism,* Middlesex, UK: Penguin Books, 1985, p. 6.
23. See Bernard S. Cohn, *Colonialism and Its Forms of Knowledge: The British in India,* Princeton, NJ: Princeton University Press, 1996, p. 5.
24. See P. J. Marshall and Glyndwr Williams, *The Great Map of Mankind: Perceptions of New Worlds in the Age of Enlightenment,* Cambridge, MA: Harvard University Press, 1982, pp. 75–77.
25. For Burke's ideas of India as an unfamiliar culture, and thus deserving of the most scrupulous moral judgment and empathy on the part of the British, see Uday Singh Mehta, *Liberalism and Empire: A Study in Nineteenth Century British Liberal Thought,* Chicago & London: University of Chicago Press, 1999, pp. 22–23.

26. Phillips, *Society and Sentiment,* p. 221.
27. Recent historiography traces the idea of a "golden age" of empire to Elizabethan times. For a balanced discussion, see James Muldoon, *Empire and Order: The Concept of Empire, 800–1800,* New York: St. Martin's Press, 1999, pp. 130–134.
28. According to Koebner, "In Great Britain and its dependencies overseas the name of Empire became overlaid with meanings which were unprecedented additions to those which had shaped its former career." See Richard Koebner, *Empire,* Cambridge, UK: Cambridge University Press, 1961, p. 60, also pp. 89–90.
29. Hilaire Belloc, *A History of England,* vol. 1, London; New York: G. P. Putnam, 1925, p. 3.
30. See Norman Vance, *The Victorians and Ancient Rome,* Oxford: Blackwell, 1997, pp. 11–12.
31. For an excellent overview see Roy Porter, *Gibbon: Making History,* New York: St. Martin's Press, 1988, p. 28.
32. On the historical relevance of the descent of Rome from republic to empire in this period, see Frank Turner, "British Politics and the Demise of the Roman Republic: 1700–1939," *The Historical Journal,* vol. 29 no. 3, 1986, pp. 577–599, also J. G. A. Pocock, "Between Machiavelli and Hume: Gibbon as Civic Humanist and Philosophical Historian," in G. W. Bowersock, John Clive, and Stephen Graubard, eds., *Edward Gibbon and the Decline and Fall of the Roman Empire,* Cambridge, MA: Harvard University Press, 1977, pp. 103–119.
33. On Gibbon's relevance for the historiography of modern Europe, see Peter Brown, "Gibbon's Views on Culture and Society in the Fifth and Sixth Centuries," in Bowersock, Clive, and Graubard, *Edward Gibbon and the Decline and Fall of the Roman Empire,* pp. 37–52.
34. William Robertson, *History of the Reign of the Emperor Charles V with a View of the Progress of Society in Europe from the Subversion of the Roman Empire to the Beginning of the Sixteenth Century,* in Dugald Stewart, ed., *The Works of William Robertson,* new ed., vol. 4, London: Cadell and Davies, et al., 1817, pp. x, 1–2. The "political system" referred directly to the "balance of power" devised by Grotius.
35. Gibbon was notably silent about the loss of Britain's American empire, and it is doubtful that his description of Rome bore a direct analogy to the contemporary expansion of England. See Stephen R. Graubard, "Contraria Sunt Complementa," in *Edward Gibbon and the Decline,* pp. 133–134.
36. See Gibbon's letter to J. B. Holroyd, May 5, 1773, in J. E. Norton, ed., *The Letters of Edward Gibbon,* New York: Macmillan, 1956, pp. 365–366. The trial is also mentioned in Georges A. Bonnard, ed., *Memoirs of My Life,* New York: Funk and Wagnall's, 1966, p. 181.
37. Bonnard, ed., *Memoirs,* p. 181.
38. He wrote to Holroyd: "the French interest is destroyed, Ragged boy (or some such name) is placed on the throne of that warlike people, and we have now more to hope than to fear from them . . . it is not impossible that Pondicherry, feebly garrisoned may at this moment be in our hands." Gibbon to Holroyd, December 9, 1778, Norton, *Letters,* vol. 2, p. 197. Gibbon was referring to Raghoba whose bid for power came to little, though this was not clear from what was being reported in England.
39. Gibbon to Holroyd, March 16, 1779, Norton, ed. *Letters,* vol. 2, p. 207.
40. Gibbon to Deyverdun, June 4, 1779, Norton ed. *Letters,* vol. 2, p. 218: "L'homme de lettres et l'homme d'Etat, qu'il vous suffise de savoir que la decadence de Deux Empires, le Romain et le Britannique s'avancent à pas egaux. J'ai contribué cependant bien plus efficacement au premier. . . ."
41. Gibbon to Deyverdun, May 20, 1783, Norton ed. *Letters,* vol. 3, p. 326: "Dans cette histoire moderne il serait [*sic*] toujours un peu question de la decadence des Empires, et autant que j'en puis juger . . . peu la puissance de l'Angleterre que celle des Romains. Notre chute cependant a eté plus douce. . . ."
42. See, esp., J. W. Johnson, *The Formation of English Neo-Classical Thought,* Princeton: Princeton University Press, 1967; and John Barrell, *The Political Theory of Painting from Reynolds to Hazlitt: "The Body of the Public,"* New Haven: Yale University Press, 1986.
43. Thompson, quoted in Preston Peardon, *The Transition in English Historical Writing, 1760–1830,* New York: Columbia University Press, 1933, pp. 64–65.
44. Robert Henry, *The History of Great Britain from the First Invasion of It by the Romans under Julius Caesar: Written on a New Plan,* vol. 1, London; Edinburgh: T. Cadell, 1771, p. 3.
45. See the "Advertisement" in William Russell, *The History of Modern Europe with an Account of the Decline and Fall of the Roman Empire, and a View of the Progress of Society, from the Rise of the Modern Kingdoms of the Peace of Paris, in 1763, in a Series of Letters from a Nobleman to his Son,* new ed. vol. 1, Philadelphia: William Young Birch and Abraham Small, 1800.
46. Ibid., p. 1.

47. Alexander Fraser Tytler, *Elements of General History, Ancient and Modern,* 76th ed., Concord, N.H.: John F. Brown, 1840, p. 11.
48. Ibid.
49. Ibid.
50. Peardon, *Transition in English Historical Writing,* p. 84.
51. William Mitford, *The History of Greece,* vol. 1, London: T. Cadell, 1822, pp. 1–2.
52. See Arthur O. Lovejoy, *The Great Chain of Being: A Study of the History of an Idea,* Cambridge, MA: Harvard University Press, 1964, p. 183.
53. For a succinct discussion of historiography during the Age of Enlightenment, Collingwood remains relevant. See R. G. Collingwood, *The Idea of History,* New York: Oxford University Press, 1956, pp. 76–85.
54. David Hume, *The History of England from the Invasion of Julius Caesar to the Abdication of James the Second, 1688,* vol. 1, New York: Harper, 1851, p. 1.
55. Henry Home, Lord Kames, *Sketches of the History of Man,* 2nd ed., Edinburgh: W. Strahan, T. Cadell and W. Creech, 1778, vol. 1, p. 1.
56. Adam Ferguson, *An Essay on the History of Civil Society,* Edinburgh: University Press [1767], 1966, p. 122.
57. Ibid.
58. Ibid., pp. 122–123.
59. Quoted in Peardon, *The Transition in English Historical Writing,* p. 64.
60. Facsimile of the dedication to the Honorable the Court of Directors of the East India Company, in Robert Orme, *Historical Fragments of the Mogul Empire and the Morattoes and of the English Concerns in Indostan,* New Delhi: Associated Publishing House [1806], 1974, p. vi.
61. William Jones, "Third Anniversary Discourse" delivered to the Asiatic Society in Calcutta, February 2, 1786, in *The Works of William Jones,* Indian reprint, Delhi: Agam Prakashan [1799], 1977, vol. 3, p. 31.
62. William Jones, "A Discourse on the Institution of a Society, for the Inquiring into the History, Civil and Natural, the Antiquities, Arts, Sciences, and Literature of Asia," in *The Works of William Jones,* vol. 3, p. 6.
63. John Millar, *The Origin of the Distinction of Ranks,* 3rd ed., Edinburgh: John Murray, 1779, reprinted in William C. Lehmann, *John Millar of Glasgow, 1735–1801: His Life and Thought and His Contributions to Sociological Analysis,* Cambridge, UK: Cambridge University Press, 1960, p. 178.
64. Ibid., pp. 280–281.
65. Kames, *Sketches of the History of Man,* vol. 1, p. 149.
66. Ibid.
67. William Robertson, *An Historical Disquisition Concerning the Knowledge which the Ancients Had of India,* in Dugald Stewart, ed., *The Works of William Robertson,* vol. 12, pp. 201–202.
68. Ferguson, *Essay on the History of Civil Society,* p. 194.
69. Robertson, *Historical Disquisition,* pp. 203, 231, 257, 285.
70. Ibid., pp. 210–211.
71. William Robertson, *The History of America,* in Stewart, ed., *The Works,* vol. 8, p. 1.
72. Ferguson, *Essay,* p. 253.
73. Ibid., p. 254.
74. Ibid.
75. Montesquieu, *Persian Letters,* trans. C. J. Betts, London: Penguin, 1973, p. 187.
76. See *The Writings and Speeches of Edmund Burke,* ed. by P. J. Marshall, Oxford: Clarendon Press, 1991, vol. 6, pp. 346–347.
77. He says further in his opening, "I do challenge the whole race of man to show me any of the Oriental Governors claiming to themselves a right to act by arbitrary will," *Writings and Speeches,* vol. 6, p. 353.
78. *Writings and Speeches,* vol. 6, p. 381.
79. Ferguson, *Essay,* p. 111.
80. Ibid.
81. Robertson, *Historical Disquisition,* p. 22.
82. Robertson, *History of the Reign of Emperor Charles V,* p. 8.
83. Burke to Robertson, June 9, 1777, in *Correspondence of Edmund Burke,* ed. Thomas Copland, Cambridge, UK: Cambridge University Press, 1958–1978, vol. 5, pp. 350–351. See also the introduction to Marshall and Williams, *The Great Map of Mankind,* p. 1.
84. See the introduction to Robert Orme, *A History of the Military Transactions of the British Nation in Indostan from the Year MDCCXLV, to which is Prefixed a Dissertation on the Establishments Made by Mahomedan Conquerors in Indostan,* London: John Nourse, 1778, vol. 1, p. 34.

85. Robert Orme, *Military Transactions,* vol. 2, part 1, p. 1.
86. Ibid., p. 4.
87. Ibid., p. 5.
88. See *DNB,* vol. 14, pp. 1150–1151. See also, A. Sinharaja Tammita Delgoda, " 'Nabob, Historian and Orientalist.' Robert Orme: The Life and Career of an East India Company Servant (1728–1801)," *Journal of the Royal Asiatic Society,* series 3, vol. 2, no. 3, 1992, pp. 364–367, and J. P. Guha, "Introducing Robert Orme," in the *Historical Fragments,* pp. ix–xv.
89. See Orme's preface to the "General Idea of the Government and People of Indostan," in his *Historical Fragments,* p. 254. Also Tammita Delgoda, " 'Nabob, Historian and Orientalist,' " p. 365.
90. Orme, *Historical Fragments,* p. 261.
91. *Military Transactions,* vol. 1, p. 2.
92. Ibid.
93. Robertson, *Historical Disquisition,* p. 1.
94. Notes to pp. 202, 203, 209, and *passim,* "Notes and Illustrations" to *Historical Disquisition,* pp. 289–384.
95. *Historical Disquisition,* p. 202.
96. See the "History of British India," in *The Asiatic Annual Register, or, the View of History of Hindustan and of the Politics, Commerce and Literature of Asia for the Year 1799,* London: J. Debrett, 1800, p. 2.
97. *Historical Fragments,* p. 271.
98. Ibid., p. 270.
99. Ibid., p. 272.
100. Ibid.
101. *Military Transactions,* vol. 1, p. 29.
102. *Historical Fragments,* p. 271.
103. Jonathan Zephania Holwell, *Interesting Historical Events Relative to the Province of Bengal and the Empire of Indostan,* London: Beckett and De Hondt, 1766.
104. Speech on the opening of the impeachment of Warren Hastings, February 15, 1788, in Marshall, ed., *Writings and Speeches,* vol. 6, p. 301.
105. Ibid., pp. 302–305.
106. For this and the following observations of Burke on the history of India, see Marshall, ed., *Writings and Speeches,* vol. 6, pp. 307–312.
107. Holwell, *Interesting Historical Events,* pp. 18–19.
108. Luke Scrafton, *Reflections on the Government of Indostan: With a Short Sketch of the History of Bengal from the Year 1739 to 1756; and an Account of English Affairs to 1758,* London: Richardson and Clark, 1763, p. 17.
109. N. B. Halhed, *Letters of Detector on the Reports of the Select Committee of the House of Commons Appointed to Consider How the British Possessions in the East Indies May Be Held and Governed with the Greatest Security and Happiness of the Natives May Best Be Promoted,* London: n.p., 1782, p. 3.
110. See Alexander Dow's preface to *The History of Hindostan,* London: Vernor and Hood et al., 1803, vol. 1, p. xi.
111. Dow, "A Dissertation Concerning the Origin of Despotism in Hindostan," in the preface to *History of Hindostan,* p. lxxxi.
112. Ibid., pp. 4–5.
113. Ibid., p. iv.
114. *Historical Disquisition,* p. 285.
115. Ibid., p. 215.
116. *Historical Fragments,* p. 257.
117. Mackintosh, "Notice of the Life, Writings and Speeches," p. xxxviii.
118. *Historical Fragments,* pp. 275–276.
119. Bernard S. Cohn, "The Recruitment and Training of Civil Servants in India, 1600–1800," in *An Anthropologist among the Historians and Other Essays,* Delhi: Oxford University Press, 1990, p. 508.
120. See, for example, the declaration of Abraham Roberts, director of the East India Company, and his nomination of John Edward Wilkinson as a writer, at the recommendation of his eldest son A. W. Roberts, the brother-in-law of the said petitioner, submitted on January 3, 1810. IOR J/1/19, p. 48. For a more extensive discussion, see Suresh Chandra Ghosh, *The Social Condition of the British Community in Bengal,* pp. 36–37. See also Anthony Farrington, *The Records of the East India College: Haileybury and Other Institutions,* London: Her Majesty's Stationery Office, 1976, pp. 4–5.

121. Ghosh, *Social Condition,* p. 40.

122. Wellesley (The Earl of Mornington) to Henry Dundas, January 25, 1800, Fort William, in Edward Ingram ed. *Two Views of British India: The Private Correspondence of Mr. Dundas and Lord Wellesley, 1798–1801,* Somerset, UK: Adams and Dart, 1970, p. 214.

123. Minute in Council at Fort William; by His Excellency the Most Noble Marquis Wellesley, containing His Reasons for the Establishment of a College in Bengal, August 18, 1800 in *The Annals of the College of Fort William from the Period of Its Foundation by His Excellency the Most Noble Richard, Marquis Wellesley on the 4th May, 1800 to the Present Time,* compiled etc. by Thomas Roebuck, Calcutta: Hindoostanee Press, 1819, p. i.

124. Ibid., p. ii.

125. Ibid., p. iv.

126. Ibid., p. xvii.

127. Ibid., p. xiv.

128. Imogen Thomas, *Haileybury 1806–1987,* Hertford, UK: Haileybury Society, 1987, p. 2.

129. "A Preliminary View of the Establishment of the Honorable East India Company in Hertofordshire for the Education of Young Persons Appointed to the Civil Service of India." Approved by the Committee of the College, December 20, 1805. Records of the East India College, IOR J/1/19, p. 448.

130. Ibid., pp. 451–452.

131. Ibid., p. 454.

132. Farrington, *Records of the East India College,* p. 5.

133. T. R. Malthus, "Statements Respecting the East-India College with an Appeal to Facts in Refutation of the Charges Brought Against it in the Court of Proprietors," in *The Pamphleteer,* Vol. IX, London: A. J. Valpy, 1817, p. 492.

134. Ibid., p. 493.

135. Ibid., p. 516.

136. "A Preliminary View of the Establishment of the Hon. EIC," IOR J/1/19, pp. 456–457.

137. Minto, quoted in Malthus, "Statements Respecting the East-India College," p. 502.

138. See letter of James Andrew of Woolwich Common, December 26, 1805; letter of William Laing, Edinburgh, March 20, 1806, IOR J/1/20.

139. Letter of C. J. Heathcote, Hackney School, January 15, 1810, IOR J/1/25, p. 118.

140. Letter of James Gregory, June 5, 1810, IOR J/1/25, pp. 189–190.

141. See Testimonials in Examination for Open Court, June 1810, IOR J/1/25, pp. 196, 219.

142. Ibid., p. 249.

143. Testimonial of Thomas Smith, Master of South Crescent, July 26, 1826, certifying that Daniel Smith was a pupil under his tuition for seven years, that the "education he has received is of a classical more than of a commercial nature," and that he has made some progress in the study of the classical authors, Ovid, Virgil, Sallust, Horace, Cicero, and in Greek, Aesop, Lucian, Plutarch, Xenophon, Anacreon, and Homer. Testimonial of John Robert Miller, Master at Blackheath Hill, January 1827, certifying that his pupil William Elliot had read Caesar's *Commentaries,* two books of the *Aneid* and the *Diatessaron,* and the first book of Euclid; testimonial of A. R. Carson, Rector of Edinburgh College, January 8, 1827, certifying that Mr. Wm. James Trotter, son of the Rt. Hon. William Trotter, Provost of Edinburgh, attended his classes in Latin, Greek and Ancient Geography, and "made highly respectable attainments in the several departments of classical literature . . ."; see also the certificate of Andrew Ross Bell from the University of Edinburgh that he had gained instruction in both *historia civilis* and *historia naturalis.* IOR J/1/91

144. Wellesley, "Minute," *Annals of the College of Fort William,* p. xi.

145. See Burke's "Observations" on the *First Report from the Select Committee, Appointed to Take into Consideration the State of the Administration of Justice in the Provinces of Bengal, Bahar and Orissa, 1782,* February 5, 1782. See Marshall, ed., *Writings and Speeches,* vol. 5, p. 144.

146. Ninth Report of Select Committee, June 25, 1783, Marshall, ed., *Writings and Speeches,* vol. 5, p. 306.

147. Speech on Fox's India Bill, December 1, 1783, Marshall, ed., *Writings and Speeches,* vol. 5, p. 402.

148. Thomas, *Haileybury,* p. 6.

149. Pratapaditya Pal and Vidya Dehejia, *From Merchants to Emperors: British Artists and India, 1757–1930,* Ithaca, NY, and London: Cornell University Press, 1986, p. 48.

150. Edmund Burke, *Reflections on the Revolution in France and On the Proceedings in Certain Societies in London Relative to that Event: In a Letter Intended to have been Sent to a Gentleman in Paris, 1790.* See *The Works of the Rt. Honorable Edmund Burke,* London: Henry G. Bohn, 1855, vol. 2, p. 410.

151. Ibid., p. 412.
152. "Remarks on the Policy of the Allies with Respect to France, Begun in October 1793." *The Works*, vol. 3, p. 456.
153. Hugh Pearson, *Memoirs of the Life and Writings of the Reverend Claudius Buchanan,* Philadelphia, PA: Benjamin and Thomas Kite, 1817, p. 154.
154. See the first volume of *The Haileybury Observer, by the Students of the East-India College,* London: W. H. Allen, 1897.
155. Editorial, *The Haileybury Observer,* October 9, 1839.
156. Henry Dundas to the Marquis Wellesley, Cheltenham, September 4, 1800, in Ingram ed. *Two Views of British India,* p. 287.
157. James Mill, *The History of British India,* 2nd ed., New Delhi: Associated Publishing House, 1972, vol. 1, p. 28.
158. Ibid., p. 30.
159. John William Kaye, *Lives of Indian Officers, Illustrative of the History of the Civil and Military Services of India,* London: A Strahan, Bell and Daldy, 1867, p. xii.
160. See the Dedication in William Hollingbery, *A History of His Late Highness Nizam Alee Khaun, Soobah of the Dekhan,* Calcutta: J. Greenway, 1805, p. iii.
161. Ibid., p. vi.
162. Ibid.
163. Ibid., p. xix.
164. Ibid., pp. 58–59.
165. Mark Wilks, *Historical Sketches of the South of India in an Attempt to Trace the History of Mysoor from the Origin of the Hindoo Government of that State to the Extinction of the Mohammedan Dynasty in 1799,* London: Longman, Hurst, Rees, Orme, and Brown, 1820, vol. 1, p. xvii.
166. Ibid., pp. 1–3.
167. Ibid., p. 22.
168. Ibid., p. 239.
169. Wilks, *Historical Sketches of the South of India,* vol. 2, p. 196.
170. *Historical Sketches,* vol. 3, p. 454.
171. Ibid., pp. 464–465.
172. Ibid., p. 467.
173. Ibid., p. 471.
174. Mackintosh, *Memoirs,* vol. 2, p. 69.
175. Ibid., p. 71.
176. Kaye, *Lives of Indian Officers,* p. 133.
177. Ibid., p. 181.
178. John Malcolm, *The History of Persia from the Most Early Period to the Present Time: Containing an Account of the Religion, Government, Usages, and Character of the Inhabitants of that Kingdom,* rev. ed., London: John Murray, 1829, vol. 1, p. 548.
179. Ibid., pp. 548–549.
180. See John Malcolm, *A Memoir of Central India, including Malwa, and Adjoining Provinces, with the History and Copious Illustrations of the Past and Present of that Country,* 3rd ed., London: Parbury, Allen & Co.: 1832, vol. 1, pp. 48–49.
181. Ibid., pp. 476–477.
182. Malcolm, *History of Persia,* vol. 2, p. 451.
183. John Malcolm, *The Political History of India, 1784 to 1823,* ed. K. N. Panikkar vol. 1, London: New Delhi: Associated Publishing House, 1970, p. 182.
184. Ibid., p. 82.
185. Ibid.
186. Kaye, *Lives of Indian Officers,* p. 307. See *DNB,* vol. 6, p. 746. Also, Mountstuart Elphinstone, *The History of India: The Hindu and Mahometan Periods,* reprint, Allahabad, India: Kitab Mahal, 1986, pp. 169–171, 182–185, 194–203.
187. Malcolm, *Political History of India,* p. 64.
188. Kaye, *Lives of Indian Officers,* pp. xiii–xiv.
189. Raphael Samuel, *Theaters of Memory,* London and New York: Verso, 1994, vol. 1, pp. x–xi.
190. See P. J. Marshall, *Problems of Empire: Britain and India, 1757–1813,* London: George Allen & Unwin, 1968, p. 54.
191. *The Annual Register* [hereafter *AR*], *Or a View of the History, Politics and Literature, for the Year 1764,* London: J. Dodsley, 1765, p. 256.
192. See P. J. Marshall, " 'Cornwallis Triumphant': War in India and the British Public in the Late Eighteenth Century," in *War, Strategy and International Politics,* ed. L. Freedman, P. Hayes, and Robert O'Neill, Oxford: Oxford University Press, 1992, pp. 67, 74.

193. Kate Teltscher, *India Inscribed: European and British Writing on India, 1600–1800,* 2nd ed., Delhi: Oxford University Press, 1997, pp. 246–247.
194. Stefan Collini, *English Pasts: Essays in History and Culture,* Oxford: Oxford University Press, 1999, p. 13.
195. Etienne Balibar, "The Nation-Form: History and Ideology," *Review,* XIII, no. 3, Summer, 1990, pp. 338–339.

NOTES TO CHAPTER 3

1. Joseph Conrad, "Geography and Some Explorers," from *Joseph Conrad: Poland's English Genius,* by Muriel C. Bradbrook, Cambridge, UK: Cambridge University Press, 1941, pp. 5–6.
2. Samuel Johnson, *The Plan of a Dictionary of the English Language,* London: Knapton, Longman, Shewell, Hitch, Millar and Dodsley, 1747, p. 33. See also Murray Cohen, *Sensible Words: Linguistic Practice in England 1640–1785,* Baltimore, MD, and London: Johns Hopkins University Press, 1977, p. 91. For both these references I am beholden to Philip Corrigan.
3. Benedict Anderson, *Imagined Communities,* London and New York: Verso, 1991, reprint, 1992. p. 163
4. Matthew H. Edney, *Mapping an Empire: The Geographical Construction of British India, 1765–1843,* Chicago: University of Chicago Press, 1997.
5. Thongchai Winichakul, *Siam Mapped: A History of the Geo-Body of a Nation,* Honolulu: University of Hawaii Press, 1994.
6. Letter addressed to Rev. Gilbert Burrington, Vicar of Chudleigh, Bengal, August 31, 1765, India Office Library and Records, Home Series Misc. Eur. D. 1073.
7. Jean Baudrillard, *Symbolic Exchange and Death,* London: Sage Publications, 1993, p. 51.
8. My use of Marx and the idea of money as fetish has been shaped to a large extent by the reading of Antonio Negri. See A. Negri, *Marx Beyond Marx: Lessons on the Grundrisse,* New York: Autonomedia, 1993, p. 35. Negri comments: "the evanescent power of money attacks things and transforms them in its own image and resemblance."
9. Michel Foucault, *The Order of Things: An Archeology of the Human Sciences,* New York: Vintage Books, 1970, pp. 132–133.
10. Ludwig Wittgenstein, *Tractatus Logico-Philosophicus,* London: Routledge & Kegan Paul [1961], 1974, p. 117. Italics in the original.
11. Barbara M. Stafford, *Voyage into Substance: Art, Science, Nature, and the Illustrated Travel Account, 1760–1840,* Cambridge, MA, and London: MIT Press, 1984, p. 40.
12. Stafford, *Voyage into Substance.*
13. André Miquel, *La Géographie Humaine du Monde Musulman jusqu'au Milieu du IIe Siècle,* Paris: Mouton & Co, 1967, p. 364. I am indebted to Faisal Devji for this reference.
14. Ibid., p. vii.
15. Francastel, Pierre, *Peinture et Société, la Naissance et la Destruction de l'Espace Plastique,* translated in part in *French Studies in History,* ed. Maurice Aymard and Harbans Mukhia, Delhi: Orient Longman, 1990, pp. 256–257.
16. Ibid., p. 259.
17. David C. Lindberg, and Nicholas H. Steneck, *Science, Medicine and Society in the Renaissance: Essays to Honor Walter Pagel,* ed. Allen G. Debus, vol. 1, New York: History Science Publications, 1972, p. 39.
18. See Svetlana Alpers, *The Art of Describing,* Chicago: University of Chicago Press, 1983, pp. 124–126.
19. Andrew Hemingway, *Landscape Imagery and Urban Culture in Early Nineteenth-Century Britain,* Cambridge, UK: Cambridge University Press, 1992, p. 17.
20. Francastel, *Peinture et Société,* pp. 259–260.
21. For a selection of various kinds of Mughal maps, see Susan Gole, *Indian Maps and Plans: From Earliest Times to the World of European Surveys,* New Delhi: Manohar Publications, 1989. The word *naqsha* can mean a sign, a motif, or a chart.
22. Victor Morgan, "Cartographic Image of 'The Country' in Early Modern England," *Transactions of the Royal Historical Society,* 5th series, 29, 1979, p. 153.
23. Victor Morgan, "Lasting Image of the Elizabethan Era," *Geographical Magazine,* 52, no. 6, 1980, p. 406. Around the same time, the antiquarian terrain of England was charted by Camden, and in his much circulated *Britannia,* Saxton's maps were included in the illustration. See H. Trevor-Roper, *Queen Elizabeth's First Historian: William Camden and the Beginning of English "Civil History,"* London: Jonathan Cape, 1971, p. 33.

24. See Drayton's *Poly-Olbion,* ed. J. William Hebel, Michael Drayton Tercentenary Edition, Vol. IV, Oxford: Basil Blackwell, 1961. p. iii. These symbols have been discussed at length in Richard, Helgerson, "The Land Speaks: Cartography, Chorography and Subversion in Renaissance England," *Representations,* 16, Fall 1986, pp. 51–85. Helgerson makes the point that maps and chorographs were much more than tools of monarchical or absolutist centralization; they were integral to other representational practices.

25. See the discussion of Petrus Apianus's *Cosmographia* of 1551, an adaptation of Ptolemy's geography, in Svetlana Alpers, *The Art of Describing,* pp. 133–134.

26. See Abu l'Fazl 'Allami's *'Ain-i Akbari,* trans. H. Blochmann, 2nd ed. revised by D. C. Phillpott, Calcutta: Royal Asiatic Society of Bengal, 1939, p. 48.

27. Sleeman, W. H. *Rambles and Recollections of an Indian Official,* vol. 1, ed. V. A. Smith, London: Archibald Constable and Company, 1893, pp. 165–166.

28. See, for example, *Haft-iqlim: The Geographical and Biographical Encyclopaedia of Amin Ahmad Razi,* ed. by A. H. Harley, Abdul Muqtadir, and Mahfuz-ul Haq, Calcutta: Bibliotheca Indica, 1939.

29. Ziauddin Alavi, *Arab Geography in the Ninth and Tenth Centuries,* Aligarh: Aligarh Muslim University, 1965, pp. 45–51.

30. *Hudud al-Alam, The Regions of the World: A Persian Geography,* translated by V. Minorsky, Karachi: Indus Publications, 1980, pp. 49–50.

31. Habib, Irfan, "Cartography in Mughal India," in *Medieval India: A Miscellany,* Bombay: Asia Publishing House, 1969, pp. 123–125.

32. See Susan Gole, *Indian Maps and Plans,* p. 95.

33. For an interesting discussion of the lack of precision in the drawing of boundaries in medieval Islamic mapping, see R. W. Bauer, *Boundaries and Frontiers in Medieval Muslim Geography,* Philadelphia, PA: American Philosophical Society, 1995, esp. pp. 1–7.

34. *Hudud al-Alam, The Regions of the World,* p. 82.

35. Chandra, Pramod, *The Tuti-Nama of the Cleveland Museum of Art and the Origins of Mughal Painting,* Graz, Austria: Akademische Druck und Verlagsanstalt, 1976, p. 183.

36. Habib, "Cartography in Mughal India," p. 128.

37. See plate 21, entitled "Jahangir's Dream," in S. C. Welch's *Imperial Mughal Painting,* New York: George Braziller, 1978. This painting was commissioned by Jahangir after he dreamt that Shah 'Abbas Safavi had appeared in a well of light to make him happy.

38. In reality, however, Kandahar on the north-western frontier of the empire was annexed by the Persians in 1622, while Jahangir was preoccupied with the rebellion of Prince Shah Jahan. Welch, *Imperial Mughal Painting,* p. 83.

39. For details see J. B. Harley, B. Petchenik, and L. W. Towner, eds., *Mapping the Revolutionary War,* Chicago and London: University of Chicago Press, 1978, p. 19. The Galerie des Plans Reliefs in France was one of the first European institutions to develop a systematic study of military field maps.

40. W. A. Seymour, *A History of the Ordnance Survey,* Kent: Dawson, 1980, pp. 5–6.

41. Charles Close, *The Early Years of the Ordnance Survey,* Devon, UK: David & Charles, 1969, pp. 27–28.

42. Archer, Mildred, *British Drawings in the India Office Library,* London: Her Majesty's Stationery Office, 1969, p. 5.

43. Luke Herrmann, *British Landscape Painting of the Eighteenth Century,* London: Faber & Faber, 1973, p. 37.

44. J. B. Harley, "Spread of Cartographic Ideas between Revolutionary Armies," in *Mapping the American Revolutionary War,* pp. 54–55.

45. Archer, Mildred, *British Drawings in the India Office Library,* p. 6.

46. For the historical and antiquarian dimensions of the geographers of empire, Rennell and Roy, see Ian Barrow, "Charted Histories in Colonial India, 1760–1900," Unpublished Ph.D. dissertation submitted to the Department of History, University of Chicago, 1998.

47. Roy, William, "An Account of the Measurement of a Base on Hounslow Heath," *Philosophical Transactions,* LXXV, p. 387. Italics mine.

48. From *A New and Complete Dictionary of Arts and Sciences,* published by the Society of Gentlemen in 1763, quoted in E. W. C. Sandes, *The Military Engineer in India,* Chatham, UK: Institute of Royal Engineers, 1933, vol. 1, p. 139.

49. Sandes, *The Military Engineer in India,* p. 180.

50. Emma Roberts, *The East India Voyager, Or the Outward Bound,* London: J. Madden, 1845, p. lx.

51. Ibid.

52. Alpers, *The Art of Describing,* pp. 144–145.

53. Luke Herrmann, *British Landscape Painting of the Eighteenth Century,* p. 38.
54. Ibid., pp. 44–45.
55. Jonathan Richardson, *The Works,* London: T. Davies, 1773, reprint Hildesheim, Germany: Georg Olms Verlag, 1969, p. 79.
56. Ibid.
57. Stephen Daniels, "Re-Visioning Britain: Mapping and Landscape Painting, 1750–1820," in Katherine Baetjer, *Glorious Nature: British Landscape Painting 1750–1850,* New York: Hudson Hills Press, 1993, pp. 61–63.
58. Adam Anderson, *An Historical and Chronological Deduction of the Origin of Commerce, from the Earliest Accounts containing an History of the Great Commercial Interests of the British Empire,"* vol. 3, London: J. White etc., 1801, p. 350.
59. Ibid.
60. Chandra Mukherjee, *From Graven Images: Patterns of Modern Materialism,* New York: Columbia University Press, 1983, pp. 118–119.
61. Michel Foucault, *Power/Knowledge: Selected Interviews and Other Writings, 1972–1977,* ed. and trans. Colin Gordon, Brighton, UK: Harvester Press, 1980, pp. 68–69. As Foucault puts it: "geography grew up in the shadow of the military."
62. Ann Birmingham, *Landscape and Ideology: The English Rustic Tradition, 1740–1860,* Berkeley, CA: University of California Press, 1986, pp. 1, 9–10, 14 and *passim.*
63. Birmingham, *Landscape and Ideology,* pp. 63–66.
64. See Ian Ousby, *The Englishman's England: Taste, Travel and the Rise of Tourism,* Cambridge, UK: Cambridge University Press, 1990.
65. Elizabeth Helsinger, "Turner and the Representation of England," in W. J. T. Mitchell, ed., *Landscape and Power,* Chicago: University of Chicago Press, 1994, pp. 105–106.
66. See Pal and Dehejia, *From Merchants to Emperors,* pp. 97–129, also Edney, *Mapping an Empire,* pp. 58–59.
67. Pal and Dehejia, *From Merchants,* pp. 100–101; also William Hodges, *Travels in India During the Years 1780, 1781, 1782, and 1783,* London: J. Edwards, 1793.
68. Pal and Dehejia, *From Merchants,* p. 105.
69. W. J. T. Mitchell, "Imperial Landscape," in Mitchell, ed., *Landscape and Power,* p. 17.
70. See, for example, Edmund Bohun, *A Geographical Dictionary: Representing the Present and Ancient Names of All the Countries, Provinces, Remarkable Cities, Universities, Ports, Towns, Mountains, Seas, Streights, Fountains, and Rivers of the Whole World: Their Distances, Longitudes, and Latitudes: With a Short Historical Account of the Same, and Their Present State, etc.* London: Charles Brome, 1691; Joseph Scott, *The New and Universal Gazetteer; or, Modern Geographical Dictionary: Containing a Full and Authentic Description of the Different Empires, Kingdoms, Republics, States, Provinces, Islands, Cities, Towns, Forts, Mountains, Caves, Capes, Canals, Rivers, Lakes, Oceans, Seas, Bays, Harbours, &c in the Known World,* . . . Philadelphia, PA: Francis & Robert Bailey, 1799; and also William Guthrie, *A New System of Modern Geography: Or, a Geographical, Historical, and Commercial Grammar,* Philadelphia: Mathew Carey, 1794–1795.
71. See preface to Bohun, *A Geographical Dictionary.*
72. Ibid.
73. Jeremy Black, *Maps and History: Constructing Images of the Past,* New Haven, CT, and London: Yale University Press, 1997, pp. 15–17.
74. See the list of necessities advertised by H. Hubert at No. 187 The Strand and Arundel, "To ladies, families, or gentlemen proceeding to India, either in the civil, military, or naval service," and also list of equipments advertised by A. D. Welch (Late Stalker and Welch), Maynard and Pyne, Silver and Company, in *The East India Register and Directory for 1827,* London: Parbury, Allen and Co., 1827, pp. 574–585.
75. R. H. Phillimore, *Historical Records of the Survey in India,* Dehra Dun: Survey Office, Government of India, 1945, vol. 1, pp. 1–2.
76. A. Dalrymple, *A Collection of Charts and Memoirs,* London: 1772, p. vii.
77. Ibid., p. 29.
78. Orme to Clive, Calcutta, September 29, 1765, quoted in Phillimore, *Historical Records of the Survey in India,* vol. 1, p. 29.
79. Phillimore, *Historical Records of the Survey in India,* vol. 1, p. 29.
80. Board to the Court of Directors, March 30, 1767, cited in Phillimore, *Historical Records of the Survey in India,* vol. 1, p. 31.
81. G. F. Heany, "Rennell and the Surveyors of India," *Geographical Journal,* vol. 134, pt. 3, September, 1968, p. 318.
82. Phillimore, *Historical Records of the Survey in India,* vol. 1, p. 34.

83. *The Journals of Major James Rennell, First Surveyor General of India, Written for the Information of the Governors of Bengal during his Surveys of the Ganges and the Brahmaputra Rivers 1764 to 1767,* ed. T. H. D. La Touche, Calcutta: Asiatic Society, 1910, pp. 61–62.

84. Ibid., p. 62.

85. Rennell to Richard Becher, Chief of the Controlling Council of Revenue at Murshidabad, Bowanygunge, December 9, 1770, quoted in *The Journals of Major James Rennell,* p. 237.

86. By the middle of the eighteenth century, maps were frequently being engraved for publications in England such as *The Universal Magazine, The Gentlemen's Magazine, The Royal Magazine,* and the *Gentlemen's Monthly Companion.* In other words, by the time Rennell's maps were available, there was a growing coterie of engravers, publishers, collectors, and armchair explorers. On this, see Susan Gole, *India within the Ganges,* New Delhi: Jayaprints, 1983, pp. 175–176. According to Edney, Rennell's maps presented the "definitive image of India" for the British and European public. See Edney, *Mapping an Empire,* p. 9.

87. Cited in Gole, *India within the Ganges,* p. 94.

88. Rennell, *Memoir of a Map of Hindoostan,* cited in Edney, *Mapping and Empire,* p. 13.

89. For a brief discussion see Mildred Archer, *India and British Portraiture,* London and New York: Sotheby Parke Bernet, 1979, p. 40.

90. Berger, John, *Ways of Seeing,* London: BBC and Penguin, 1972, pp. 96–97.

91. I am grateful to Urmilla Dé for this reference from the Harris Art Gallery and Museum in Lancashire. Biographical information on Devis can be found in Mildred Archer, *British Drawings in the India Office Library: Volume II, Official and Professional Artists,* London: Her Majesty's Stationery Office, 1969, pp. 417–18.

92. Bickham George, *The British Monarchy, or a New Chorographical Description of All the Dominions Subject to the King of Great Britain,* London: Bunhill-Fields, 1743, reprint, Newcastle upon Tyne: Frank Graham, 1967.

93. Bickham, *The British Monarchy,* p. 3.

94. Haskell, Framcis, *History and its Images: Art and the Interpretation of the Past,* London and New Haven: Yale University Press, 1993, pp. 148–150.

95. Edney, *Mapping an Empire,* pp. 11–13.

96. Bickham, *The British Monarchy,* p. 187.

97. Phillimore, *Historical Records of the Survey in India,* vol. 1, p. 4.

98. Ibid., p. 8–9.

99. Archer, *India and British Portraiture,* pp. 307–308.

100. Lambton, William, "An Account of a Method for Extending a Geographical Survey across the Peninsula of India," *Asiatick Researches,* vol. 7, 3rd ed. 1807, p. p. 312. Italics mine.

101. Heany, "Rennell and the Surveyors of India," p. 320.

102. Phillimore, *Historical Records of the Survey in India,* vol. 2, p. 3.

103. Phillimore, *Historical Records of the Survey in India,* vol. 3, p. 2.

104. Black, *Maps and History,* p. 49.

105. Edney, *Mapping an Empire,* pp. 287–289.

106. "Computation of the Area of the Kingdoms and Principalities of India," *Journal of the Asiatic Society of Bengal,* no. 20, August 1833, pp. 488–491.

107. Ibid., pp. 489–490.

108. "Progress of the Indian Trigonometrical Survey," *Journal of the Asiatic Society of Bengal,* ed. J. Prinsep, vol. 1, no. 2, 1832, p. 71. The report says: "An elegant breakfast was laid out in the tents after the ceremonies of the morning were concluded. . . . [we were] contemplating with admiration the order and precision with which the whole process was conducted."

109. Sleeman, *Rambles and Recollections,* vol. 1, p. 244.

110. Ibid.

111. A more or less clear articulation of this is made by Foucault in the context of the Panopticon, where he suggests that the homgenity of power lies in the particularity of the distribution of bodies, surfaces, lights, and gazes. Michel Foucault, *Discipline and Punish: The Birth of the Prison,* New York: Vintage Books, 1979, p. 202.

NOTES TO CHAPTER 4

1. T. B. Macaulay, *Critical, Historical and Miscellaneous Essays and Poems,* Boston: Estes and Lauriat, 1880, vol. 2, pp. 566–567.

2. Stevens, quoted in Nirad C. Chaudhuri, *Thy Hand, Great Anarch! India: 1921–1952,* Reading, UK: Addison-Wesley, 1987, p. 673.

3. William Tennant, *Thoughts on the Effects of the British Government on the State of India: Accompanied with Hints Concerning the Means of Conveying Civil and Religious Instruction to the Natives of that Country.* Edinburgh: Edinburgh University Press, 1807, p. 252.

4. Ibid., p. 59.

5. Mackintosh, "Notice of the Life, Writings and Speeches," p. xxxviii.

6. Judith Butler, *Bodies that Matter,* New York and London: Routledge, 1993, p. 219.

7. See, for instance, Ronald Hyam, *Empire and Sexuality: The British Experience,* Manchester and New York: Manchester University Press, 1990, pp. 211–212.

8. For the in-depth study of one family on this very question, see John Tosh, "Domesticity and Manliness in the Victorian Middle Class: The Family of Edward White Benson," in Michael Roper and John Tosh, eds., *Manful Assertions: Masculinities in Britain Since 1800,* London and New York: Routledge, 1991, pp. 44–73. See also Leonore Davidoff and Catherine Hall, *Family Fortunes,* and Jonathan Barry and Christopher Brooks eds., *The Middling Sort of People: Culture, Society, and Politics in England, 1550–1800,* New York: St. Martin's Press, 1994.

9. Tosh, *Domesticity and Manliness,* pp. 44–45.

10. Immanuel Kant, "Von den Vershidenen Racen der Menschen, 1775," in *This Is Race,* ed. by Earl W. Count, New York: Henry Schuman, 1950, p. 74.

11. Linda Kerber, *Women of the Republic: Intellect and Ideology in Revolutionary America,* New York and London: W. W. Norton, 1986, pp. 27–28.

12. Keith Tribe, "The 'Histories' of Economic Discourse," *Economy and Society,* vol. 6, 1977, pp. 326–329. See also his *Genealogies of Capitalism,* London: Macmillan, 1981, *passim.*

13. Philip Corrigan and Derek Sayer, *The Great Arch: English State Formation as Cultural Revolution,* Oxford: Basil Blackwell, 1985, p. 12.

14. J. Steuart, *Inquiry into the Principles of Political Economy,* Edinburgh: Oliver and Boyd [1767], 1966, p. 16.

15. John Bennet, *The National Merchant: Or Discourses on Commerce and Colonies; Being an Essay for Regulating and Improving the Trade and Plantations of Great Britain by Uniting the National and Mercatorial Interests,* London: J. Walthoe and T. Osborn, 1736, p. 6.

16. Lawrence Stone, *The Family, Sex and Marriage in England,* 1500–1800, New York: Harper and Row, 1979, p. 146.

17. See Jonathan Barry, "Bourgeois Collectivism? Urban Association and the Middling Sort," in Barry and Brooks eds., *Middling Sort of People,* pp. 84–112.

18. William Blackstone, *The Sovereignty of the Law: Selections from Blackstone's Commentaries on the Laws of England,* ed. Gareth Steadman Jones, Toronto: University of Toronto Press, 1973, p. 126.

19. Henry Home, Lord Kames, *Principles of Equity,* Edinburgh: Bell, Bradforte and W. Creech, 1800, p. 507.

20. Blackstone, *Sovereignty of the Law,* p. 118.

21. I am obligated to Philip Corrigan for this valuable insight.

22. Habakkuk, "England," in *The European Nobility in the Eighteenth Century,* ed. Albert Goodwin, New York and Evanston: Harper and Row, 1967.

23. Daniel Defoe, *Atlantis Major,* Los Angeles: William Andrews Clark Memorial Library [1711], 1979, p. 37.

24. Susan Dwyer Amussen, *An Ordered Society: Gender and Class in Early Modern England,* New York: Columbia University Press, 1993, pp. 63–65; see also Margaret R. Hunt, *The Middling Sort: Commerce, Gender, and the Family in England, 1680–1780,* Berkeley: University of California Press, 1996, esp. Chap. 8.

25. Oliver Goldsmith, *The Vicar of Wakefield,* ed. Arthur Friedman, London: Oxford University Press, 1974, pp. 20–21.

26. Ibid., pp. 97–98.

27. Henry Home, Lord Kames, *Sketches of the History of Man,* Edinburgh: Bell, Bradforte and W. Creech, 1774, vol. 1, p. 169.

28. Leonore Davidoff and Catherine Hall, *Family Fortunes: Men and Women of the English Middle Class, 1780–1850,* Chicago: University of Chicago Press, 1987, pp. 229–231.

29. Albert O. Hirschman, *The Passions and the Interests: Political Arguments for Capitalism before Its Triumph,* Princeton, NJ: Princeton University Press, 1997, pp. 8–9.

30. Ibid., pp. 69–70.

31. Adam Anderson, *An Historical and Chronological Deduction of the Origin of Commerce, From the Earliest Accounts Containing an History of the Great Commercial Interests of the British Empire,* London: J. White and Company, 1801, vol. 3, p. 3.

32. See Alexander Dalrymple, *Heads of an Agreement between the Parliament and the East India Company,* London: s.n., 1780, pp. 4, 179.

33. Edmund Burke, *Reflections on the Revolution in France,* Philadelphia: Young, Dobson, Carey, and Rice, MDCCXCII, p. 53.
34. Thomas Pownall, *The Right, Interest, and Duty of the State as Concerned in the Affairs of the East Indies,* London: S. Bladon, 1773, p. 19.
35. Ranajit Guha, *A Rule of Property for Bengal: An Essay on the Idea of Permanent Settlement,* Durham, NC, and London: Duke University Press, 1996, pp. 8–9.
36. E. P. Thompson, *Customs in Common: Studies in Traditional Popular Culture,* New York: New Press, 1993, p. 170.
37. Alexander Dalrymple, *A General View of the East India Company,* London: J. Nourse, 1772, pp. 19–21.
38. Indrani Chatterjee, *Gender, Slavery and Law in Colonial India,* New Delhi: Oxford University Press, 1999, pp. 225–226.
39. Gilles Deleuze and Felix Guattari, *Anti-Oedipus: Capitalism and Schizophrenia,* Minneapolis, MN: University of Minnesota Press, 1983, pp. 194–196.
40. See, for example, James Muldoon, "The Indian as Irishman," *Essex Institute Historical Collections,* vol. 3, no. 4, October 1975, pp. 284–285.
41. Anon. *A Demonstration of the Necessity and Advantages of a Free Trade to the East Indies,* London: C. Chapple, 1807, pp. 138–139.
42. Francis Fowke to F. Fowke, Benares, India, March 22, 1775. IOR/Mss EUR E3, p. 44.
43. Ibid., John Walsh to Ms. Fowke, June 30, 1777.
44. F. Fowke to M. Fowke, Benares, July 18, 1776. IOR/Mss. Eur. F2, p. 70.
45. Ibid., Francis Fowke to F. Fowke, April 30, 1977, p. 64.
46. Rev. William Tennant, *Indian Recreations: Consisting Chiefly of Strictures on the Domestic and Rural Economy of the Mahommedans and Hindoos,* Edinburgh: C. Stewart, 1803, vol. 1, p. 79.
47. *Sketches of India: Or, Observations Descriptive of the Scenery, &c., in Bengal, with Notes on the Cape of Good-Hope and St. Helena,* London: s. n., 1816, pp. 166–168.
48. Ibid., p. 171.
49. Emma Roberts, *East India Voyager,* p. 177.
50. Ibid.
51. *Sketches of India,* p. 111.
52. Tennant, *Indian Recreations,* vol. 1, p. 14.
53. Ibid., p. 13.
54. Ibid., p. 128.
55. Dalrymple, Alexander, *Measures to be Pursued in India for Ensuring the Permanency, and Augmenting the Commerce of the Company,* London: J. Nourse, 1772, p. 3.
56. Ibid.
57. Law, Thomas, *Sketch of Some Late Arrangements and a View of the Rising Resources in Bengal,* London: John Stockdale, 1792, p. 127.
58. Tennant, *Indian Recreations,* p. 129.
59. Ibid., pp. 135–136.
60. Alexander Dow, "Dissertation on the Origin of Despotism in Hindostan," in *The History of Hindostan,* p. lxxxi.
61. Tennant, *Indian Recreations,* p. 128.
62. J. Bennet, *The National Merchant,* pp. 125–126.
63. A. J. Barker, *The African Link,* London: Frank Cass, 1978, pp. 59, 66.
64. William Watts, *Memoirs of the Revolution in Bengal,* reprint, Calcutta: K. P. Bagchi, [1760], 1983, pp. 2–3.
65. Dow, "Dissertation on the Origin of Despotism," p. lxxv.
66. Ibid., pp. lxxv–lxxvi.
67. Ibid.
68. Ibid., p. lxxi.
69. Ibid., p. lxxii.
70. Ibid.
71. Orme, *Historical Fragments,* p. 262.
72. Ibid., pp. 298–299.
73. Colebrooke, *Remarks on the Present State of the Husbandry and Commerce of Bengal,* 1795, p. 6.
74. Elphinstone, *History of India,* pp. 169–170.
75. Ibid., p. 194.
76. Ibid., p. 195.
77. Ibid., p. 197.
78. Kames, *Sketches,* vol. 2, pp. 5–7.

79. *Indian Antiquities or Dissertations Relative to the Ancient Geographical Divisions, the Pure System of Primeval Theology, the Grand Code of Civil Laws, the Original Form of Government, and the Various and Profound Literature of Hindostan,* London: W. Richardson, 1792, vol. 1, part 1, pp. 825–856.
80. Tennant, *Indian Recreations,* p. 4.
81. See Rev. William C. Holden, *The Past and Future of the Kaffir Races,* facsimile reprint, Cape Town: C. Struik [1866], 1963, p. 3.
82. See *The Word "Hotttentot": Articles Extracted from the Transactions of the Philosophical Society,* London, 1866, Pretoria: Pretoria State Library, 1971, pp. 15–16.
83. See A. J. Tancred, *Letters to Sir Peregrine Maitland, Governor of the Colony of the Cape of Good Hope on the Present Kafir War,* Cape Town: De Zuid-Afrikaan, 1846, p. 96.
84. See Brian D. Osborne's "Introduction" in Thomas Pennant, *A Tour in Scotland, 1769,* Edinburgh: Birlinn, 2000, p. xii.
85. Orme, *Historical Fragments,* p. 265.
86. Ibid.
87. Tennant, *Indian Recreations,* p. 345.
88. Ibid.
89. Ibid., pp. 355–356.
90. Colebrooke, *Remarks,* vol. 2, p. 4.
91. Ibid., pp. 4–5.
92. Ibid., p. 25.
93. Ibid., p. 27.
94. Ibid., p. 15.
95. Ibid., pp. 16–17.
96. Ibid.
97. Ibid., p. 11.
98. Ibid., pp. 18–19.
99. Colebrooke, p. 28.
100. Ibid.
101. Ibid., p. 29.
102. Ibid.
103. Ibid., p. 30.
104. Tennant, *Indian Recreations,* pp. 102–103.
105. Ibid., p. 103.
106. Ibid., p. 104.
107. Ibid., pp. 104–105.
108. See, for example, Karen Ordahl Kupperman, *Settling with the Indians: The Meeting of English and Indian Cultures in America, 1580–1640,* Totowa, NJ: Rowman and Littlefield, 1980, pp. 2–3.
109. Ibid., p. 25.
110. Ibid., pp. 104–105, 121–125.
111. Ibid., p. 128.
112. James Boswell, *Journal of a Tour to the Hebrides with Samuel Johnson,* London: Office of the National Illustrated Library [1746], 1852, p. 120.
113. Ibid., p. 129, trans. Robert Carruthers.
114. Pennant, *Tour in Scotland,* p. 127.
115. Ibid., p. 128.
116. Ibid., p. 84.
117. John Carr, *The Stranger in Ireland: Or, a Tour in the Southern and Western Parts of that Country, in the Year 1805,* Philadelphia: Samuel F. Bradford, John Conrad etc. 1806, p. 45.
118. Ibid., p. 181.
119. Ibid.
120. Ibid., p.182.
121. Alexander Dalrymple, *General Remarks on the System of Government in India; With Farther Considerations on the Present State of the Company at Home and Abroad,* London: J. Nourse, 1773, p. 68.
122. Ibid., p. 65.
123. Blathazar Solvyns, quoted in Mildred Archer and R. Lightbown, *India Observed: India as Viewed by British Artists, 1760–1860,* London: Victoria and Albert Museum, 1982, p. 84.
124. Quoted in Mildred Archer, *Early Views of India: The Picturesque Journeys of Thomas and William Daniell, 1786–1794,* London: Thames and Hudson, 1980, p. 224.

125. See William Foster, "British Artists in India, 1760–1820," in *The Nineteenth Volume of the Walpole Society, 1930–1931,* Oxford: Oxford University Press, 1931, p. 22.

126. See Pal and Dehejia, *From Merchants to Emperors,* p. 98.

127. See William Gilpin, *Three Essays on Picturesque Beauty: On Picturesque Travel and on Sketching Landscape,* 2nd ed., London: R. Blamire, 1794.

128. See Warren Hasting's handwritten notes on Gilpin, *Three Essays,* Houghton Library, Harvard University, p. 3.

129. I am indebted to Dr. Urmila Dé for bringing Devis to my attention.

130. See Stephen Whittle's introduction to Stephen Whittle ed. *Arthur William Devis, 1762–1822,* Preston, Lancashire: Harris Museum and Art Gallery, 2000, p. 10.

131. Foster, "British Artists in India," p. 24.

132. George Keate, *An Account of the Pelew Islands Situated in the Western Part of the Pacific Ocean, Composed from the Journals and Communications of Captain Henry Wilson, and Some of His Officers, Who in August 1783, were there Shipwrecked,* Philadelphia, PA: Joseph Crukshank, 1789, p. 194.

133. Mildred Archer, *India and British Portraiture, 1770–1825,* London, New York, Karachi, and Delhi: Oxford University Press, 1979, p. 238.

134. Keate, *An Account of the Pelew Islands,* p. 209.

135. Whittle, in *Arthur William Devis,* p. 14.

136. Sydney H. Pavière, "Biographical Notes on the Devis Family of Painters," in *The Twenty-Fifth Volume of the Walpole Society, 1936–1937,* Oxford: Oxford University Press, 1937, p. 141.

137. *A Descriptive Catalogue of a few Asiatic Subjects, Illustrative of the Agriculture, Arts and Manufactures of Hindoostan, Being Part of a More Extensive Work, Painted by A. W. Devis,* Westminster: G. Smeeton, 1821; see also Pavière, "Biographical Notes," p. 142.

138. Pavière, "Biographical Notes," pp. 159–161.

139. *A Descriptive Catalogue,* p. 3.

140. Ibid., p. 15.

141. Ibid., p. 14.

142. Ibid., p. 15.

143. Cohn, *Colonialism and Its Forms of Knowledge,* p. 12.

144. Sir John Sinclair, *Analysis of the Statistical Account of Scotland with a General View of the History of that Country and Discourses on Some Important Branches of Political Economy,* Edinburgh: Arch. Constable and Company, 1825, reprint, New York and London: Johnson Reprint Corporation, 1970, pp. 6, 59.

145. See C. E. A. W. Oldham's "Introduction," in *Journal of Francis Buchanan, Kept During the Survey of the District of Shahabad in 1812–1813,* Patna: Superintendent, Government Printing, Bihar and Orissa, 1926, p. ii. See also Sir David Prain, "Sketch of the Life of Francis Hamilton," *Annals of the Royal Botanical Garden,* Calcutta, vol. 10, 1905.

146. See the Introduction, in Francis Buchanan, *An Account of the Districts of Bihar and Patna in 1811–1812,* Patna: Bihar and Orissa Research Society, 1936, p. 1.

147. Ibid., pp. i–ii.

148. Ibid., p. ii.

149. Ibid., p. iii.

150. C. Oldham, "Introduction," *Journal of Francis Buchanan, Shahabad,* p. v.

151. See the introduction to the *Journal of Francis Buchanan (Afterwards Hamilton) Kept During the Survey of the Districts of Patna and Gaya in 1811–1812,* ed. by V. H. Jackson, Patna: Superintendent, Government Printing, Bihar and Orissa, 1925, pp. xi–xii.

152. C. Oldham, "Introduction," *Journal of Francis Buchanan, Shahabad,* p. xi.

153. Mary Poovey, *Making a Social Body: British Cultural Formation, 1830–1864,* Chicago and London: University of Chicago Press, 1995, pp. 6–7.

154. Chloe Chard, *Pleasure and Guilt on the Grand Tour: Travel Writing and Imaginative Geography, 1600–1830,* Manchester and New York: Manchester University Press, 1999, p. 37 For a study of travel as integral to the vision of empire and its negotiation of cultural difference, see Mary Louise Pratt, *Imperial Eyes: Travel Writing and Transculturation,* London and New York: Routledge, 1991.

155. Anthony Fletcher, *Gender, Sex, and Subordination in England, 1500–1800,* New Haven, CT: Yale University Press, 1995, esp. chap. 16.

156. *The Art of Governing a Wife: With Rules for Batchelors,* London: J. Robinson, 1747; Thomas Gisborne, *An Enquiry Into the Duties of the Female Sex,* reprint, Philadelphia: James Humphreys, [1797], 1798.

157. On this, see Catherine Hall, "The Early Formation of Victorian Domestic Ideology," in her *White, Male and Middle Class: Explorations in Feminism and History,* New York: Routledge, 1992; for a contrary perspective, see Amanda Vickery, "Golden Age to Separate Spheres? A Review of the Categories and Chronology of English Women's History," *Historical Journal,* no. 36, 1993, pp. 383–414.

158. John Tosh, *A Man's Place: Masculinity and the Middle-Class Home in Victorian England,* New Haven and London: Yale University Press, 1999, pp. 13, 102–122.

NOTES TO CHAPTER 5

1. *Imperial Parliament, House of Commons* (publication details missing), p. 1. Phillips Library, Peabody Essex Museum, Salem.

2. Mackintosh, "Notice of the Life, Writings and Speeches," p. xxxix.

3. Ivan Hannaford, *Race: The History of an Idea in the West,* Washington, DC: Woodrow Wilson Center Press, 1996, pp. 147–148.

4. Lovejoy, *Great Chain of Being,* p. 244.

5. Richard H. Popkin, "The Philosophical Bases of Modern Racism," in Craig Walton and John P. Anton eds., *Philosophy and the Civilizing Arts: Essays Presented to Herbert W. Schneider,* Athens, OH: Ohio University Press, 1974, p. 132.

6. Kames, *Sketches of the History of Man,* pp. 11–22.

7. Ibid., pp. 64–65.

8. Popkin, "The Philosophical Bases of Modern Racism," p. 138.

9. Stephen J. Gould, *The Mismeasure of Man,* New York and London: Norton, 1981, pp. 31–39.

10. Ronald Hyam, *Empire and Sexuality: The British Experience,* Manchester and New York, *Manchester University Press,* p. 211.

11. Ann Laura Stoler, *Race and the Education of Desire: Foucault's* History of Sexuality *and the Colonial Order of Things,* Durham, NC, and London: Duke University Press, 1995.

12. Robert Young, *Colonial Desire: Hybridity in Theory, Culture, and Race,* London and New York: Routledge, 1995, pp. 25–26.

13. See the introduction to Michael Roper and John Tosh, *Manful Assertions,* pp. 13–14.

14. See, for instance, Percival Spear, *The Nabobs: A Study of the Social Life of the English in Eighteenth Century India,* London: Curzon Press, 1980; Kenneth Ballhatchet, *Race, Sex and Class under the Raj: Imperial Attitudes and Policies and their Critics, 1793–1905,* New York: St. Martin's Press, 1980; and, more recently, Ronald Hyam, *Empire and Sexuality,* pp. 115–116.

15. A. B. Keith, ed., *Speeches & Documents on Indian Policy,* vol. 1, New Delhi: Anmol Publications, 1985, p. 146.

16. Speech at the Hastings trial, February 15, 1788. Keith, *Speeches and Documents,* p. 128.

17. Francis Hutchins, *The Illusion of Permanence: British Imperialism in India,* Princeton, NJ: Princeton University Press, 1967, p. 19.

18. Cited in Dennis Kincaid, *British Social Life in India, 1608–1937,* London: Routledge, 1938, p. 79.

19. Mildred Archer, *India and British Portraiture, 1770–1825,* London, New York, Karachi, and Delhi: Oxford University Press, 1979, p. 39.

20. Kincaid, *British Social Life,* p. 80.

21. Pal and Dehejia, *From Merchants to Emperors,* pp. 55–56.

22. Ibid., pp. 57, 61.

23. Keith, *Speeches and Documents,* pp. 143–145.

24. J. R. Martin, *Notes on the Medical Topography of Calcutta,* Calcutta: Departments of State and Public Institutions, Medical Board, 1837, p. 45.

25. Hennen, quoted by Martin. See Dr. John Hennen, *Sketches of the Medical Topography of the Mediterranean: Comprising an Account of Gibraltar, the Ionian Islands, and Malta,* ed. J. Hennen, London: s.n., 1830; and also his *Principles of Military Surgery, Comprising Observations on the Arrangement, Police, and Practice of Hospitals, and on the History, Treatment and Anomalies of Variola and Syphilis,* 2nd ed., Edinburgh, s.n., 1820.

26. Nancy Leys Stepan, *Picturing Tropical Nature,* Ithaca, NY: Cornell University Press, 2001, p. 31.

27. Ibid.

28. Ibid., p. 36.

29. Ibid., pp. 88–94.

30. Tennant, *Indian Recreations,* vol. 1, p. 76.

31. Ibid., pp. 77–78.

32. Martin, *Notes on the Medical Topography of Calcutta,* p. 155.

33. Jackson quoted in Martin, *Notes on the Medical Topography,* pp. 156–157.
34. Martin, *Notes,* p. 163.
35. Ibid.
36. Ibid. See also Alexander Hamilton, *A New Account of the East Indies,* Edinburgh: J. Mosman, 1727.
37. "On the Yearly Mortality at Calcutta," in *The East India Register and Directory for 1803,* London: Black, Kingsbury, Parbury and Allen, 1803, p. 59.
38. Ibid., p. 60.
39. Tennant, *Thoughts on the Effects of the British Government on the State of India,* pp. 57–58.
40. For a recent and in-depth study and reevaluation of this subject, see Durba Ghosh, "Colonial Companions: Bibis, Begums, and Concubines of the British North India, 1760–1830" Ph.D. Dissertation submitted to the University of California, Berkeley, 2000.
41. Capt. Thomas Williamson, *The East India Vade Mecum,* 1810, quoted in M. Archer, *India and British Portraiture,* p. 51. For an extended discussion of Williamson's attitude, see Durba Ghosh, "Colonial Companions," pp. 45–46.
42. See S. C. Hill, ed., *List of Europeans and Others in Bengal in 1756 at the Time of the Siege in Calcutta,* pp. 1–99.
43. Williamson, cited in S. C. Ghosh, *Social Condition,* p. 61.
44. J. Blackiston, *Twelve Years' Military Adventure in Three Quarters of the Globe: Or, Memoirs of an Officer Who Served in the Armies of His Majesty and of the East India Company, Between the Years 1802 and 1814,* London: Henry Colburn, 1829, pp. 49–50.
45. Ibid., p. 51.
46. Kincaid, *British Social Life,* p. 51.
47. Harry Hobbs, "Old-Time European Women," in H. S. Bhatia, ed., *European Women in India: Their Life and Adventures,* New Delhi: Deep and Deep, 1979, p. 15.
48. Percival Spear, *The Nabobs,* p. 62.
49. Spear, *The Nabobs,* p. 63.
50. William Hickey, *Memoirs of William Hickey,* vol. 4, London: Hurst and Blackett, 1913–25, pp. 140–141.
51. S. C. Ghosh, *Social Condition,* pp. 73–74.
52. D. Ghosh, "Colonial Companions," pp. 79, 173–174.
53. S. C. Ghosh, *Social Condition,* p. 77.
54. Williamson, *East India Vade Mecum,* vol. 1, p. 452.
55. Ketaki Kushari Dyson, *A Various Universe: A Study of the Journals and Memoirs of British Men and Women in the Indian Subcontinent, 1765–1856,* Delhi: Oxford University Press, 1978, p. 81.
56. See Qurratulain Hyder Foreword, in Hasan Shah, *The Dancing Girl: A Novel,* New York: New Directions, 1993, pp. ix–xii.
57. See Muhammad Hasan Shah, *Nishtar,* Lahore: Majlis Tavagi-yi Adab, 1923.
58. Capt. Thomas Williamson, *East India Vade Mecum or Complete Guide to Gentlemen Intended for the Civil, Military or Naval Service of the Honourable East India Company,* London: Black, Parry, and Kingsbury, 1810, vol. 1, p. 451.
59. J. Blackiston, *Twelve Years' Military Adventure,* p. 29.
60. Keith, *Speeches and Documents,* p. 138.
61. Thomas Motte, "A Narrative of a Journey to the Diamond Mines of Sumbhulpoor, in the Province of Orissa," in *The Asiatic Annual Register for the Year 1799,* London: J. Debrett, 1800, p. 56.
62. Ibid., p. 57.
63. James Forbes, *Oriental Memoirs: A Narrative of Seventeen Years Residence in India,* London: Richard Bentley, 1834, vol. 2, p. 52.
64. Tennant, *Thoughts on the Effects of the British Government on the State of India,* p. 62.
65. Ibid., pp. 62–63.
66. For an interesting discussion of the role of servants in the lives of the British in India, see R. V. Vernède, ed., *British Life in India: An Anthology of Humorous and Other Writings Perpetrated by the British in India, 1750–1950,* p. 97.
67. Ibid., pp. 98–99.
68. Emma Roberts, "The East India Voyager," *Oriental Herald,* vol. 3, no. 13, 1839 British Library 1509/1014, p. 181.
69. Ibid., p. 184.
70. See, esp., Kenneth Ballhatchet, *Race, Sex and Class,* pp. 96–97; and Spear, *The Nabobs,* pp. 140–141.
71. Catherine Hall, *White, Male and Middle Class: Explorations in Feminism and History,* New York: Routledge, 1992, pp. 205–207.

72. Bishop Heber describes a similar number of servants in his travel narrative. See Reginald Heber, *Narrative of a Journey through the Upper Provinces of India, from Calcutta to Bombay, 1824–1825,* 3rd edition, London: J. Murray, 1828, p. 25.

73. Colesworthy Grant, *An Anglo-Indian Domestic Sketch: A Letter from an Artist in India to His Mother in England,* Calcutta: Thacker and Company, 1849, p. 87.

74. Ibid.

75. Winthrop D. Jordan, *White over Black: American Attitudes toward the Negro, 1550–1812,* Chapel Hill, NC: University of North Carolina Press, 1968, p. 163.

76. Ibid., p. 168.

77. Kathleen Brown, "Native Americans and Early Modern Concepts of Race," in Martin Daunton and Rick Halpern, eds., *Empire and Others: British Encounters with Indigenous Peoples, 1600–1850,* Philadelphia, PA: University of Pennsylvania Press, 1999.

78. Kathleen Brown, *Good Wives, Nasty Wenches, and Anxious Patriarchs: Gender, Race, and Power in Colonial Virginia,* Chapel Hill, NC: University of North Carolina Press, 1996, pp. 66–67, 131–134.

79. Ibid., pp. 181–186.

80. Peter Marshall, "The Whites of British India, 1780–1830: A Failed Colonial Society?" in *Trade and Conquest: Studies on the Rise of British Dominance in India,* Hampshire, UK: Varorium, 1993, pp. 26–44.

81. Valencia, quoted in Herbert Alick Stark, *John Ricketts and His Times, Being a Narrative Account of Anglo-Indian Affairs during the Eventful Years from 1791 to 1835,* Calcutta: Wilsone, 1934, pp. 19–20.

82. C. J. Hawes, *Poor Relations: The Making of a Eurasian Community in British India,* Surrey, UK: Curzon Press, 1996, pp. 71–72.

83. This is the position of S. C. Ghosh, contrary to that of H. A. Stark. See *Social Condition,* p. 87.

84. H. A. Stark, *Hostages to India, or; The Life Story of the Anglo-Indian Race,* Calcutta: Fine Art Cottage, 1926, pp. 56–57.

85. Will of Francis Fowke, July 18, 1781, IOR/Mss EUR F3, pp. 30–31.

86. Stark, *Hostages to India.,* p. 60.

87. Hawes, *Poor Relations,* p. 55; also S. C. Ghosh, *Social Condition,* p. 83.

88. Charles Ross, ed., *Correspondence of Charles, First Marquis Cornwallis,* vol. 2, London: John Murray, 1859, p. 570.

89. Ibid., p. 576.

90. S. C. Ghosh, *Social Condition,* p. 84.

91. "Funds for the Maintenance of the Orphans of the Company's Military Officers," IOR, HM 85, pp. 49, 52.

92. IOR, HM 730, p. 82.

93. Extract, military letter from Fort St. George, September 8, 1805, Board's Collection (hereafter BC), India Office Library and Records, London (hereafter IOR), F/4/211, no. 4716.

94. For example, Mary Christie, the widow of one Sergeant James Dick, was identified as a "native of India" from her marriage certificate, and her claim on her late husband's pension was denied. Similarly, the widow of Sgt. Samuel Vinon, although legally married, was not allowed a share in her husband's assets as she appeared to be a "Malabar woman" and a "native of India." (Extract, military letter to Fort Saint George, September 7, 1808), BC, IOR, F/4/360, no. 8774.

95. Stark, *John Ricketts,* p. 27; Hawes, *Poor Relations,* pp. 66–67.

96. Extract, military letter to Bombay, January 17, 1810. The proposals were adopted in 1816; see extract, military letter to Bombay, May 4, 1816, BC, IOR, F/4/538, no. 12948.

97. See Ghosh, "Colonial Companions," pp. 244–245.

98. See H. Torrance's letter of August 21, 1820, and extract, military letter from Bengal, July 7, 1817, IOR, L/MIL/5/376, pp. 231–232, 238–239.

99. Ibid., p. 233.

100. Ibid., pp. 252–253. Thus Elizabeth Sheeliah and Mary Ann Putnam were placed in the Lower Orphan School in Calcutta: Jane and Amelia Flack, Mary Crawford, Mary Fit, Elizabeth Blannagan, and Sarah Barron went to the Public Seminary in Calcutta.

101. Extract, military letter of July 21, 1818, and separate military letter from Bengal, February 15, 1819, IOR, L/MIL/5/376, pp. 239, 242.

102. See extract, military letter from Madras, October 17, 1812, and extract, Bengal military consultations, March 25, 1817, L/MIL/5/376, pp. 246–247.

103. See, for instance, David Arnold, "European Orphans and Vagrants in India in the Nineteenth Century," *Journal of Imperial and Commonwealth History,* no. 7, 1978, pp. 109–127; D. Ghosh, "Colonial Companions," Chap. 5.

104. Minutes of evidence by J. W. Ricketts before the Select Committee of the House of Lords on East India Affairs, March 31, 1830, cited in S. C. Ghosh, *Social Condition,* p. 89.
105. Minutes of evidence by J. W. Ricketts before the Select Committee of the House of Commons on East India Affairs, June 21, 1830, cited in S. C. Ghosh, *Social Condition,* p. 89.
106. Martin, *Notes,* p. 44.
107. See extract, military letter from Madras, August 11, 1817, BC, IOR, F/4/557, no. 13666.
108. Female orphans in the Bengal Military Orphan Society were instructed in the arts of milliners and staymakers. Their relatives, guardians, or trustees received an annual sum of £40 for their upkeep until they could find their own husbands and homes. See "Memorial of the General Management of the Bengal Military Orphan Society," BC, IOR, F/4/712, no. 19454.
109. Capt. Albert Hervey, *A Soldier of the Company: Life of an Indian Ensign, 1833–43,* ed. Charles Allen London: Michael Joseph, 1988, p. 77.
110. Hervey, *A Soldier of the Company,* p. 79.
111. "On a Beautiful East Indian," in *The Asiatic Journal and Monthly Register for British India and its Dependencies,* vol. 2, June-December, 1816, p. 581.
112. Orme, *Fragments,* p. 301.
113. *Sketches of India,* pp. 167–168.
114. *Bengal Hurkaru,* March 26, 1825 quoted in Stark, *John Ricketts,* p. 23.
115. *Sketches of India,* pp. 164–165.
116. Ibid., p. 166.
117. Robert Grant, *The Expediency Maintained of Continuing the System by which the Trade and Government of India are now Regulated,* London: Black, Parry and Co., 1813, p. 226.
118. Ibid., p. 227.
119. Ibid., pp. 227–228.
120. This is the breakdown given in the contemporary account of the Moravian missionary to the Virgin Islands. See C. G. A. Oldendorf, "On the Various Colors of the Inhabitants of the Three Islands and Health Conditions among the Whites" in *St. Thomas in Early Danish Times: A General Description of all the Danish, American, or West Indian Islands,* trans. Arnold Highfield, St. Croix: Virgin Islands Humanities Council, 1997, p. 137. See also Johan J. Bossart, *C. G. A. Oldendorps Geschichte der Mission der Evangelischen Brüder auf den Caraibischen Inseln S. Thomas, S. Croix and S. Jan,* Barby: Christian Friedrich Laux, 1777.
121. For more extensive discussion, see B. W. Higman, *Slave Populations of the British Caribbean, 1807–1834,* Baltimore, MD: Johns Hopkins University Press, 1984.
122. H. T. Colebrooke, *Remarks,* pp. 91–92.
123. Marshall, "The Whites of British India,", p. 32.
124. "British India and its Mal-Administration (A Review of Auber, Rise and Progress of the British Power in India, London: Allen, 1837)," in *Parbury's Oriental Herald and Colonial Intelligencer,* London: Parbury, 1838, vol. 1, p. 142.
125. Grant, *The Expediency Maintained,* p. 182.
126. Stark, *John Ricketts,* pp. 37–38.
127. Memorial of the General Management of the Bengal Military Orphan Society, 1783, BC, IOR, F/4/712, no. 19454.
128. *The Asiatic Journal* 1825, quoted in Stark, *John Ricketts,* pp. 38–39.
129. Ibid., p. 76.
130. See military letter to Bombay, February 8, 1832, military letter from Bombay, December 4, 1833, Directors of the Military Fund to Chief Secretary Norris, August 15, 1833, and "Petition of the East Indians to the Court of Directors," BC, IOR, F/4/1454, no. 57236.
131. "Petition of the East Indians." Emphasis in the original.
132. "Petition of the East Indians."
133. Stark, *Hostages to India,* p. 65.
134. "Petition of the East Indians to the Honorable Commons of the United Kingdom of Great Britain and Ireland in Parliament Assembles." See Appendix A, Stark, *John Ricketts,* p. 5.
135. "Petition of the Christian Natives of India," in *Hansard's Parliamentary Debates,* London: Baldwin and Cradock; J. Booker; Longman, Rees, and Orme etc., 1830, new series, vol. 23, p. 962.
136. Ibid., p. 963.
137. "Parliamentary Debate on the occasion of the presentation of the East Indian's Petition to the House of Commons by the Right Honorable Mr. William Wynn, MP, on the 4th May, 1830." Appendix D, Stark, *John Ricketts,* p. 34.

138. "Proceedings of the Public Meeting held on the 28th March, 1831 in the Town Hall, Calcutta, to receive the Report of Mr. J. W. Ricketts, the Agent of the East Indians, just returned from his Deputation with their Petition to the British Parliament." Appendix F, Stark, *John Ricketts*, p. 49.
139. Ibid., p. 88.
140. Heber, *Narrative*, p. 57.
141. "Sketches in India," quoted in Stark, *Hostages to India*, p. 119.
142. "Proceedings of the Public Meeting," Stark, *John Ricketts*, p. 49.
143. *Sketches*, p. 165.
144. Ibid.
145. William Carey, (1794), quoted in Spear, *The Nabobs*, p. 197.
146. Tennant, *Recreations*, p. 101.
147. James Muldoon, "The Indian as Irishman," *Essex Institute Historical Collections*, vol. 3, no. 4, 1975, pp. 284–285.
148. *A Demonstration of the Necessity and Advantages of a Free Trade to the East Indies*, London: C. Chapple, 1807, pp. 138–139.
149. Alexander Dalrymple, *Measures to be Pursued in India for Ensuring the Permanency, and Augmenting the Commerce of the Company*, London: J. Nourse, 1772, p. 3.
150. A. J. Barker, *The African Link*, London: Frank Cass, 1978, pp. 59, 66.
151. Kant, "Von den vershidenen racen der Menschen," pp. 17–18.
152. Popkin, *The Philosophical Bases of Modern Racism*, pp. 134–135.
153. Ibid. See also another version of this essay, "The Philosophical Basis of Eighteenth Century Racism," in *Racism in the Eighteenth Century*, ed. Harold E. Pagliaro, Cleveland and London: Case Western Reserve University Press, 1973, pp. 245–262.
154. Georges Cuvier, "The Animal Kingdom," in *This Is Race*, pp. 44–45.
155. Chevalier de Lamarck, "Zoological Philosophy," in *This Is Race*, pp. 40–43.
156. Robert Orme, *Historical Fragments of the Mogul Empire*, ed. J. P. Guha, New Delhi: Associated Publishing House [1782], 1974, p. 262.
157. Orme, *Historical Fragments*, pp. 298–299.
158. Martin, *Notes on the Medical Topography*, p. 43.
159. Ibid., p. 52; emphasis in the original.
160. Grant, *Expediency Maintained*, p. 236.
161. Ibid.
162. J. Crawfurd, "Free Trade Pamphlet," quoted in *The Political Commercial & Financial Condition of the Anglo-Eastern Empire in 1832*, London: Parbury, Allen and Co., 1832, p. 37.
163. *Political Commercial & Financial Condition of the Anglo-Eastern Empire*, p. 50.
164. Grant, *Expediency Maintained*, p. 174.
165. Martin, *Notes on the Medical Topography of Calcutta*, pp. 173, 175.
166. Emma Roberts, "The East India Voyager," *Oriental Herald*, vol. 1, no. 3, British Library 1509/1014, p. 397.
167. Ibid., pp. 397–398.
168. "The East India Company's Army," *Calcutta Gazette*, October 26, 1797, in W. S. Seton-Karr, *Selections from the Calcutta Gazettes*, vol. 3, Calcutta: Microform Publication, 1987, pp. 115–119.
169. John Briggs, *Letters Addressed to a Young Person in India*, London: John Murray, 1828, p. 14.
170. Rozina Visram, *Ayahs, Lascars and Princes*, pp. 13–17.
171. Ibid., p. 11.
172. Heber, *Narrative*, p. 57.
173. Letter of Monday, April 5, 1830 to the editor of the Government Gazette, in Anil Chandra Das Gupta, ed., *The Days of John Company: Selections from the Calcutta Gazette, 1824–1832*, Calcutta: Government Printing, West Bengal, 1959, pp. 492–493.
174. J. Blackiston, *Twelve Years' Military Adventure*, p. 51.
175. Hervey, *A Soldier of the Company*, p. 79.
176. For ideas of technological superiority and global hegemony of European nations, see M. Adas, *Machines as the Measure of Men*, Ithaca, NY: Cornell University Press, 1989.
177. See Nancy Leys Stepan, *The Idea of Race in Science: Great Britain 1800–1960*, Connecticut: Archon Books, 1982, "Introduction."
178. For a discussion of the idea of race as a formative force, see Hannaford, *Race: The History of an Idea in the West*, Washington, DC: Woodrow Wilson Center Press, 1996, pp. 189, 232.
179. Hannaford, *Race*, pp. 213–214.
180. I borrow the term from Richard Godbeer's "Eroticizing the Middle Ground: Anglo-Indian Sexual Relations," in Martha Hodes, ed., *Sex, Love, Race: Crossing Boundaries in North American History*, New York, New York University Press, 1999, p. 92.

NOTES TO AFTERWORD

1. J. R. Seely, *Expansion of England*, p. 206.
2. Ibid., p. 135.
3. Ibid., p. 143.
4. Colley, *Britons*, p. 145.
5. Wahrman, "The English Problem of Identity," pp. 5–6; also Breen, "Ideology and Nationalism," pp. 28–29.
6. Armitage, *Ideological Origins*, pp. 10–11.
7. Seely, *Expansion of England*, p. 202.
8. For a study of the Anglo-Irish that is relevant to this very point, see John Hutchinson, *The Dynamics of Cultural Nationalism: The Gaelic Revival and the Creation of the Irish Nation State*, London: Allen and Unwin, 1987, pp. 50–53.
9. Samuel Johnson, *Journey to the Western Islands of Scotland*, London: Oxford University Press Humphrey Milford, 1934, p. 42.
10. Pitt, quoted in Seely, *Expansion of England*, p. 198
11. Ibid., p. 198.
12. Lawrence James, *The Rise and Fall of the British Empire*, New York: St. Martin's Press, 1994, p. 135.
13. For comparison, see Thomas Douglas, Earl of Selkirk, *Observations on the Present State of the Highlands of Scotland with a View of the Causes and Probable Consequences of Emigration*, 2nd ed., Edinburgh: A. Constable, 1806. On Ireland, see Nicholas Canny, *Kingdom and Colony: Ireland, in the Atlantic World, 1560–1800*, Baltimore, MD: Johns Hopkins University Press, 1988; Canny, "Identity Formation in Ireland: Emergence of the Anglo-Irish," in Nicholas Canny and Anthony Pagden, eds., *Colonial Identity in the Atlantic World, 1500–1800*, Princeton, NJ: Princeton University Press, 1987; and also R. B. MacDowell, *Ireland in the Age of Imperialism and Revolution, 1760–1801*, Oxford: Clarendon Press, 1979. For a much more nuanced study of lyrical nationalism in literature, see Katie Trumpener, *Bardic Nationalism: The Romantic Novel and the British Empire*, Princeton, NJ: Princeton University Press, 1997, esp. pp. 22–23.
14. S. C. Ghosh, *Social Condition*, p. 155.
15. See Douglas Peers, *Between Mars and Mammon: Colonial Armies and the Garrison State in India, 1819–35*, London: Aldershot, 1995; and Seema Alavi, *The Sepoys and the Company: Tradition and Transition in Northern India, 1770–1830*, Delhi: Oxford University Press, 1995.
16. See IOR K/2/1.
17. See the entry "Lunatics of the Indian Naval and Military Services," in Memo book 1/4/78. See also the dispatch to India Public Department June 28, 1820. IOR K/2/34.
18. *Blackwood's Edinburgh Magazine*, no. xlviii, vol. 8, March 1821, pp. 665–667.
19. R. Farmer, *The Soldier: An Historical Poem, in Three Parts, Containing an Epitome of the Wars Entered into by Great Britain, from the Year 1739 to the Present Time*, London: Lackington, Allen Co.; Crosby and Letterman, etc., 1802, part 1, p. 21.

Select Bibliography

Adas, Michael. *Machines as the Measure of Men*. Ithaca, NY: Cornell University Press, 1989.

Alavi, Seema. *The Sepoys and the Company: Tradition and Transition in Northern India, 1770–1830*. Delhi: Oxford University Press, 1995.

Alavi, Ziauddin. *Arab Geography in the Ninth and Tenth Centuries*. Aligarh: Aligarh Muslim University, 1965.

Allen, Charles, ed. *A Soldier of the Company: Life of an Indian Ensign, 1833–43*. London: Michael Joseph, 1988.

Alpers, Svetlana. *The Art of Describing*. Chicago: University of Chicago Press, 1983.

Amussen, Susan Dwyer. *An Ordered Society: Gender and Class in Early Modern England*. New York: Columbia University Press, 1993.

Anderson, Adam. *An Historical and Chronological Deduction of the Origin of Commerce, from the Earliest Accounts Containing an History of the Great Commercial Interests of the British Empire*. Vol. 3. London: J. White and Company, 1801.

Anderson, Benedict. *Imagined Communities*. London and New York: Verso, 1991. Reprint, 1992.

Anonymous. *A Descriptive Catalogue of a Few Asiatic Subjects, Illustrative of the Agriculture, Arts, and Manufactures of Hindoostan, Painted by A. W. Devis*. Westminster, UK: G. Smeeton, 1821.

———. *Articles Extracted from the Transactions of the Philosophical Society*. London, 1866; Pretoria: Pretoria State Library, 1971.

———. *Chartered Rights*. London: A. McPherson, n.d.

———. *The Art of Governing a Wife: With Rules for Batchelors*. London: J. Robinson, 1747.

———. *Thoughts on the Present East India Bill: Passed into a Law, August 1784*. London: John Stockdale, 1784.

———. *Indian Antiquities or Dissertations Relative to the Ancient Geographical Divisions, the Pure System of Primeval Theology, the Grand Code of Civil Laws, the Original Form of Government, and the Various and Profound Literature of Hindostan*. Vol. 1. London: W. Richardson, 1792.

———. *A Demonstration of the Necessity and Advantages of a Free Trade to the East Indies*. London: C. Chapple, 1807.

———. *Sketches of India: Or, Observations Descriptive of the Scenery, &c., in Bengal, with Notes on the Cape of Good-Hope and St. Helena*. London: s.n., 1816.

Archer, Mildred. *British Drawings in the India Office Library.* London: Her Majesty's Stationery Office, 1969.

———. *India and British Portraiture, 1770–1825.* London, New York, Karachi, and Delhi: Oxford University Press, 1979.

———. *Early Views of India: The Picturesque Journeys of Thomas and William Daniell, 1786–1794.* London: Thames and Hudson, 1980.

Archer, Mildred, and Lightbown, R. *India Observed: India as Viewed by British Artists, 1760–1860.* London: Victoria and Albert Museum, 1982.

Armitage, David. *The Ideological Origins of the British Empire.* Cambridge and New York: Cambridge University Press, 2000.

Aylmer, G. E. "The Peculiarities of the English State." *Journal of Historical Sociology* 3, no. 2 (1990): 91–108.

Aymard, Maurice, and Harbans Mukhia, eds. and trans. *French Studies in History.* Delhi: Orient Longman. 1990.

Baetjer, Katherine. *Glorious Nature: British Landscape Painting 1750–1850.* New York: Hudson Hills Press, 1993.

Bagehot. Walter. *The English Constitution.* Oxford: Oxford University Press, [1867] 2001.

Bailyn, Bernard. "The Challenge of Modern Historiography." *American Historical Review* 87, no. 1 (1982): 1–24.

Balibar, Etienne. "The Nation-Form: History and Ideology," *Review* XIII 3 (Summer 1990): 338–339.

Ball, Upendra Nath. *Rammohun Roy: A Study of His Life, Works and Thoughts.* Calcutta: U. Ray, 1933.

Ballhatchet, Kenneth. *Race, Sex and Class under the Raj: Imperial Attitudes and Policies and Their Critics.* New York: St. Martin's Press, 1980.

Barker, A. J. *The African Link.* London: Frank Cass, 1978.

Barrell, John. *The Political Theory of Painting from Reynolds to Hazlitt: "The Body of the Public."* New Haven, CT: Yale University Press, 1986.

Barrow, Ian. "Charted Histories in Colonial India, 1760–1900." Unpublished Ph.D. dissertation, University of Chicago, 1998.

Barry, Jonathan, and Christopher Brooks, eds. *The Middling Sort of People: Culture, Society, and Politics in England, 1550–1800.* New York: St. Martin's Press, 1994.

Baudrillard, Jean. *Symbolic Exchange and Death.* London: Sage Publications, 1993.

Bauer, R. W. *Boundaries and Frontiers in Medieval Muslim Geography.* Philadelphia, PA: American Philosophical Society, 1995.

Bayly, C. A. *Origins of Nationality in South Asia: Patriotism and Ethical Government in the Making of Modern India.* Delhi: Oxford University Press, 1998.

———. *Imperial Meridian: The British Empire and the World.* London and New York: Longman, 1989.

Beames, John. *Memoirs of a Bengal Civilian.* London, Chatto & Windus, 1961. Reprint, Delhi: South Asia Books, 1984.

Belloc, Hilaire. *A History of England.* Vol. 1. London and New York: G.P. Putnam, 1925.

Bennet, George, ed., *The Concept of Empire: Burke to Atlee.* London: Adam and Charles Black, 1953.

Bennet, John. *The National Merchant: Or Discourses on Commerce and Colonies; Being an Essay for Regulating and Improving the Trade and Plantations of Great Britain by Uniting the National and Mercatorial Interests.* London: J. Walthoe and T. Osborn, 1736.

Berger, John. *Ways of Seeing.* London: BBC and Penguin, 1972.

Bhaba, Homi. *Location of Culture.* London and New York: Routledge, 1994.

Bhatia, H. S., ed. *European Women in India: Their Life and Adventures.* New Delhi: Deep and Deep, 1979.

Bickham, George. *The British Monarchy, or a New Chorographical Description of All the Dominions Subject to the King of Great Britain.* London: Bunhill-Fields, 1743. Reprint, Newcastle upon Tyne, UK: Frank Graham, 1967.

Birmingham, Ann. *Landscape and Ideology: The English Rustic Tradition, 1740–1860.* Berkeley, CA: University of California Press, 1986.

Black, Jeremy. *Maps and History: Constructing Images of the Past.* New Haven, CT, and London: Yale University Press, 1997.

Blackiston, John. *Twelve Years' Military Adventure in Three Quarters of the Globe: Or, Memoirs of an Officer Who Served in the Armies of His Majesty and of the East India Company, between the Years 1802 and 1814.* London: Henry Colburn, 1829.

Blackstone, William. *The Sovereignty of the Law: Selections from Blackstone's Commentaries on the Laws of England.* Ed. Gareth Steadman Jones. Toronto: University of Toronto Press, 1973.

Bohun, Edmund. *A Geographical Dictionary: Representing the Present and Ancient Names of All the Countries, Provinces, Remarkable Cities, Universities, Ports, Towns, Mountains, Seas, Streights, Fountains, and Rivers of the Whole World: Their Distances, Longitudes, and Latitudes: With a Short Historical Account of the Same, and Their Present State.* . . . London: Charles Brome, 1691.

Bonnard, Georges A., ed. *Memoirs of My Life.* New York: Funk and Wagnall's 1966.

Bossart, Johan J. *C. G. A. Oldendorps Geschichte der Mission der Evangelischen Brüder auf den Caraibischen Inseln S. Thomas, S. Croix and S. Jan.* Barby: Bey Christian Friedrich Laux, 1777.

Boswell, James. *Journal of a Tour to the Hebrides with Samuel Johnson (1746).* London: Office of the National Illustrated Library, 1852.

Bowen, Huw V. "A Question of Sovereignty? The Bengal Land Revenue Issue, 1765–67." *Journal of Imperial and Commonwealth History* 16 (1988): 155–176.

———. *Revenue and Reform: The Indian Problem in British Politics, 1757–1773.* Cambridge, UK: Cambridge University Press, 1991.

Bowersock, G. W., Clive, John, and Graubard, Stephen, eds. *Edward Gibbon and the Decline and Fall of the Roman Empire.* Cambridge, MA: Harvard University Press, 1977.

Bradbrook, Muriel C. *Joseph Conrad: Poland's English Genius.* Cambridge: Cambridge University Press, 1941.

Braddick, Michael J. *The Nerves of State: Taxation and the Financing of the English State, 1558–1714.* Manchester and New York: Manchester University Press; New York: St. Martin's Press, 1996.

Breen, T. H. "Ideology and Nationalism on the Eve of the American Revolution: Revisions *Once More* in Need of Revising." *Journal of American History* no. 84 (June 1997): 13–39.

Brewer, John. *Sinews of Power.* New York: Alfred A. Knopf, 1989.

Brown, Kathleen. *Good Wives, Nasty Wenches, and Anxious Patriarchs: Gender, Race, and Power in Colonial Virginia.* Chapel Hill, NC: University of North Carolina Press, 1996.

Buchanan, Francis. *Journal of Francis Buchanan (Afterwards Hamilton) Kept During the Survey of the Districts of Patna and Gaya in 1811–1812.* Ed. V. H. Jackson. Patna: Superintendent, Government Printing, Bihar and Orissa, 1925.

———. *Journal of Francis Buchanan, Kept During the Survey of the District of Shahabad in 1812–1813.* Patna: Superintendent, Government Printing, Bihar and Orissa, 1926.

———. *An Account of the Districts of Bihar and Patna in 1811–1812.* Patna: Bihar and Orissa Research Society, 1936.

Burke, Edmund. *Reflections on the Revolution in France.* Philadelphia: Young, Dobson, Carey, and Rue, 1792.

———. *The Works of the Rt. Honorable Edmund Burke.* vols. 2–3. London: Henry G. Bohn, 1854–55.

Burton, Antoinette. "Who Needs the Nation? Interrogating 'British' History." *Journal of Historical Sociology* 10, no. 3 (September 1997): 227–248.

———. *At the Heart of Empire: Indians and the Colonial Encounter in Late-Victorian Britain.* Berkeley, CA: University of California Press, 1998.

Butler, Judith. *Bodies that Matter.* New York and London: Routledge, 1993.

Cannon, John. "The Survival of British Monarchy" (Prothero Lecture, July 3, 1985). *Transactions of the Royal Historical Society* 36 (1986): 143–164.

Canny, Nicholas. *Kingdom and Colony: Ireland in the Atlantic World, 1560–1800.* Baltimore, MD: Johns Hopkins University Press, 1988.

Canny, Nicholas, and Anthony Pagden, eds. *Colonial Identity in the Atlantic World, 1500–1800.* Princeton, NJ: Princeton University Press, 1987.

Carr, John. *The Stranger in Ireland: Or, a Tour in the Southern and Western Parts of that Country, in the Year 1805.* Philadelphia, PA: Samuel F. Bradford, John Conrad, etc. 1806.

Cavendish, Henry. *Debates of the House of Commons during the Thirteenth Parliament of Great Britain.* Vol. 1. London: Longman, Orme, Brown, Green & Longmans, 1840–1843.

Chambers, Ian, and Curtis, Lidia, eds. *The Post-Colonial Question: Common Skies, Divided Horizons.* New York: Routledge, 1996.

Chandra, Pramod. *The Tuti-Nama of the Cleveland Museum of Art and the Origins of Mughal Painting,* Graz, Austria: Akademische Druck und Verlagsanstalt, 1976.

Chard, Chloe. *Pleasure and Guilt on the Grand Tour: Travel Writing and Imaginative Geography, 1600–1830.* Manchester and New York: Manchester University Press, 1999.

Chatterjee, Indrani. *Gender, Slavery, and Law in Colonial India.* New Delhi: Oxford University Press, 1999.

Chatterjee, Partha. *The Nation and its Fragments: Colonial and Postcolonial Histories.* Princeton: Princeton University Press, 1964.

Chaudhuri, Nirad C. *Thy Hand, Great Anarch! India: 1921–1952.* Reading, UK: Addison-Wesley, 1987.

Clifford, James. *The Predicament of Culture.* Cambridge, MA: Harvard University Press, 1988.

Close, Charles. *The Early Years of the Ordnance Survey.* Devon, UK: David & Charles, 1969.

Cobbett, John M. and James P. eds. *Selections from Cobbett's Political Works.* Vol. 4. London: Anne Cobbett, 1835.

Cohen, Murray. *Sensible Words: Linguistic Practice in England 1640–1785.* Baltimore and London: Johns Hopkins University Press, 1977.

Cohn, Bernard S. "Representing Authority in Victorian India," in *An Anthropologist among the Historians and Other Essays.* Delhi: Oxford University Press, 1990.

———. "The Recruitment and Training of Civil Servants in India, 1600–1800," in *An Anthropologist among the Historians and Other Essays.* Delhi: Oxford University Press, 1990.

———. *Colonialism and Its Forms of Knowledge: The British in India.* Princeton, NJ: Princeton University Press, 1996.

Colebrooke, T. H. *Remarks on the Present State of the Husbandry and Commerce of Bengal.* Calcutta: s. n., 1795.

Colesworthy, Grant. *An Anglo-Indian Domestic Sketch: A Letter from an Artist in India to His Mother in England.* Calcutta: Thacker and Company, 1849.

Colley, Linda. "The Apotheosis of George III: Loyalty, Royalty and the British Nation 1760–1820." *Past and Present* 102 (1984): 94–129.

———. "Whose Nation? Class and National Consciousness in Britain, 1750–1830." *Past and Present* 113 (1986): 97–117.

———. *Britons: Forging a Nation, 1707–1837.* New Haven, CT: Yale University Press, 1992.

Collingwood, R. G. *The Idea of History.* New York: Oxford University Press, 1956.

Collini, Stefan. *English Pasts: Essays in History and Culture.* Oxford: Oxford University Press, 1999.

Copland, Thomas, ed. *Correspondence of Edmund Burke.* Cambridge, UK: Cambridge University Press, 1958–1978.

Corrigan, Philip. "Feudal Relics or Capitalist Monuments?" *Sociology* 11 (1977): 35–63.

Corrigan, Philip, and Sayer, Derek. *The Great Arch: English State Formation as Cultural Revolution.* Oxford: Basil Blackwell, 1985.

Count, Earl W. *This Is Race.* New York: Henry Schuman, 1950.

Crawfurd, J. *The Political Commercial & Financial Condition of the Anglo-Eastern Empire in 1832.* London: Parbury, Allen and Co., 1832.

Curtin, Philip. *The Image of Africa: British Ideas and Action, 1780–1850.* Madison: The University of Wisconsin Press, 1964.

Dalton, Charles. *Memoir of Captain Dalton, Defender of Trichinopoly, 1752–1753.* London: W. H. Allen, 1886.

Dalrymple, Alexander. *A General View of the East India Company.* London: s. n., 1772.

———. *Measures to Be Pursued in India for Ensuring the Permanency, and Augmenting the Commerce of the Company,* London: J. Nourse, 1772.

———. *A Collection of Charts and Memoirs.* London: s. n., 1772.

———. *General Remarks on the System of Government in India; With Farther Considerations on the Present State of the Company at Home and Abroad.* London: J. Nourse, 1773.

———. *Heads of an Agreement between the Parliament and the East India Company.* London: s. n., 1780.

Das Gupta, Anil Chandra, ed. *The Days of John Company: Selections from the Calcutta Gazette, 1824–1832.* Calcutta: Government Printing, West Bengal, 1959.

Daunton, Martin, and Halpern, Rick, eds. *Empire and Others: British Encounters with Indigenous Peoples, 1600–1850.* Philadelphia, PA: University of Pennsylvania Press, 1999.

Davidoff, Leonore, and Hall, Catharine. *Family Fortunes: Men and Women of the English Middle Class, 1780–1850.* Chicago: University of Chicago Press, 1987.

Davies, Rees. "The English State and 'Celtic' Peoples." *Journal of Historical Sociology* 6, no. 1 (1993): 1–14.

Debus, Allen G. *Science, Medicine and Society in the Renaissance: Essays to Honor Walter Page.* Vol. 1. New York: History Science Publications, 1972.

Defoe, Daniel. *Atlantis Major.* Los Angeles: William Andrews Clark Memorial Library [1711], 1979.

Deleuze, Gilles, and Guattari, Felix. *Anti-Oedipus: Capitalism and Schizophrenia.* Minneapolis, MN: University of Minnesota Press, 1983.

Dow, Alexander. *The History of Hindostan,* London: Vernor and Hood, Cuthell and Martin, J. Walker, Wynne and Scholey, John Debrett, Blacks and Parry, T. Kay, and J. Asperne, 1803.

Drayton, Michael. *Poly-Olbion.* Vol. 4. Ed. J. William Hebel. Oxford: Basil Blackwell, 1961.

Dryden, John. *Aureng-Zebe.* Ed. Frederick M. Link. Lincoln, NE: University of Nebraska Press, 1971.

Duffy, Michael. *The Englishman and the Foreigner.* Cambridge, U.K. and Alexandria, VA: Chadwyck-Healey, 1986.

Dyson, Ketaki Kushari. *A Various Universe: A Study of the Journals and Memoirs of British Men and Women in the Indian Subcontinent, 1765–1856.* Delhi: Oxford University Press, 1978.

Edney, Matthew H. *Mapping and Empire: The Geographical Construction of British India, 1765–1843.* Chicago: University of Chicago Press, 1997.

Elphinstone, Mountstuart. *The History of India: The Hindu and Mahometan Periods.* Reprint, Allahabad, India: Kitab Mahal, 1986.

Fanon, Franz. *Black Skin, White Masks.* New York: Grove and Weidenfeld, 1967.

Farmer, R. *The Soldier: An Historical Poem, in Three Parts, Containing an Epitome of the Wars Entered into by Great Britain, from the Year 1739 to the Present Time.* London: Lackington and Allen; Crosby and Letterman, etc., 1802.

Farrington, Anthony. *The Records of the East India College: Haileybury and Other Institutions.* London: Her Majesty's Stationery Office, 1976.

Ferguson, Adam. *An Essay on the History of Civil Society.* Edinburgh: University Press [1767], 1966.

Fieldhouse, D. K. *The Colonial Empires: A Comparative Survey from the Eighteenth Century.* New York: Delacorte Press, 1967.

Firminger, Walter Kelly, ed. *The Fifth Report from the Select Committee of the House of Commons on the Affairs of the East India Company.* Vols. 1–2. Calcutta: R. Cambray & Co., 1917.

Fletcher, Anthony. *Gender, Sex, and Subordination in England, 1500–1800.* New Haven, CT: Yale University Press, 1995.

Forbes, James. *Oriental Memoirs: A Narrative of Seventeen Years Residence in India.* London: Richard Bentley, 1834.

Foster, William. "British Artists in India, 1760–1820" in *The Nineteenth Volume of the Walpole Society, 1930–1931.* Oxford: Oxford University Press, 1931, 1–88.

Foucault, Michel. *The Order of Things: An Archaeology of the Human Sciences.* New York: Vintage, 1970. Reprint, 1973.

———. *Discipline and Punish: The Birth of the Prison.* New York: Vintage Books, 1979.

———. *Power/Knowledge: Selected Interviews and Other Writings, 1972–1977.* Ed. and trans. Colin Gordon. Brighton, UK: Harvester Press, 1980.

Freedman, L., Hayes, P., and O'Neill, Robert. eds. *War, Strategy and International Politics: Essays in Honor of Sir Michael Howard.* Oxford and New York: Oxford University Press, 1992.

Fry, Michael. *The Dundas Despotism.* Edinburgh: Edinburgh University Press, 1992.

Furber, Holden. *Henry Dundas, First Viscount Melville, 1742–1811: Political Manager of Scotland, Statesman, Administrator of British India.* London: Oxford University Press, 1931.

Gellner, Ernest. *Nations and Nationalism.* Ithaca: Cornell University Press, 1983.

Ghosh, Durba. "Colonial Companions: Bibis, Begums, and Concubines of the British North India, 1760–1830." Ph.D. dissertation, University of California, Berkeley, CA, 2000.

Ghosh, Suresh Chandra. *The Social Condition of the British Community in Bengal 1757–1800.* Leiden, Holland: E. J. Brill, 1970.

Gillingham, John. "The Beginning of English Imperialism," *Journal of Historical Sociology* 5, no. 4 (1992): 392–409.

Gilpin, William. *Three Essays on Picturesque Beauty: On Picturesque Travel and on Sketching Landscape.* 2nd ed. London: R. Blamire, 1794.

Gisborne, Thomas. *An Enquiry into the Duties of the Female Sex.* 1797; Reprint, Philadelphia, PA: James Humphreys, 1798.

Goldsmith, Oliver. *The Vicar of Wakefield.* New York: Century, 1902.

Gole, Susan. *India within the Ganges.* New Delhi: Jayaprints, 1983.

———. *Indian Maps and Plans: From Earliest Times to the World of European Surveys.* New Delhi: Manohar Publications, 1989.

Goodwin, Albert, ed. *The European Nobility in the Eighteenth Century.* New York and Evanston: Harper and Row, 1967.

Gould, Stephen J. *The Mismeasure of Man.* New York and London: Norton, 1981.

Grant, Colesworthy. *An Anglo-Indian Domestic Sketch: A Letter from an Artist in India to His Mother in England.* Calcutta: Thacker and Company, 1849.

Grant, Robert. *The Expediency Maintained of Continuing the System by which the Trade and Government of India Are now Regulated.* London: Black, Parry and Co., 1813.

Greenblatt, Stephen. *Marvelous Possessions: The Wonder of the New World.* Chicago: University of Chicago Press, 1991.

Griffiths, Percival. *A Licence to Trade: The History of English Chartered Companies.* London and Tonbridge: Ernest Benn, 1974.

Guha, Ranajit. *A Rule of Property for Bengal: An Essay on the Idea of the Permanent Settlement.* Paris: Mouton, 1963.

———. *A Rule of Property for Bengal: An Essay on the Idea of Permanent Settlement.* Durham and London: Duke University Press, 1996.

Guthrie, William. *A New System of Modern Geography: Or, A Geographical, Historical, and Commercial Grammar.* Philadelphia, PA: Mathew Carey, 1794–1795.

Habib, Irfan. "Cartography in Mughal India." *Medieval India: A Miscellany.* Vol. 4. Bombay: Asia Publishing House, 1969: 122–134.

Halhed, N. B. *Letters of Detector on the Reports of the Select Committee of the House of Commons Appointed to Consider How the British Possessions in the East Indies May Be Held and Governed with the Greatest Security and Happiness of the Natives May Best Be Promoted.* London: s. n., 1782.

Hall, Catherine. *White, Male, and Middle Class: Explorations in Feminism and History.* New York: Routledge, 1992.

Hallam, Henry. *The Constitutional History of England from the Accession of Henry II to the Death of George II.* 5th ed. New York: Harper and Brothers, 1870.

Hamilton, Alexander. *A New Account of the East Indies.* Edinburgh: J. Mosman, 1727.

Hannaford, Ivan. *Race: The History of an Idea in the West.* Washington, DC: Woodrow Wilson Center Press, 1996.

Hansard, T. C., ed. *The Parliamentary Debates, from the Year 1803 to the Present Time.* Vol. 4. London: Longman, Hurst, Rees, Orme, Brown etc., 1805.

———, ed. *Hansard's Parliamentary Debates.* Vol. 23. New Series. London: Baldwin and Cradock; J. Booker; Longman, Rees, and Orme etc., 1830.

Harley, J. B., Petchenik, B., and Towner, L. W., eds. *Mapping the Revolutionary War.* Chicago and London: University of Chicago Press, 1978.

Hasan Shah, Muhammad. *Nishtar.* Lahore: 1923.

Haskell, Framcis. *History and Its Images: Art and the Interpretation of the Past.* London and New Haven, CT: Yale University Press, 1993.

Hawes, C. J. *Poor Relations: The Making of a Eurasian Community in British India.* Surrey, UK: Curzon Press, 1996.

Heany, G. F. "Rennell and the Surveyors of India." *Geographical Journal* 134, pt. 3 (September, 1968): 318–327.

Heber, Reginald. *Narrative of a Journey through the Upper Provinces of India, from Calcutta to Bombay, 1824–1825.* 3rd ed. London: J. Murray, 1828.

Helgerson, Richard. "The Land Speaks: Cartography, Chorography and Subversion in Renaissance England." *Representations* 16 (Fall 1986): 51–85.

Hemingway, Andrew. *Landscape Imagery and Urban Culture in Early Nineteenth-Century Britain.* Cambridge, UK: Cambridge University Press, 1992.

Hennen, John. *Sketches of the Medical Topography of the Mediterranean: Comprising an Account of Gibraltar, the Ionian Islands, and Malta.* Ed. J. Hennen. London: s. n., 1830.

———. *Principles of Military Surgery, Comprising Observations on the Arrangement, Police, and Practice of Hospitals, and on the History, Treatment and Anomalies of Variola and Syphilis.* 2nd ed. Edinburgh: s. n., 1820.

Henry, Robert. *The History of Great Britain from the First Invasion of It by the Roman Under Julius Caesar: Written on a New Plan.* Vol. 1. London and Edinburgh: T. Cadell, 1771.

Herrmann, Luke. *British Landscape Painting of the Eighteenth Century.* London: Faber & Faber, 1973.

Herrup, Cynthia. "Beyond Personality and Pomp: Recent Works on Early Modern Monarchies." *Journal of British Studies* 28 (1989): 175–180.

Hickey, William. *Memoirs of William Hickey.* 4 vols. London: Hurst and Blackett, 1913–25.

Higman, B. W. *Slave Populations of the British Caribbean, 1807–1834.* Baltimore: Johns Hopkins University Press, 1984.

Hill, S. C., ed. *List of Europeans and Others in Bengal in 1756 at the Time of the Siege in Calcutta in the year 1756.* Calcutta: Office of the Superintendent of Government Printing, India, 1902.

Hirschman, Albert O. *The Passions and the Interests: Political Arguments for Capitalism before its Triumph.* Princeton, NJ: Princeton University Press, 1997.

Hodes, Martha, ed. *Sex, Love, Race: Crossing Boundaries in North American History.* New York: New York University Press, 1999.

Holden, William C. *The Past and Future of the Kaffir Races.* Facsimile Reprint. Cape Town: C. Struik [1866], 1963.

Hollingbery, William. *A History of His Late Highness Nizam Alee Khaun, Soobah of the Dekhan.* Calcutta: J. Greenway, 1805.

Holwell, Jonathan Zephania. *Interesting Historical Events Relative to the Province of Bengal and the Empire of Indostan.* London: Beckett and De Hondt, 1766.

Hume, David. *The History of England from the Invasion of Julius Caesar to the Abdication of James the Second, 1688.* Vol. 1. New York: Harper, 1851.

Hunt, Margaret R. *The Middling Sort: Commerce, Gender, and the Family in England, 1680–1780.* Berkeley, CA: University of California Press, 1996.

Hutchins, Francis. *Illusion of Permanence:* Princeton, NJ: Princeton University Press, 1967.

Hutchinson, John. *The Dynamics of Cultural Nationalism: The Gaelic Revival and the Creation of the Irish Nation State.* London: Allen and Unwin, 1987.

Hyam, Ronald. *Empire and Sexuality: The British Experience.* Manchester and New York: Manchester University Press, 1990.

Ignatiev, Noel. *How the Irish Became White.* Routledge: New York and London, 1995.

Ingram, Edward, ed. *Two Views of British India: The Private Correspondence of Mr. Dundas and Lord Wellesley, 1798–1801.* Somerset, UK: Adams and Dart, 1970.

James, Lawrence. *The Rise and Fall of the British Empire.* New York: St. Martin's Press, 1994.

Johnson, J. W. *The Formation of English Neo-Classical Thought.* Princeton, NJ: Princeton University Press, 1967.

Johnson, Samuel. *The Plan of a Dictionary of the English Language.* London: Knapton, Longman, Shewell, Hitch, Millar and Dodsley, 1747.

————. *Journey to the Western Islands of Scotland.* London: Oxford University Press, Humphrey Milford, 1934.

Jones, Gareth S., ed. *Sovereignty of the Law: Selections from Blackstone's Commentaries on the Laws of England.* Toronto: University of Toronto Press, 1973.

Jones, William. *The Works of William Jones.* Vols. 11–12. Delhi: Agam Prakashan [1799], 1977–.

Jordan, Winthrop D. *White over Black: American Attitudes toward the Negro, 1550–1812.* Chapel Hill, NC: University of North Carolina Press, 1968.

Kames, Lord Henry Home. *Sketches of the History of Man.* Vols. 1–2. 2nd ed. Edinburgh: W. Strahan, T. Cadell and W. Creech, 1778.

————. *Principles of Equity.* Edinburgh: Bell, Bradforte and W. Creech, 1800.

Kantorowicz, Ernest. *The King's Two Bodies: A Study in Medieval Political Theology.* Princeton, NJ: Princeton University Press, 1957.

Kaye, John William. *Lives of Indian Officers, Illustrative of the History of the Civil and Military Services of India.* London: A Strahan, Bell and Daldy, 1867.

Kaye, John W., and Malleson, G. B. *Kaye's and Malleson's History of the India Mutiny.* 2nd ed. London: W. H. Allen 1892.

Keate, George. *An Account of the Pelew Islands Situated in the Western Part of the Pacific Ocean, Composed from the Journals and Communications of Captain Henry Wilson, and Some of His Officers, Who in August 1783, Were There Shipwrecked.* Philadelphia, PA: Joseph Crukshank, 1789.

Kedourie, Elie. *Nationalism.* 4th ed. Oxford: Blackwell, 1993.

Keith, A. B., ed. *Speeches & Documents on Indian Policy.* Vol. 1. New Delhi: Anmol Publications, 1985.

Kenyon, John. *The History Men: The Historical Profession in England since the Renaissance.* Pittsburgh, PA: University of Pittsburgh Press, 1984.

Kerber, Linda. *Women of the Republic: Intellect and Ideology in Revolutionary America.* New York and London: W.W. Norton, 1986.

Khan, Seid Gholam Hossein. *The Seir Mutaqherin or Review of Modern Times.* Reprint, Lahore: Oriental Publishers and Booksellers [1789], 1975.

Kincaid, Dennis. *British Social Life in India, 1608–1937.* London: Routledge, 1938.

Koebner, Richard. *Empire.* Cambridge, UK: Cambridge University Press, 1961.

Krieger, Leonard. *An Essay on the Theory of Enlightened Despotism.* Chicago and London: University of Chicago Press, 1975.

Kupperman, Karen Ordahl. *Settling with the Indians: The Meeting of English and Indian Cultures in America, 1580–1640.* Totowa, NJ: Rowman and Littlefield, 1980.

La Touche, T. H. D., ed. *The Journals of Major James Rennell, First Surveyor General of India, Written for the Information of the Governors of Bengal during His Surveys of the Ganges and the Brahmaputra Rivers 1764 to 1767,* Calcutta: Asiatic Society, 1910.

Lambton, William. "An Account of a Method for Extending a Geographical Survey across the Peninsula of India." *Asiatick Researches* 7, 3rd ed. (1807): 312–335.

Law, Thomas. *Sketch of Some Late Arrangements and a View of the Rising Resources in Bengal.* London: John Stockdale, 1792.

Lawson, Philip. *The East India Company: A History.* London and New York: Longman, 1993.

Lehmann, William C. *John Millar of Glasgow, 1735–1801: His Life and Thought and His Contributions to Sociological Analysis.* Cambridge, UK: Cambridge University Press, 1960.

Levine, Phillipa. "Re-reading the 1890s: Venereal Disease as 'Constitutional Crisis' in Britain and British India." *Journal of Asian Studies* 55, no. 3 (1996): 585–612.

Lindberg, David C., and Nicholas H. Steneck, *Science, Medicine, and Society in the Renaissance: Essay to Honor Walter Pagel.* Ed., Allen G. Debus. Vol. 1. New York: History Science Publications, 1972.

Lovejoy, Arthur O. *The Great Chain of Being: A Study of the History of an Idea.* Cambridge, MA: Harvard University Press, 1964.

Macaulay, T. B. *Critical, Historical and Miscellaneous Essays and Poems.* Vol. 2. Boston: Estes and Lauriat, 1880.

MacDowell, R. B. *Ireland in the Age of Imperialism and Revolution, 1760–1801.* Oxford: Clarendon Press, 1979.

Mackenzie, John M. *Orientalism: History, Theory and the Arts,* Manchester: Manchester University Press, 1995.

Mackintosh, Robert J., ed. *Memoirs of the Life of Sir James Mackintosh.* 2 Vols. 2nd ed. London: Edward Moxon, 1836.

Mackintosh, James. *History of the Revolution in England in 1688.* London: Longman, Rees, Orme et al., 1834.

Maitland, W. F. *The Constitutional History of England: A Course of Lectures Delivered.* Cambridge, UK: Cambridge University Press, 1920.

Malcolm, John. *Persia: A Poem.* 2nd ed. London: John Murray, 1814.

———. *The History of Persia from the Most Early Period to the Present Time: Containing an Account of the Religion, Government, Usages, and Character of the Inhabitants of that Kingdom.* Rev. ed. Vol. 2. London: John Murray, 1829.

———. *A Memoir of Central India, Including Malwa, and Adjoining Provinces, with the History and Copious Illustrations of the Past and Present of that Country.* 3rd ed. London: Parbury, Allen & Co., 1832.

Malcolm, John. *The Political History of India 1784 to 1823.* Ed. K. N. Panikkar. New Delhi: American Publishing House, 1970.

Marshall, P. J. *Problems of Empire: Britain and India, 1757–1813.* London: George Allen & Unwin, 1968.

———, ed. *The Writings and Speeches of Edmund Burke.* Vol. 6. Oxford: Clarendon Press, 1991.

———. "The Whites of British India, 1780–1830: A Failed Colonial Society?" in *Trade and Conquest: Studies on the Rise of British Dominance in India.* Hampshire, UK: Varorium, 1993.

Marshall, P. J., and Williams, Glyndwr. *The Great Map of Mankind: Perceptions of New Worlds in the Age of Enlightenment.* Cambridge, MA: Harvard University Press, 1982.

Mauss, M. *Manuel d'Ethnographie.* Paris: Payot, 1974.

Meek, Ronald. *Social Science and the Ignoble Savage.* Cambridge, UK: Cambridge University Press, 1976.

Mehta, Uday Singh. *Liberalism and Empire: A Study in Nineteenth Century British Liberal Thought.* Chicago and London: University of Chicago Press, 1999.

Metcalf, Thomas. *Ideologies of the Raj.* Cambridge and New York: Cambridge University Press, 1994.

Minorsky, V., trans. *Hudud al-Alam, The Regions of the World: A Persian Geography.* Karachi: Indus Publications, 1980.

Miquel, André. *La Géographie Humaine du Monde Musulman jusqu'au Milieu du 11e Siècle.* Paris: Mouton & Co, 1967.

Mitchell, W. J. T., ed. *Landscape and Power.* Chicago: University of Chicago Press, 1994.

Mitford, William. *The History of Greece.* Vol. 1. London: T. Cadell, 1822.

Montesquieu. *Persian Letters,* trans. C. J. Betts. London: Penguin, 1973.

Morgan, Victor, "Cartographic Image of the 'The Country' in Early Modern England." *Transactions of the Royal Historical Society.* 5th Series, 29 (1979): 129–154.

———. "Lasting Image of the Elizabethan Era." *Geographical Magazine* 52, no. 6 (1980): 401–408.

Morris, Marilyn. *The British Monarchy and the French Revolution.* New Haven, CT, and London: Yale University Press, 1998.

Mosse, George, L. *The Struggle for Sovereignty in England: From the Reign of Queen Elizabeth to the Petition of Right.* New York: Octagon Books, 1968.

Motte, Thomas. "A Narrative of a Journey to the Diamond Mines of Sumbhulpoor, in the Province of Orissa," in *The Asiatic Annual Register for the Year 1799.* London: J. Debrett, 1800.

Mountnorris, George Annesley. *Voyages and Travels in India, Ceylon, the Red Sea, Abyssinia, and Egypt, in the Years 1802, 1803, 1804, 1805, and 1806, by George Viscount Valentia.* London: W. Butmer, 1809.

Mukherjee, Chandra. *From Graven Images: Patterns of Modern Materialism.* New York: Columbia University Press, 1983.

Muldoon, James. "The Indian as Irishman." *Essex Institute Historical Collections* 3, no.4. (October 1975): 267–289.

———. *Empire and Order: The Concept of Empire, 800–1800.* New York: St. Martin's Press, 1999.

Nandy, Ashish. *The Intimate Enemy: Loss and Recovery of the Self Under Colonialism.* Delhi: Oxford University Press, 1983.

Negri, A. *Marx beyond Marx: Lessons on the Grundnisse.* New York: Autonomedia, 1993.

Norton, J. E., ed. *The Letters of Edward Gibbon.* Vols. 2–3. New York: Macmillan, 1956.

Oldendorf, C. G. A. *St. Thomas in Early Danish Times: A General Description of all the Danish, American, or West Indian Islands.* Trans. Arnold Highfield. St. Croix: Virgin Islands Humanities Council, 1997.

O'Leary, Patrick. *Sir James Mackintosh: The Whig Cicero.* Aberdeen: Aberdeen University Press, 1989.

Orme, Robert. *Historical Fragments of the Mogul Empire and the Morattoes and of the English Concerns in Indostan.* New Delhi: Associated Publishing House [1806], 1974.

———. *A History of the Military Transactions of the British Nation in Indostan from the Year MDC-CXLV, to which Is Prefixed a Dissertation on the Establishments Made by Mahomedan Conquerors in Indostan.* London: John Nourse, 1778.

Ousby, Ian. *The Englishman's England: Taste, Travel and the Rise of Tourism.* Cambridge, UK: Cambridge University Press, 1990.

Pagden, Anthony. *The Fall of Natural Man.* Cambridge, UK: Cambridge University Press, 1986.

———. *Lords of All the World: Ideologies of Empire in Spain, Britain and France c. 1500–c. 1800.* New Haven, CT, and London: Yale University Press, 1995.

Pagliaro, Harold E., ed. *Racism in the Eighteenth Century.* Cleveland and London: Case Western Reserve University Press, 1973.

Pal, Pratapaditya, and Dehejia, Vidja. *From Merchants to Emperors: British Artists and India, 1757–1930.* Ithaca, NY, and London: Cornell University Press, 1986.

Parbury's Oriental Herald and Colonial Intelligencer. Vol. 1. London: Parbury, 1838.

Pavière, Sydney H. "Biographical Notes on the Devis Family of Painters," in *The Twenty-Fifth Volume of the Walpole Society, 1936–1937.* Oxford: Oxford University Press, 1937, 115–166.

Peardon, Preston. *The Transition in English Historical Writing, 1760–1830.* New York: Columbia University Press, 1933.

Pearson, Hugh. *Memoirs of the Life and Writings of the Reverend Claudius Buchanan*. Philadelphia, PA: Benjamin and Thomas Kite, 1817.

Peers, Douglas. *Between Mars and Mammon: Colonial Armies and the Garrison State in India, 1819–35*. London: Aldershot, 1995.

Pennant, Thomas. *A Tour in Scotland, 1769*. Edinburgh: Birlinn, 2000.

Phillimore, R. H. *Historical Records of the Survey in India*. Vols. 1–3. Dehra Dun, India: Survey Office, Government of India, 1945.

Phillips, Mark S. *Society and Sentiment: Genres of Historical Writing in Britain, 1740–1820*. Princeton, NJ: Princeton University Press, 2000.

Pocock, J. G. A. "The Limits and Divisions of British History: In Search of the Unknown Subject." *American Historical Review* 87, no. 2 (1982): 311–336.

Poovey, Mary. *Making a Social Body: British Cultural Formation, 1830–1864*. Chicago and London: University of Chicago Press, 1995.

Popkin, Richard H. "The Philosophical Bases of Modern Racism," in Craig Walton and John P. Anton, eds. *Philosophy and the Civilizing Arts: Essays Presented to Herbert W. Schneider*. Athens, OH: Ohio University Press, 1974.

Porter, Roy. *Gibbon: Making History*. New York: St. Martin's Press, 1988.

Pownall, Thomas. *The Right, Interest, and Duty of the State as Concerned in the Affairs of the East Indies*. London: S. Bladon, 1773.

Pratt, Mary Louise. *Imperial Eyes: Travel Writing and Transculturation*. London; New York: Routledge, 1991.

Princep, J., ed. "Progress of the Indian Trigonometrical Survey." *Journal of the Asiatic Society of Bengal* 1, no. 2, (1832): 71–72.

———. "Computation of the Area of the Kingdoms and Principalities of India." *Journal of the Asiatic Society of Bengal* no. 20 (August 1833): 488–491.

Raynal, Abbe. *Philosophical and Political History of the Settlements and Trade of the Europeans in the East and West Indies*. Trans. J. O. Justamond. Vol. 1. 2nd ed. Reprint, New York: Negro Universities Press, 1969.

Razi, Amin Ahmed. *Haft-iqlim: The Geographical and Biographical Encyclopaedia of Amin Ahmad Razi*. Ed. by A. H. Harley, Abdul Muqtadir, and Mahfuz-ul Haq. Calcutta: Bibliotheca Indica, 1939.

Rennell, James. *The Geographical System of Herodotus Examined and Explained by a Comparison with those of Other Ancient Authors, and with Modern Geography*. London: G. and W. Nicol, 1800.

Richardson, Jonathan. *The Works*. London: T. Davies, 1773. Reprint, Hildesheim, Germany: Georg Olms Verlag, 1969.

Roberts, Emma. *The East India Voyager, Or the Outward Bound*. London: J. Madden, 1845.

Robertson, William. *The Works of William Robertson*. Ed. Dugald Stewart. Vol. 4. New edition, London: Cadell and Davies, et al., 1817.

Roebuck, Thomas, compiled. *The Annals of the College of Fort William from the Period of Its Foundation by His Excellency the Most Noble Richard, Marquis Wellesley on the 4th May, 1800 to the Present Time*. Calcutta: Hindoostanee Press, 1819.

Ross, Charles, ed. *Correspondence of Charles, First Marquis Cornwallis*. London: John Murray, 1859.

Roy, William. "An Account of the Measurement of a Base on Hounslow Heath." *Philosophical Transactions of the Royal Society* 75: 385–480.

———. *The Military Antiquities of the Romans in Britain*. London: W. Bulmer, 1793.

Russell, William. *The History of Modern Europe with an Account of the Decline and Fall of the Roman Empire, and a View of the Progress of Society, from the Rise of the Modern Kingdoms of the Peace of Paris, in 1763, in a Series of Letters from a Nobleman to his Son.* Vol. 1. New ed., Philadelphia, PA: William Young Birch and Abraham Small, 1800.

Sack, James J. *From Jacobite to Conservative: Reaction and Orthodoxy in Britain, c. 1760–1832.* Cambridge, UK: Cambridge University Press, 1993.

Said, Edward. *Orientalism.* Middlesex, UK: Penguin Books, 1985.

Samuel, Raphael. *Theaters of Memory.* London and New York: Verso, 1994.

Sandes, E. W. C. *The Military Engineer in India.* Vol. 1. Chatham, UK: Institute of Royal Engineers, 1933.

Saville, J., ed. *Democracy and the Labour Movement.* London: Lawrence and Wishart, 1954.

Sayer, Derek. "A Notable Administration: English State Formation and the Rise of Capitalism." *American Journal of Sociology* 97, no. 5 (March 1992): 1382–1415.

Scott, Jonathan. *England's Troubles: Seventeenth-Century English Political Instability in European Context,* Cambridge, UK, and New York: Cambridge University Press, 2000.

Scott, Joseph. *The New and Universal Gazetteer; or, Modern Geographical Dictionary Containing a Full and Authentic Description of the Different Empires, Kingdoms, Republics, States, Provinces, Islands, Cities, Towns, Forts, Mountains, Caves, Capes, Canals, Rivers, Lakes, Oceans, Seas, Bays, Harbours, &c in the Known World.* Philadelphia, PA: Francis & Robert Bailey, 1799.

Scrafton, Luke. *Reflections on the Government of Indostan: With a Short Sketch of the History of Bengal from the Year 1739 to 1756; and an Account of English Affairs to 1758.* London: Richardson and Clark, 1763.

Seely, J. R. *The Expansion of England.* Ed. John Gross. Chicago and London: University of Chicago Press, 1971.

Selkirk, Earl of, Thomas Douglas. *Observations on the Present State of the Highlands of Scotland with a View of the Causes and Probable Consequences of Emigration.* 2nd ed. Edinburgh: A. Constable, 1806.

Sen, Sudipta, "Colonial Frontiers of the Georgian State." *Journal of Historical Sociology* 7, no. 4 (December 1994): 368–392.

——. *Empire of Free Trade: The East India Company and the Making of the Colonial Marketplace.* Philadelphia, PA: University of Pennsylvania Press, 1998.

Seton-Karr, W. S. *Selections from the Calcutta Gazettes.* Vol. 3. Calcutta: Microform Publication, 1987.

Seymour, W. A. *A History of the Ordnance Survey.* Kent, UK: Dawson, 1980.

Sharpe, Jenny. *Allegories of Empire: The Figure of Woman in the Colonial Text.* Minneapolis, MN: University of Minnesota Press, 1993.

Sheridan, Richard Brinsley. *A General Dictionary of the English Language.* 2nd ed. London: Charles Dilly, 1789.

Sinclair, Sir John. *Analysis of the Statistical Account of Scotland with a General View of the History of that Country and Discourses on Some Important Branches of Political Economy.* Edinburgh: Arch. Constable and Company, 1825. Reprint, New York and London: Johnson Reprint Corporation, 1970.

Sinha, Mrinalini. *Colonial Masculinity: The "Manly Englishman" and the "Effeminate Bengali" in the Late Nineteenth Century.* Manchester: Manchester University Press, 1995.

Sleeman, W. H. *Rambles and Recollections of an Indian Official.* Ed. V. A. Smith. Vol. 1. London: Archibald Constable, 1893.

Spear, Percival. *The Nabobs: A Study of the Social Life of the English in Eighteenth Century India.* London: Curzon Press, 1963.

Stafford, Barbara M. *Voyage into Substance: Art, Science, Nature, and the Illustrated Travel Account, 1760–1840.* Cambridge, MA, and London: MIT Press, 1984.

Stark, Herbert Alick. *Hostages to India: or the Life Story of the Anglo-Indian Race.* Calcutta: Fine Art Cottage, 1926.

————. *John Ricketts and His Times, Being a Narrative Account of Anglo-Indian Affairs during the Eventful Years from 1791 to 1835.* Calcutta: Wilsone, 1934.

Stepan, Nancy Leys. *The Idea of Race in Science: Great Britain 1800–1960.* Connecticut: Archon Books, 1982.

————. *Picturing Tropical Nature,* Ithaca, NY: Cornell University Press, 2001.

Stephen, Leslie, and Lee, Sidney. *The Dictionary of National Biography.* London: Oxford University Press, 1917–.

Steuart, J. *Inquiry into the Principles of Political Economy.* Edinburgh: Oliver and Boyd [1767], 1966.

Stokes, Eric. *The English Utilitarians and India.* Oxford: Oxford University Press, 1959.

Stoler, Ann. *Race and the Education of Desire, Foucault's History of Sexuality and the Colonial Order of Things.* Durham, NC: Duke University Press, 1995.

Stone, Lawrence. *The Family, Sex and Marriage in England, 1500–1800.* New York: Harper and Row, 1979.

Sutherland, Dame Lucy. *East India Company in Eighteenth Century Politics.* Oxford: Oxford University Press, 1952.

Tamita Delgoda, A. Sinharaja, " 'Nabob, Historian and Orientalist.' Robert Orme: The life and Career of an East India Company Servant (1728–1801)." *Journal of the Royal Asiatic Society,* Series 3, vol. 2, no. 3 (1992): 363–376.

Tancred, A. J. *Letters to Sir Peregrine Maitland, Governor of the Colony of the Cape of Good Hope on the Present Kafir War.* Cape Town: De Zuid-Afrikaan, 1846.

Teltscher, Kate. *India Inscribed: European and British Writing on India, 1600–1800.* 2nd ed. Delhi: Oxford University Press, 1997.

Tennant, William. *Indian Recreations: Consisting Chiefly of Strictures on the Domestic and Rural Economy of the Mahommedans and Hindoos.* Vol. 1. Edinburgh: C. Stewart, 1803.

————. *Thoughts on the Effects of the British Government on the State of India: Accompanied with Hints Concerning the Means of Conveying Civil and Religious Instruction to the Natives of that Country.* Edinburgh: Edinburgh University Press, 1807.

The Asiatic Annual Register, or, the View of History of Hindustan and of the Politics, Commerce and Literature of Asia for the Year 1799. London: J. Debrett, 1800.

The Pamphleteer, Vol. IX, London: A. J. Valpy, 1817.

The Speech of Mr. Hardinge as Counsel for the Directors of the East India Company. London: J. Stockdale, 1784.

Thomas, Imogen. *Haileybury 1806–1987.* Hertford, UK: Haileybury Society, 1987.

Thomas, Law. *Sketch of Some Late Arrangements and a View of the Rising Resources in Bengal.* London: John Stockdale, 1792.

Thompson, E. P. *Customs in Common: Studies in Traditional Popular Culture.* New York: New Press. 1993.

Tosh, John. *A Man's Place: Masculinity and the Middle-Class Home in Victorian England.* New Haven, CT, and London: Yale University Press, 1999.

Tosh, John, and Roper, Michael, eds. *Manful Assertions: Masculinities in Britain since 1800.* London and New York: Routledge, 1991.

Trevor-Roper, H. *Queen Elizabeth's First Historian: William Camden and the Beginning of English "Civil History."* London: Jonathan Cape, 1971.

Tribe, Keith. "The 'Histories' of Economic Discourse." *Economy and Society* 6 (1977): 315–343.

————. *Genealogies of Capitalism.* London: Macmillan, 1981.

Trumpener, Katie. *Bardic Nationalism: The Romantic Novel and the British Empire.* Princeton, NJ: Princeton University Press, 1997.

Tucker, Henry St. George. *Memorials of Indian Government.* Ed. by John William Kaye. London: Richard Bentley, 1853.

Turner, Frank. "British Politics and the Demise of the Roman Republic: 1700–1939." *Historical Journal* no. 3 (1986): 577–599.

Tytler, Alexander Fraser. *Elements of General History, Ancient and Modern.* 76th ed. Concord, NH: John F. Brown, 1840.

Vance, Norman. *The Victorians and Ancient Rome.* Oxford: Blackwell, 1997.

Vickery, Amanda. "Golden Age to Separate Spheres? A Review of the Categories and Chronology of English Women's History." *Historical Journal,* no. 36 (1993): 383–414.

Visram, Rozina. *Ayahs, Lascars and Princes: Indians in Britain 1700–1947.* London: Pluto Press, 1986.

Wahrman, Dror. "The English Problem of Identity in the American Revolution." *American Historical Review* 106, no. 4 (October 2001): 1236–1262.

Walvin, J. *England, Slaves and Freedom, 1776–1838.* Jackson, MS, and London: University Press of Mississippi, 1986.

———. *Slaves and Slavery: The British Colonial Experience,* Manchester and New York: Manchester University Press, 1992.

Watts, William. *Memoirs of the Revolution in Bengal.* Reprint. Calcutta: K. P. Bagchi [1760], 1988.

Welch, S. C. *Imperial Mughal Painting.* New York: George Raziller, 1978.

Whittle, Stephen, ed. *Arthur William Devis, 1762–1822.* Preston, Lancashire, U.K.: Harris Museum and Art Gallery, 2000.

Wilks, Mark. *Historical Sketches of the South of India in an Attempt to Trace the History of Mysoor from the Origin of the Hindoo Government of that State to the Extinction of the Mohammedan Dynasty in 1799.* Vol. 3. London: Longman, Hurst, Rees, Orme, and Brown, 1817–1820.

Williamson, Capt. Thomas. *East India Vade Mecum or Complete Guide to Gentlemen Intended for the Civil, Military or Naval Service of the Honourable East India Company.* 2 vols. London: Black, Parry, and Kingsbury, 1810.

Wilson, Kathleen. *The Sense of the People: Politics, Culture and Imperialism in England, 1715–1785.* Cambridge: Cambridge University Press, 1995.

Winichakul, Thongchai. *Siam Mapped: A History of the Geo-Body of a Nation.* Honolulu: University of Hawaii Press, 1994.

Wittgenstein, Ludwig. *Tractatus Logico-Philosophicus.* London: Routledge & Kegan Paul [1961], 1974.

Young, Robert. *Colonial Desire: Hybridity in Theory, Culture, and Race.* London and New York: Routledge, 1995.

INDEX

A

Abbas Shah, 64

Absolute monarchy, xviii, xix, xxiii

Absolutism, political, xxiii, 19. *See also* Despotism

Adadh, nawab of, 79

Adam, Robert, 76

Adams, Samuel, 68

Africa/Africans, 3, 14, 17, 43, 126, 147, 148
  description of subject populations, 104
  interracial unions and mixed-race children, 134, 139–140
  racial attributes, 144–145
  theories of race, 16–17

Agrarian bourgeoisie, English, 94

Agrarian poor, domestic rule, 25–26

Agriculture, 20, 89, 106–107, 115–116

Akbar (Mughal emperor), 41, 43, 53, 105

Alam, Shah, xii, xxi, 79

Albion, 62

Alexander, 40

Alexander, William, 65

Ali Khan, Fateh, 53

Allegory, history as, 33

Alpers, Svetlana, 68

American Indians, 108, 109, 134

American Revolution, 4, 7, 34, 59, 151–152

Anderson, Adam, 20, 68–69, 92

Anderson, Benedict, 58

Anglo-Indians. *See* Indo-British/Eurasians

Anne, Queen, xiv, 4

Annexation, 7, 80

Anthropology, 15–16, 148

Arab geographers, 63–64

Archer, Mildred, 74, 111–112

Archetypes/stereotypes. *See* Hindu and Muslim stereotypes; Race and ethnicity

Architecture, 47–48, 65, 68

Aristotle, 88

Armitage, David, xxvi

Arrian, 40, 104

Art, xxi–xxii, 60, 80
  depiction of Indian life, 110–111
  landscape painting, 61, 67–68, 69–70
  military education and training, 65, 67–68
  Mughal versus British cartography, 64
  portraiture and drama, xxi–xxiv
  Roman architecture and sculpture, 47–48

Artisans, Indian, 104–108

Arts and sciences in India, 37

Aryan ancestry, 148–149

Asiatic governments, historiography, 28

Asiatics, 36, 145, 148

Assimilation/transculturation, xxv–xxvi, 56, 96–97, 128, 103, 134, 153

Astrology, 63

Astronomy, 70

Atlantic merchants, 15

Atlases, title pages of, 74, 75, 76f

Auber, Peter, 140

Aurangzeb, xxii, 37, 42, 50, 53

Authoritarian family, 13–14

Authoritarian rule, 2, 19, 23

Authority. *See also* Rule/ruler
  class and, 25–26
  of Company, xv, 11
  constitution, xviii
  deterritorialization of, 95